Nicholas Wolterstorff interprets and discusses the ethics of belief which Locke developed in the latter part of Book IV of his *Essay Concerning Human Understanding*. After lengthy discussions on the origin of ideas, the nature of language, and the nature of knowledge, Locke got around to arguing what he indicated in the opening Epistle to the Reader to be his overarching aim: how we ought to govern our belief, especially (though by no means only) on matters of religion and morality. Professor Wolterstorff shows that what above all placed this topic on Locke's agenda was the collapse, in his day, of a once-unified moral and religious tradition in Europe into warring factions. Locke's epistemology was thus a culturally and socially engaged one; it was his response to the great cultural crisis of his day. Convinced also that of genuine knowledge we human beings have very little, Locke argued that instead of following tradition we ought to turn "to the things themselves" and let "Reason be your guide." This view of Locke, in which centrality is given to the last book of the *Essay*, invites an interpretation of the origins of modern philosophy different from most of the current ones. Accordingly, after discussing Hume's powerful attack on Locke's recommended practice, Wolterstorff argues for Locke's originality and discusses his contribution to the "modernity" of post-sixteenth-century philosophy.

CAMBRIDGE STUDIES IN RELIGION AND CRITICAL THOUGHT 2

COLLEGIUM

CHRISTI REGIS

FROM THE COLLECTION OF

GEORGE SCHNER, S.J.
1946 - 2000

CAMBRIDGE STUDIES IN RELIGION
AND CRITICAL THOUGHT

Edited by
Wayne Proudfoot (Columbia University),
Jeffrey L. Stout (Princeton University),
and Nicholas Wolterstorff (Yale University)

Since the Enlightenment, there has been debate, at times heated, over the implications of critical thought for our understanding of religious ideas and institutions. Disciplinary boundaries have always mattered less to the debate than certain acknowledged exemplars of critical thinking. Locke, Hume, Kant, Marx, Feuerbach, Nietzsche, Freud, and Durkheim long ago became canonical figures, but the list of model critics has never been stable, and continues to proliferate. Struggles against sexism, racism, and imperialism have all produced prominent critics of their own. Now, complicating matters further, the idea of critical thought is itself under attack. At the same time, many scholars are returning to religious traditions in search of resources for their critique of contemporary society and culture. Cambridge Studies in Religion and Critical Thought is a series of books intended to address the various interactions of critical thinking and religious tradition in this rapidly changing context. The series will take up the following questions, either by reflecting on them philosophically or by pursuing their ramifications in studies of specific figures and movements: Is a coherent critical perspective on religion desirable or even possible? If so, what would it look like, and how might it answer charges of reductionism, relativism, and nihilism? Should it aspire to take the form of a systematic theory? What sort of relationship to religious tradition ought a critic to have? One of detachment? Of active opposition? Of empathy? Of identification? What, if anything, is worth saving from the Enlightenment legacy or from critics of religion like Hume and Feuerbach? Where else should we look for guidance in critically appraising religious traditions? To premodern philosophers? To postmodern texts? To the religious traditions themselves? When we turn to specific religious traditions, what resources for criticizing modern society and culture do we find? The answers offered will be varied, but will uniformly constitute distinguished, philosophically informed, critical analyses of particular religious topics.

A list of books in the series is given at the end of the book.

JOHN LOCKE AND THE ETHICS OF BELIEF

NICHOLAS WOLTERSTORFF

Noah Porter Professor of Philosophical Theology, Yale University

CAMBRIDGE
UNIVERSITY PRESS

Published by the Press Syndicate of the University of Cambridge
The Pitt Building, Trumpington Street, Cambridge CB2 1RP
40 West 20th Street, New York, NY 10011-4211, USA
10 Stamford Road, Oakleigh, Melbourne 3166, Australia

First published 1996

Printed in Great Britain at the University Press, Cambridge

A catalogue record for this book is available from the British Library

Library of Congress cataloguing in publication data
Wolterstorff, Nicholas.
John Locke and the ethics of belief
Nicholas Wolterstorff.
p.   cm. – (Cambridge studies in religion and critical thought; 2)
Includes index.
ISBN 0 521 55118 8 (hardback)
1. Locke, John, 1632–1704. *Essay concerning human understanding.*
2. Locke, John, 1632–1704 – Religion. I. Title. II. Series.
B1298. R4W65   1996
121–dc20   95–7256   CIP

ISBN 0 521 55118 8 hardback
ISBN 0 521 55909 X paperback

Contents

Preface

There's a story making the rounds today about the beginnings of modern philosophy in which John Locke is either villain or tragic hero – take your pick. According to this story, the core of modern philosophy was epistemology, "theory of knowledge"; and epistemology was the project of discovering the nature, foundations, and scope of knowledge.

Philosophy as a discipline thus [saw] itself as the attempt to underwrite or debunk claims to knowledge made by science, morality, art, or religion. It [purported] to do this on the basis of its special understanding of the nature of knowledge and of mind. Philosophy can be foundational in respect to the rest of culture because culture is the assemblage of claims to knowledge, and philosophy adjudicates such claims. It can do so because it understands the foundations of knowledge, and it finds these foundations in a study of man-as-knower, of the "mental processes" or the "activity of representation" which make knowledge possible . . . Philosophy's central concern [was] to be a general theory of representation, a theory which will divide culture up into the areas which represent reality well, those which represent it less well, and those which do not represent it at all (despite their pretense of doing so).[1]

It is to the seventeenth century in general, but "especially to Locke" that "we owe the notion of [philosophy as] a "theory of knowledge" based on an understanding of "mental processes.""[2]

Locke is villain or tragic hero in that story because the story itself has turned out to be either pathetic or tragic: We now know it to have been an illusion that philosophy-as-epistemology could be "an autonomous discipline . . . distinct from and sitting in judgment upon"[3] religion and art, science and morality.

In this book I tell a different story about the same events. In this

---

[1] Richard Rorty, *Philosophy and the Mirror of Nature* (Princeton, Princeton University Press, 1979), p. 3.   [2] *Ibid.*, p. 131.   [3] *Loc.cit.*

ix

alternative story Locke is not the philosopher in the tower rendering judgments on who knows what and how, but the philosopher in the street offering advice to his anxious combative compatriots on how to overcome the cultural crisis engulfing them. Locke was as much a cultural philosopher in his epistemology as he was a social philosopher in his political theory. For centuries European humanity had resolved its moral and religious quandaries by appealing to its intellectual inheritance – its tradition. By Locke's day and in Locke's place this tradition had split into warring fragments. Thus on the cultural agenda there was the question: How should we form our beliefs on fundamental matters of religion and morality so as to live together in social harmony, when we can no longer appeal to a shared and unified tradition? This anxious question motivated Locke's *Essay Concerning Human Understanding*. Locke does indeed offer a "theory of knowledge." But that theory of knowledge, though important in its own right, and no doubt regarded by Locke as important in its own right, is placed in the *Essay* as a step on the path toward answering that other question which Locke regarded as much more important. Knowledge, said he, is "short and scanty." How are we to pick our way when we find ourselves forced, as we all are, to leave the small clearing of knowledge and enter the twilight of belief and disbelief?

I did not *set out* to tell a different story about the origins of modern philosophy; I set out to understand better the traditional story so as to resolve some of my own perplexities. The alternative story emerged unexpectedly, slowly, fitfully – begging a reluctant author to tell it, like Pirandello's characters in search of an author.

It is about twenty-five years ago now that I first became perplexed over the challenge so widely issued to religious people that they must have evidence for their religious beliefs – evidence consisting of other beliefs. It was insisted that at bottom a person might not *reason from* his or her religious beliefs but had to *reason to* them from other beliefs. Why was this? I asked. Nobody assumed, for example, that all our perceptual beliefs had to be based on other beliefs; what was it about one and all religious beliefs that made them different? Eventually I (along with colleagues of mine at Calvin College) concluded that the culprit in the matter was the assumption that foundationalism, specifically, "classically modern" foundationalism, states the truth of the matter concerning proper belief-formation.[4] So I reflected on the

---

[4] By a *classical* foundationalist I mean one who holds that the only *immediate* (*basic*) beliefs which possess whatever be the doxastic merit in question are those whose content is either a

tenability of this epistemological position, eventually concluding that, when clearly formulated and then held up to the light, it is decisively mistaken – and it makes no difference whether it is offered as a criterion for acceptance of scientific theories, as a criterion for entitlement to ordinary beliefs about the world and religious matters, or whatever. Almost two decades ago, then, I published my objections; and along with my then-colleague, Alvin Plantinga, worked out an alternative in the domain of religious belief which we called "Reformed epistemology."[5]

But my attack, and that of others of which I was aware, left me feeling uneasy. If classical and near-classical foundationalism, in the versions of it which I and others had attacked, seemed to me so obviously unacceptable, why had so many great philosophers found it compelling? Why did my own students so often find the prospect of surrendering it disturbing? Apparently something deep was at stake. Our attack remained too superficial; the depths had not yet been probed, the motivation and attraction not yet laid bare. So I looked for exponents of (classical and near-classical) foundationalism in whom what was deep came to the surface. This led me eventually to Locke. Not to Descartes; though I looked there first. But I became persuaded – I shall present my case in the pages that follow – that Descartes's foundationalism was far more restricted and traditional in its scope than was Locke's. Descartes espoused a foundationalist account of *scientia* (science) and only of that – though it must at once be added that he had expansive expectations concerning the potential scope of *scientia*. Locke's foundationalism was meant for all human beings, whether or not they were engaged in science. It is that wider Lockian foundationalism which has shaped the modern mind. More important for me: In Locke's foundationalism there is revealed, more clearly than in Descartes's, that depth for which I was looking. What lures and inspires the typical foundationalist is the conviction that it is possible for us human beings to have direct insight into certain of the facts of reality – to have direct awareness. An added benefit was that

---

proposition self-evident to the person, or a proposition which is an incorrigible report of a mental act or object of the person.

[5] We called it (not very felicitously) "Reformed epistemology" because we took it to be characteristic of the Reformed tradition of Christianity. My earliest objections to classical foundationalism can be found in *Reason within the Bounds of Religion* (Grand Rapids, Eerdmans, 1976). The best statement of Reformed epistemology was given in the essays by Alston, Plantinga, and myself in Alvin Plantinga and Nicholas Wolterstorff (eds.), *Faith and Rationality* (Notre Dame, University of Notre Dame Press, 1983).

with great care and articulateness Locke drew out of his foundationalism its evidentialist implications for religious belief.

I had to overcome strong prejudices. In the philosophical world I inhabit, Locke has the reputation of being boringly chatty and philosophically careless – having been too busy with the practical matters of making money and participating in revolutionary politics to have thought with profundity. Quite some time ago I had read Books I and II of Locke's *Essay*. The reputation seemed to me eminently just. The prose itself seemed plodding and lustreless, compared to the quick glittery sheen of Descartes's writing. But now I leaped over the first three books of the *Essay* and plunged into Book IV, concentrating on its second half. I felt myself present at the making of the modern mind.

A second path led me to Locke. It is widely assumed nowadays that anti-foundationalism in epistemology requires anti-realism in meta-physics – requires embracing the view that there is no way the world is except relative to some conceptual scheme. In fact there is no such requirement. I remain a thorough-going metaphysical realist who is also an anti-foundationalist. One day I happened to read some pages of Thomas Reid; I do not remember why. Reid, in spite of his eighteenth-century fame and nineteenth-century influence, has fallen out of the canon of modern philosophy. At once I recognized a soul-mate, a metaphysical realist who was an anti-foundationalist. Indeed, Reid was the first great anti-foundationalist of the modern tradition; intervening centuries have dimmed neither the rhetorical brilliance nor the philosophical power of his attack. So I resolved to write a book on Thomas Reid, not only to rescue him from his undeserved oblivion but to give presence in the current discussion to this overlooked option of anti-foundationalist realism. But I found I could not lay out Reid's thought without first laying out Locke's thought. Reid's thought on epistemological matters was shaped by his polemic against what he called "The Way of Ideas"; and though Reid regarded Descartes, Malebranche, Locke, Berkeley, and Hume as all espousing The Way of Ideas, it came to seem to me that Locke was the central formative figure. So I planned an introductory chapter on Locke's epistemology. That chapter insisted on becoming a book.

There was yet a third path which led me to Locke. In an essay I had written defending religious belief against foundationalist critique,[6] I

---

[6] "Can Religion be Rational if it has no Foundations?," in Plantinga and Wolterstorff, *Faith and Rationality*.

had joined a wide range of epistemologists in speaking of us human beings as having responsibilities for our beliefs; and I had announced that I would make it my practice to use "rational" as a synonym for "permissible": The rational belief is the permissible belief, i.e., the belief which does not violate the relevant norms. I thought of myself, in this resolution, as following established linguistic practice. What had struck me was the fact that discussions concerning what we *ought to* believe were regularly conducted in the language of what it was rational to believe. I noticed that there was a powerful impulse toward saying of everything judged acceptable for believing that it was rational to believe it, and of everything judged unacceptable, that it was not rational to believe it. "Rational," I concluded, was a synonym of "permissible" in these discussions.

Then doubts set in. Does not rationality, at its core, have to do with reasons, or reasoning, or Reason? If so, then surely rationality is not simply to be *identified* with the root idea behind such words as "should," "permissible," "ought," and "responsible." In the interweaving of the language of rationality with the language of obligation we are dealing with something deeper than mere linguistic practice. Coming to the surface is the unspoken assumption that what we ought to believe has something intimate to do with reasons, and/or reasoning, and/or Reason. But why make that assumption? There is more to human life, more even to the life of the mind, than reasons, reasoning, and Reason. So why give rationality such exalted status? Obviously a look into the literature on rationality was called for.

I immersed myself for a while. But the immersion had on me the opposite effect of that hoped for. I had hoped to understand why rationality was assumed to have something special to do with what we ought to believe. Instead of illumination I experienced bewilderment. Obviously those participating in the discussions saw themselves as having sharp disagreements with each other. Often intense passions were attached to those disagreements. One thinker saw rationality as an instrument of oppression; another, as a source of enlightenment and liberation. One lamented the spread of rationality in the modern world; another, its lack. But were they talking about the same phenomenon? And those who offered theories of rationality: Were they offering competing analyses of the same concept and competing theories as to the conditions under which that concept has application, or were they working with different concepts and thus just missing each other?

There are fundamentally two ways of extricating oneself from an intellectual predicament of this sort. One can compose a taxonomy in which one distinguishes the issues under discussion and lays out the structurally distinct options on those issues. Or one can engage in the archaeology of cultural memory, with the aim of telling the story of how we got to where we are in our thinking – in this case, in our thinking about rationality and our assuming that what we ought to believe has something special to do with rationality. A good telling of the story would uncover the assumptions behind our way of thinking, some of which have perhaps fallen out of consciousness; and would uncover the purposes which those ways of thinking once served or were thought to serve. Thus it would help us understand our confusion: We would see that concepts which may once have had a function in a certain intellectual and social milieu no longer have that in ours. We would see the whole to which the shards once belonged. Thus the taxonomic and archaeological approaches ideally serve the same end, that of illuminating our predicament and inviting suggestions as to how to extricate ourselves from it.

I decided to practice the archaeology of cultural memory so as to tell the story of how we got to where we are in our thinking. To my considerable surprise I was once again led to John Locke. Locke was the first to develop with profundity and defend the thesis that we are all responsible for our believings, and that to do one's duty with respect to one's believings one must, at appropriate junctures and in appropriate ways, listen to the voice of Reason. Reason must be one's guide. Locke had forebears and cohorts in this line of thought; I want not only to concede but to insist on this. Nonetheless, Locke was the great genius behind our modern ways of thinking of rationality and responsibility in beliefs. And Locke's vision became classic: for many, compelling; by some, contested; by no one, ignored. Locke, *on this issue*, is the father of modernity.

In short, three different paths of inquiry led me to Locke's epistemology. His thought has proved maddeningly elusive, however. Over and over, lines of interpretation which initially seemed promising led to dead ends. Rather soon I concluded, along with other recent commentators, that the traditional school-book interpretation of Locke, which places the *Essay*'s center of gravity in Book II, must be rejected. The center of gravity is Book IV; that is clear from Locke's own comments about the *Essay*. It's true that issues of intrinsic interest are raised in the other three books, issues intrinsically interesting to

Locke himself. Nonetheless, these books *as a whole* are to be read as preparation for Book IV. The traditional neo-Hegelian interpretation of Locke as an empiricist is based on emphasizing Books I and II and all but ignoring Book IV. When Book IV is given its due and intended weight, it becomes clear that Locke is one of the great rationalists of the Western philosophical tradition. More precisely: In his discussion concerning the origin of "ideas" in Book II, Locke is an empiricist; but in his discussion of the nature of knowledge and the proper governance of belief in Book IV, Locke gives to Reason a central role. It is not hard to see how the neo-Hegelian misinterpretation, once it arose, got perpetuated. Most readers, by the time they get to the end of Book II, have run out of time and patience; they move on to something else. Long books in which the main point gets developed only toward the end inevitably run the great risk of being misunderstood!

Another feature of the *Essay* proved to be a far greater obstacle to interpretation. Eventually I concluded that to make sense of Locke, I had to distinguish between what in the following exposition I call the *visionary* passages of the *Essay* and the *craftsmanly* passages. A typical strategy of Locke, when discussing a topic, is first to present his thought in eloquent visionary unqualified language, then to elaborate and articulate his thought with great philosophical craftsmanship, and then to close by returning to the visionary. Unfortunately, he never brings these two sides of his genius into harmony with each other. For what he says in the detailed working out of his thought regularly undercuts the visionary statement; the qualifications and elaborations not only amplify but deconstruct the official formulations. Locke is to be counted among Locke's most acute critics. Thus arise many, though indeed not all, of the oft-remarked "inconsistencies" in Locke. Obviously this pattern confronts the interpreter with a serious problem. The solution must consist of keeping both sides of Locke's genius in view – the visionary and the craftsmanly. But it takes a long time before one feels able to draw the line with any confidence.

The difficulty of getting hold of Locke's thought proved, in my own case, to have a source deeper yet than either of these. As will be evident from the foregoing, I came to Locke with my own questions and assumptions. So it always is. I concluded after a while that Locke's main aim in Book IV was to offer a theory of entitled (i.e., permitted, responsible) belief. His picture, so I concluded, was that there are norms for believing and that beliefs are entitled if they do not violate those norms. I saw him as endeavoring to formulate those norms and defend his formulation. I recognized that he also proposed a theory of knowledge earlier in Book IV, and the rudiments of a theory of rationality. But these, though important, were situated as components in his larger endeavor of offering a theory of entitled belief.

More generally, I saw Locke as primarily engaged in *regulative*, as opposed to *analytic*, epistemology. In analytic epistemology one explores the conditions under which one or another merit is present in beliefs. Theories of knowledge and theories of rationality belong to analytic epistemology. They are not meant to offer guidance, except, of course, guidance in analysis for those who wish to pick out knowledge from non-knowledge and rationality from non-rationality. In regulative epistemology, on the other hand, one discusses how we ought to conduct our understandings – what we ought to do by way of forming beliefs. The title of one of Locke's small books, *The Conduct of the Understanding*, was for me the clue that his concern was regulative epistemology – that, plus the fact that he so regularly spoke about our *obligation* to govern our belief-forming faculties.

Only recently did I see that I was mistaken. Not mistaken in my conviction that regulative epistemology was Locke's over-riding concern, and that his excursions into analytic epistemology are ancillary to that. Mistaken in assuming that his intent was to offer a criterion for entitled belief. For one thing, I had quite early concluded that one of the main motivations of Locke's endeavor was his wish to address the cultural crisis of his day; I have already spoken of that. But a criterion of entitled belief would not be a response to this crisis. It would not address this anxiety. It took me a long time to acknowledge this.

Secondly, though the recommendations Locke offers for one's conduct of one's understanding are typically couched in universalistic language, it gradually became clear to me that he did not intend them to be interpreted universalistically – that I had to draw the line between the visionary and the craftsmanly passages differently from how I had been drawing it. "Listen to the voice of Reason," Locke says; "let Reason be your guide." But in the course of explaining what this listening and guidance come to, Locke makes clear his view that one is obligated to do this only for propositions which are of maximal "concernment" to one, as he calls it. Only if a proposition is of maximal "concernment" to one does entitlement to believe require listening to the voice of Reason. Concerning all other cases, Locke has nothing to say. For a long time I tried to make him say something about all those other cases. But he has nothing to say. Locke has no general theory of belief-entitlement.

I think we can best understand what Locke was doing by employing the concept of a *doxastic practice* (Greek *doxa* = belief). Locke was proposing a reform in the doxastic practices of his day. Those practices, he thought, were incapable of coping with the cultural crisis engulfing Europe in general and England in particular; they had, in fact, contributed to that crisis. Sometimes the issue of whether or not to believe a certain proposition is of such importance to one – such "concernment" – that one is obligated to try seriously to do one's best to get in touch with reality on this point. Locke's proposals, I came to see, were proposals as to what *doing one's best* consists of. Locke is indeed a near-classical foundationalist – but not with respect to *scientia*, or knowledge, or warrant, or justification, or entitlement – or any of the other merits in belief so regularly discussed in present-day epistemology. Locke was a near-classical foundationalist concerning doing one's best to get in touch with reality. And since Locke regarded his fellow citizens as not doing their best, when they should be, and not believing with a firmness appropriate to the results of that endeavor, his proposals had the status of proposals for reform. Locke was urging on his fellows that they reform their doxastic practices; he was persuaded that if they did reform them, in accordance with his advice, the cultural crisis would be overcome. For doing one's best, as Locke understood it, consists of setting aside all unverified tradition and getting down to "the things themselves."

I have borrowed the term "doxastic practice" from William P. Alston.[7] By a doxastic practice I mean, and Alston means, a certain mode of belief-formation. However, the sort of mode I have in mind differs a bit from that which Alston has in mind. For Alston, a doxastic practice is a *habit* – or rather, a system of habits. He says that

The term "practices" will be misleading if it is taken to be restricted to voluntary activity; for I do not take belief-formation to be voluntary. I am using "practice" in such a way that it stretches over, e.g., psychological processes such as perception, thought, fantasy, and belief-formation, as well as voluntary action. A doxastic practice can be thought of as a system or constellation of *dispositions* or habits, or, to use a currently fashionable term, *mechanisms*, each of which yields a belief as output that is related in a certain

---

[7] Wm. P. Alston, "A 'Doxastic Practice' Approach to Epistemology," in M. Clay and K. Lehrer (eds.), *Knowledge and Skepticism* (Boulder, Colo., Westview Press, 1989).

way to an "input." The sense perceptual doxastic practice . . . is a constellation of habits of forming beliefs in a certain way on the basis of inputs that consist of sense experiences. (p. 5)

Alston emphasizes that, on his understanding of doxastic practices, we all "engage in a plurality of doxastic practices, each with its own sources of belief, its own conditions of justification, its own fundamental beliefs, and, in some cases, its own subject matter, its own conceptual framework, and its own repertoire of possible 'overriders.'"[8] Likewise he emphasizes that "These practices are acquired and engaged in well before one is explicitly aware of them and critically reflects on them";[9] that they "are set in the context of wider spheres of practice";[10] and that the habits in question "are thoroughly *social*: socially established by socially monitored learning, and socially shared." He goes on to say that "This is not to deny that innate mechanisms and tendencies play a role here. We still have much to learn about the relative contribution of innate structures and social learning in the development of doxastic practices . . . But whatever the details, both have a role to play; and the final outcome is socially organized, reinforced, monitored and shared."[11]

Though I have found the notion of doxastic practices indispensable to understanding and explaining what Locke was up to, I shall not be understanding them quite as *habits* or *constellations of habits*. As Alston remarks, the activation of a habit is not a case of voluntarily doing something. But the doxastic practice which Locke promotes as doing one's best incorporates various types of voluntary action – gathering evidence, appraising that evidence so as to determine probability, etc. The picture which Locke takes for granted is not just that we all possess habits of belief-formation which get activated by certain experiences, these habits being the product of innate dispositions which have undergone conditioning, but that we have all been tutored – self-tutored and socially tutored – in how to put these habits to use. We learn how to use our sense-perceptual habits; we learn, for example, when to be suspicious of what our eyes tell us and what to do to overcome the suspicion, how to move about so as best to determine the shape of an object, how to go about judging whether the light is right for determining the "real" color of an object, and so on.

So let us for our purposes think of doxastic practices as ways of using our belief-forming habits. A doxastic practice, thus understood, is a

---

[8] *Ibid.*, p. 5. [9] *Ibid.*, p. 7. [10] *Ibid.*, p. 8. [11] *Ibid.*

way of *using* what *Alston* calls "doxastic practices." Locke was persuaded that there was something seriously amiss in how his compatriots were using their belief-forming dispositions. Their tutoring in how to use this equipment was deficient. He outlined a new practice which, so he argued, had the merit of constituting doing one's best to bring it about, for some proposition, that one believes it if and only if it is true. Whenever one wants to do one's best, this is the practice to try to implement; whenever one *ought to* try seriously to do one's best, this is the practice that one *ought to* try to implement. As we shall see, Locke recognized that the implementation of his proposal would require more than preachments; it would require tutoring – even *school* tutoring. European men and women would have to be tutored differently in the use of their belief-forming dispositions if the cultural crisis was to be overcome – the crisis, namely, of a people schooled to consult tradition who now find their tradition fractured. Locke's epistemology is the epistemology of a culturally engaged philosopher.

I said that I wanted to tell a story. But all I have done in this book is talk about the role of Locke and Descartes in the first half of the story. And as to the second half, I only talk about Hume; in particular, I never get to Reid. We all know Kant's famous statement that Hume awakened him from his dogmatic slumbers. The school-book narratives of modern philosophy, stemming ultimately from the neo-Hegelian historians, go straight from Hume to Kant, usually with the moralism attached that Hume exhibited the bankruptcy of empiricism, whereupon Kant showed that the way ahead was a synthesis of continental rationalism with British empiricism. The story has to be revised. Reid and Kant are *together* the great eighteenth-century responses to Hume's mode of challenging Locke's vision. Not only that; even their modes of response, and sometimes their language, are strikingly similar. In words which immediately bring to mind Kant's remark, Reid says that Hume shocked him out of his unquestioning acceptance of "The Way of Ideas."

I hope at some later time to continue the story begun here, a story of tradition, awareness, and interpretation. That larger story within which the present one is framed is more important. For it speaks not only to our intellectual, but also to our social, concerns. The issue which Locke addressed, of how to govern one's beliefs when tradition has been fragmented and pluralized, so far from disappearing, has become more pressing and insistent than ever. It remains on our cultural agenda. And the proposed answers all turn up again. We in our century have been replaying the intellectual drama that unfolded from Locke to Hegel. With these two big differences: God is now regularly missing from the picture, and it is now widely believed that everything is contingent. For the present, though, it will be enough to articulate Locke's vision, show its originality, appraise its tenability, and defend this reading of one strand within the beginnings of modern philosophy. Reid will have to remain in the waiting room for a while yet.

A final word: In the last couple of decades there has merged, from the seedbed of analytic philosophy, a truly admirable flowering of studies in the philosophers of the past, including studies in Locke. Once upon a time the engagement of the analytic philosopher with the history of philosophy – I caricature a bit – was of the mode: Thoughts that occurred to me one day upon reading a sentence in an English translation of Descartes. The result, unsurprisingly, was that the philosophers of the past all looked rather like analytic philosophers, albeit befuddled ones. By contrast, the practitioners of the new wave bring an admirably wide range of learning to bear on determining *what the philosopher himself was saying*. The results, in my judgment, are vastly more interesting – sometimes strange, often provocative, frequently instructive. I have consulted all such studies as I could discover that were relevant to the topics I discuss here – though it remains the case, in my judgment, that the latter part of Book IV of the *Essay* is a relatively neglected part of Locke. Not neglected, as before; but still *relatively* neglected. I have benefited from many of those studies. What follows, though, is not a typical specimen of this new wave of historical studies.

It differs in at least four respects from typical specimens. First, I pay relatively little attention to matters of influence and development – little attention to philosophical and other forms of intellectual influence on or by Locke, and little attention to the development of Locke's own thought. My concern is to understand Locke's thought on the matters at hand in its final form. And though I claim that Locke's thought on these matters was extraordinarily influential, I don't here defend that claim.[12]

---

[12] Let me refer any reader who might be dubious on the matter to Hans Aarsleff, "Locke's Influence," in Vere Chappell (ed.), *The Cambridge Companion to Locke* (Cambridge, Cambridge University Press, 1994).

Secondly, my explication of Locke's thought in its final form is defended almost exclusively by citations from the texts of Locke in which that thought finds expression – those being, let me add, a rather wide range of Locke's texts, not just the *Essay*. I have profited from the endeavors of such historians as John Yolton and Michael Ayers to illuminate Locke's thought by setting him within the philosophical debates and traditions of his day; but I have not myself tried to add to what they and others have done on this score. Mainly I have used other texts of Locke himself to illuminate obscure passages in the Lockian text.

Thirdly, I do rather less than most historians by way of explicitly interacting, either in agreement or disagreement, with the historians who have discussed the same topics. For example: There is a well-known article by J. A. Passmore titled "Locke and the Ethics of Belief" on Locke's views as to the relation of belief to the will. It will be evident to everyone who reads what Passmore says on this topic, and then what I say, that I think Passmore's interpretation is seriously misguided; but I don't detail our differences of interpretation.

Lastly, my attempt throughout is to get beyond the words of Locke and down to what he was getting at. The best of the new historians do the same. But my attempt to do so takes a form closer to "rational reconstruction" than is typical of the historians. I have no interest in submitting Locke to what is nowadays blandly called by some a strong reading. But I do see Locke as a dialogue partner for contemporary epistemology; and that shapes my discussion.

It is my judgment that in his late writings, especially in the second part of Book IV of his *Essay*, Locke developed a line of thought on the governance of belief which has played an extraordinarily prominent role in subsequent culture and which remains fascinating to this day. Locke was by no means the only one thinking along those lines at that time; he was, though, the most profound and influential. I have done my best to understand and explicate that line of thought without letting much else get in the way – other than citations from the texts which express that line of thought.

My quotations from Locke's *Essay Concerning Human Understanding* are all from the edition by Peter Nidditch (Oxford, Clarendon Press, 1975). I have modernized most of the spelling, and followed modern practices of capitalization. The edition of Locke's *Works* that I have used is the twelfth edition (London, 1824).

CHAPTER I

Rationality in everyday life

"We should not judge of things by men's opinions, but of opinions by things."

(Conduct of the Understanding, §24; Works II, 363).

"God has made the intellectual world harmonious and beautiful without us; but it will never come into our heads all at once; we must bring it home piece-meal, and there set it up by our own industry, or else we shall have nothing but darkness and a chaos within, whatever order and light there be in things without us."

(Conduct of the Understanding, §38; Works II, 385)

I THE VISION: LET REASON BE YOUR GUIDE IN BELIEVING

(a) Introduction

Early in 1671, John Locke had a discussion with some five or six friends in his apartment at Exeter House in London on matters of morality and revealed religion.[1] The discussants, says Locke, "found themselves quickly at a stand by the difficulties that arose on every side. After we had awhile puzzled ourselves, without coming any nearer a resolution of those doubts which perplexed us, it came into my thoughts that we took a wrong course, and that before we set ourselves upon enquiries of that nature it was necessary to examine our own abilities, and see what objects our understandings were or were not fitted to deal with" (*Essay*, Epistle to the Reader). This thought, says Locke, "was that which gave the first rise to this Essay concerning the Understanding" (i,i,7).

---

[1] See Maurice Cranston, *John Locke: A Biography* (London, Longman, 1957), pp. 140–1.

Locke's resolution was also a rejection. He did not propose consulting the textual tradition so as to be nourished on its wisdom. Neither did he propose reading Sacred Scripture. For about a thousand years Western intellectuals had been schooled to consult the texts bequeathed them, when they found themselves in quandaries as to what to believe on matters of morality and religion, and more besides, so as to extract from those texts answers to their quandaries. Ever since Abelard's *Sic et Non* (*Yes and No*), every European intellectual had been vividly aware of the appearance of significant contradictions in the textual tradition. Almost all remained convinced, however, that on a wide range of issues, this was only appearance. Of course, it was recognized that there were heresies, errors, and disputed questions; some, such as the followers of the *Via Moderna*, were more inclined than were the Thomists and Scotists to identify errors in the tradition. Nonetheless, the conviction remained that if one assigned the proper priorities among the texts (with the Bible being preeminent), selected the right senses, used the appropriate strategies of interpretation, and made the right distinctions, a richly articulated body of truth would come to light. St. Paul and Virgil, Aristotle and Augustine, would all be seen to fit together. Where once the texts had appeared contradictory, now they would be seen as getting at different facets of the complex truth. Many medievals also held that a dialectical appropriation of this tradition was the best preparation for engaging in that highest of intellectual activities, the practice of *scientia*.

In the sixteenth century, this view of the textual tradition was battered from all sides; as a consequence, by Locke's time and in Locke's situation, the latter half of the seventeenth century in England and the Netherlands, no one was any longer espousing it. Nobody supposed that Protestants in their various sects were all getting at different aspects of one complex truth, let alone that Protestants and Catholics together were doing so. And even the view that the *pre-Reformation Christian tradition* presented a unified body of truth had fewer and fewer defenders. What was handed down was fractured and seen as such. Here is Locke:

since traditions vary so much the world over and men's opinions are so obviously opposed to one another and mutually destructive, and that not only among different nations but in one and the same state – for each single opinion we learn from others becomes a tradition – and finally since everybody contends so fiercely for his own opinion and demands that he be believed, it would plainly be impossible – supposing tradition alone lays down the ground of our duty – to find out what that tradition is, or to pick out truth from among such a variety, because no ground can be assigned why one man of the old generation, rather than another maintaining quite the opposite, should be credited with the authority of tradition or be more worthy of trust; except it be that reason discovers a difference in the things themselves that are transmitted, and embraces one opinion while rejecting another, just because it detects more evidence recognizable by the light of nature for the one than for the other. Such a procedure, surely, is not the same as to believe in tradition, but is an attempt to form a considered opinion about things themselves; and this brings all the authority of tradition to naught.[2]

Thus a chasm, wrought by the revolutionary developments of the sixteenth century, yawns between Locke and the medievals in their attitude toward the textual tradition. Locke was modern, alienated from that tradition. He did his philosophizing, and perceived himself as doing his philosophizing, in a situation of cultural crisis, a crisis induced by the widespread consensus that the European moral and religious tradition was fractured and that new "foundations" for knowledge and belief had to be discovered. The wisdom of a (supposedly) unified tradition could no longer be consulted to resolve one's quandaries. Inescapably there was on the cultural agenda the question, "How do we go about deciding what to believe?" "How do we conduct our understandings?" That is one of the fundamental questions to which Locke addressed himself in his epistemology. Locke was not an academic addressing academics on purely academic topics but an intellectual addressing intellectuals in a situation where they could no longer say: Let the wisdom of the unified tradition be your guide.[3] Let *Reason* be your guide, said Locke; in everything, be guided by Reason.

It must be added that in the *Essay* Locke repeatedly expresses the conviction that all traditions up to his time, *unified or not*, are infected with a disease which makes them incapable of serving as satisfactory guides. Selecting *some particular tradition* is not the solution to the crisis

---

[2] *Essays on the Law of Nature*, ed. W. von Leyden (Oxford, Clarendon Press, 1958), pp. 129–31.

[3] The writer who has most clearly seen the social and political intentions of Locke in his *Essay* is Neal Wood in *The Politics of Locke's Philosophy* (Berkeley, University of California Press, 1983). Wood remarks that "Far from being an arcane manual for a restricted audience of academicians and experts, the *Essay* was intended for ordinary educated readers of common sense: peers, landed gentry, merchants, manufacturers, administrators, physicians, lawyers, clerics, men of letters. The *Essay* was conceived primarily to aid them in their everyday lives, to guide them in the great practical concerns of religion, morality, politics, and law, and in normal intercourse" (p. 2). That is exactly correct!

caused by the fracturing of the tradition. That fracturing is not itself the disease, but a symptom. The disease is that people have not conducted their understandings properly; as a consequence, all traditions are repositories more of error than of wisdom. That "by which men most commonly regulate their assent, and upon which they pin their faith more than anything else . . . is, *the opinion of others*; though there cannot be a more dangerous thing to rely on, nor more likely to mislead one; since there is much more falsehood and errour amongst men, than truth and knowledge. And if the opinions and persuasions of others, whom we know and think well of, be a ground of assent, men have reason to be heathens in Japan, Mahumetans in Turkey, Papists in Spain, Protestants in England, and Lutherans in Sweden" (iv,xv,6).

We can specify more precisely the crisis which Locke addressed.[4] It was not merely that the grand textual tradition was no longer perceived as presenting a unified body of wisdom on moral and religious matters. In their situation of fractured tradition, people were being schooled into becoming unreflective partisans *of their own party and of its particular tradition*. They were being schooled into uncritical acceptance on sayso of the deliverances of the leaders of their own faction. Traditions had replaced tradition; the religious wars were a consequence: "if anyone should a little catechize the greatest part of the partisans of most of the sects in the world, he would not find, concerning those matters they are so zealous for, that they have any opinions of their own: much less would he have reason to think, that they took them upon the examination of arguments, and appearance of probability. They are resolved to stick to a party, that education or interest has engaged them in; and there, like the common soldiers of an army, show their courage and warmth, as their leaders direct, without ever examining, or so much as knowing the cause they contend for" (iv,xx,18).

Locke did not view the existence of these schooled practices as inadvertent. If we dig beneath the practices so as to uncover the

---

[4] In thus interpreting Locke as responding to a crisis, I agree with James Tully, "Governing Conduct," in Edmund Leites (ed.), *Conscience and Casuistry in Early Modern Europe* (Cambridge, Cambridge University Press, 1988). The crisis to which Leites points was social as well as cultural; he calls the whole a "legitimation crisis." I entirely agree that in the totality of his work Locke was responding to a social, as well as to a cultural, crisis. I furthermore agree that the cultural crisis to which he was responding contributed to the social crisis; there was indeed a "legitimation crisis." But in my discussion I shall be focusing my attention almost entirely on Locke's response to the great cultural crisis threatening his society, that of intense partisanship in a situation of fractured tradition.

motives of those who urge and inculcate them, we regularly discover
that the practices are instruments of power:

> it was of no small advantage to those who affected to be masters and
> teachers, to make this the principle of principles, that principles must not be
> questioned: For having once established this tenet, that there are innate
> principles, it put their followers upon a necessity of receiving some doctrines
> as such; which was to take them off from the use of their own reason and
> judgment, and put them upon believing and taking them upon trust,
> without farther examination: In which posture of blind credulity, they might
> be more easily governed by, and made useful to some sort of men, who had
> the skill and office to principle and guide them. Nor is it a small power it gives
> one man over another, to have the authority to be the dictator of principles,
> and teacher of unquestionable truths; and to make a man swallow that for an
> innate principle, which may serve to his purpose, who teacheth them.
> (I,iv,24; cf. I,iii,22–7; and *Conduct*, §41; *Works* II,389)

We must look to historians for a detailed account of why European
humanity in the sixteenth century came to see its textual tradition as
always having been fractured and why the fracturing became
rampant. But a few brief observations may be in order. The
increasing contact of Europeans with non-Europeans certainly played
a role in loosening the grip of their own tradition on Europeans and in
suggesting alternative ways of thinking, as one can see from the
writings of Montaigne. But it didn't, as such, lead Europeans to see
their own tradition as always having been riddled with inconsistencies.
And for those contacts to play even the role that they played in
Montaigne, a fundamental change of attitude toward The Other was
required. There had always been contacts with other peoples, though
few, indeed, compared with the number now occurring; but seldom
were these contacts experienced as unsettling. The "others" whom
the Europeans met were regarded as pagans or infidels and their
traditions accordingly rejected as inferior – compatible at certain
points with the European tradition, but otherwise, misguided.
Seldom did travelers return home loosened from their own religious
and moral convictions.

It was principally internal factors which caused the perception of
disunity; likewise, it was principally internal factors which caused the
increasing fragmentation. At the very heart of medieval European
intellectual life were the Christian Scriptures, along with the tradition
of councils, popes, and church Fathers. It was the perception of *that
core of the tradition* as contradictory that was principally responsible for

the crisis in the minds and hearts of Europeans, this perception itself leading to further and obvious fracturing. In turn, it was especially Luther's rebellion against the magisterium that caused this new perception and fracturing. Luther succeeded in persuading a great many Europeans that the tradition of the councils, popes, and Fathers was filled with fault lines.

Initially Luther defended his theological convictions from within the tradition by offering a new interpretation of Scripture and tradition. Those who first answered him also did so in the traditional way; they contested his interpretation by citing other Fathers and other passages from Scripture and dialectically weaving a different interpretation. Though Luther's attack on the standard interpretation of Scripture and tradition was aimed at a very deep point, he might nonetheless eventually have won this exegetical debate, at least if the debate had been purely intellectual. Of course it was not; Luther was attacking the powers. But in any case, rather than continuing the debate in the traditional fashion, Luther broke things wide open in his rejoinder: He asserted that the magisterial tradition was in *fact contradictory*, not just apparently so; and that many of its real contradictions were not trivial but fundamental. The tradition was filled with fundamental falsehood. It was, accordingly, merely human; we ought to renounce our dependence on it and return to *God's* book – the Bible.[5] Probably the new reading habits cultivated by the humanists, habits and attitudes which broke with the practices of exegesis, distinction, interpretation, and so on which had been developed by the medievals for extracting unified truth from disparate texts, helped to make Luther's claim persuasive.

We must recall that the traditional understanding of the textual tradition itself invited Luther's call to return to the Bible; for the tradition of councils, popes, and Fathers was officially a hermeneutic of the Bible. Thus the Catholic response to Luther's move was not that it was wrong to go back to the Bible, but that it was useless to do so unless one also had available an authoritative interpretation of the Bible. And so it was that there arose the bitter debate between Catholics and Protestants over the so-called "rule of faith": Is the Bible alone to be our authority, or is the Bible as authoritatively interpreted by the church to be that?

Luther was branded a heretic. Many people before him had been

[5] See Richard Popkin, *The History of Scepticism from Erasmus to Spinoza* (Berkeley, University of California Press, 1979), chap. 1.

branded heretics. What made Luther's heresy different was that he had powerful political support at the right times, and that the defenders of the tradition were widely perceived as corrupt.

But though it was the emergence of Protestantism, incited by Luther's rebellion, that was mainly responsible for leading Europeans to conclude that their textual tradition had never contained a unified body of moral and religious thought, there were other movements as well which contributed significantly to the increasing fragmentation – in addition, that is, to the tendency, already noted, to see more worth in the thought and practices of other peoples than had been typical of the Europeans. There was, for one thing, the increasing dissatisfaction with Aristotelian natural philosophy and science, and the emergence of new methods and new science in the hands of – to mention only a few major figures – Galileo, Bacon, and Descartes. And there was the recovery and publication, at the hands of the humanists, of many lost and forgotten texts from antiquity, with the consequence that Platonism, Epicureanism, skepticism, and Stoicism all began to make their presence felt on the intellectual scene.

The consequence of all these developments together was that by the middle of the seventeenth century there was available to the European intellectual a wide variety of more or less internally coherent, but mutually incompatible, modes of thought. Some, such as the new mechanistic and mathematical sciences, were in ascendency, others were in decline; and flashpoints of tension leaped about from place to place.

The England of Locke's day was a special case. In some parts of Europe, the Netherlands in particular, a social *modus vivendi* had emerged by the early part of the seventeenth century among parties adhering to different frameworks of conviction. Not so in England. Here the religious antagonisms erupted into civil war. After a period of intense hostility between Protestants and Catholics, a variety of Protestant sects began to do battle not only with the established Church of England but with each other – some, though not all, of these sects exemplifying the "enthusiasm" which Locke and his Latitudinarian friends found so alarming. In the background of Locke's epistemology was the general European crisis to which I have pointed; in the foreground was the specific, intensely antagonistic, form which that crisis was taking in English culture and society in Locke's day.

To this fragmentation Locke's attitude was, in one way, eminently

"Protestant": We must not follow the Catholic strategy of trying to recover the authoritative position of one tradition and of one interpretation of that tradition, but must appeal to something outside all tradition. For Locke, however, that "something" was not the Word of God, but Reason, coupled with insight in general – and the Bible when, but only when, Reason supports it; for Reason and insight take us to the things themselves. Locke regarded the new natural philosophy coming to birth in his day as a concrete paradigm of how we should conduct our understandings; there one saw, already in place, the practice which bore the promise of resolving our anxiety.

But before we construct, we must engage in critique, so as to discover how much of a "fit" there is between our abilities and the things themselves. Otherwise human beings, "extending their enquiries beyond their capacities, and letting their thoughts wander into those depths, where they can find no sure footing; 'tis no wonder, that they raise questions, and multiply disputes, which never coming to any clear resolution, are proper only to continue and increase their doubts, and to confirm them in absolute scepticism" (I,i,7).

Skepticism as to the possibility of getting to the things themselves seems not to have caused Locke any personal anxiety. Nonetheless, the existence of skepticism as a cultural movement played an important role in the shaping of his strategy: No longer can we simply assume a nice fit between reality and our capacities for discovering reality. We must stand back and *ask whether there is* such a fit. Skepticism encouraged Locke to place *the self* on center stage; that is the significance of the resolution he took when the discussion with his friends came to a standstill. Though he urged that we conduct our understandings so as to get to the things themselves, his own talk was more of us than of the things.[6]

Locke's *Essay Concerning Human Understanding* was, for one thing, an enquiry into human knowledge – into its certainty, grounds, and extent, and into the origin of the ideas which (on Locke's view) make up our knowledge. As to the scope of our knowledge, Locke's conclusion was that, compared to "the vast extent of things" (I,i,5), our knowledge is, and must forever remain, "very short and scanty" (IV,xiv,I).

---

[6] As already mentioned, skepticism also played a role in bringing about that cultural anxiety which Locke addressed. A full account of the contribution of the resurgence of skepticism to that anxiety, under the stimulus of the recovery of the ancient skeptical writings, would trace the interaction between "the problem of the criterion" posed by the skeptics, and the disputes by religious parties over "the rule of faith." (See Popkin, *ibid.*)

Locke realized that complaint and lament over the absurdity of our fate would be seen by many as the appropriate response to this measured skepticism concerning the scope of knowledge. His own reaction was different. *Contentment* is the appropriate response: "to sit down in a quiet ignorance of those things, which, upon examination, are found to be beyond reach of our capacities," to "learn to content ourselves with what is attainable by us in this state" (1,i,4). Part of the rationale for such contentment is that discontent with not doing what one knows one cannot do makes no sense. Close scrutiny of the contours of our knowledge uncovers, however, a more specific rationale for contentment: Our knowledge is adequate for our fundamental moral and religious concerns. God our Maker has placed within the scope of the knowledge of human beings "the knowledge of their Maker, and the sight of their own duties"(1,i,5). Contentment with the adequacy of our knowledge is thus appropriately accompanied by gratitude to our Maker: we "have cause enough to magnify the bountiful author of our being, for that portion and degree of knowledge he has bestowed on us . . ."(1,i,5). In short,

We shall not have much reason to complain of the narrowness of our minds, if we will but employ them about what may be of use to us; for of that they are very capable: And it will be unpardonable, as well as childish peevishness, if we undervalue the advantages of our knowledge, and neglect to improve it to the ends for which it was given us, because there are some things that are set out of the reach of it . . . If we will disbelieve everything, because we cannot certainly know all things; we shall do much-what as wisely as he, who would not use his legs, but sit still and perish, because he had no wings to fly . . . 'Tis of great use to the sailor to know the length of his line, though he cannot with it fathom all the depths of the ocean. 'Tis well he knows, that it is long enough to reach the bottom, at such places, as are necessary to direct his voyage, and caution him against running upon shoals, that may ruin him. Our business here is not to know all things, but those which concern our conduct. (1,i,5-6)

Recommending grateful contentment with our limits, on the ground that our knowledge is sufficient for our needs, was not, however, Locke's only response to what he saw as the limited scope of human knowledge. He recommended contentment as well because, where knowledge is absent, God has graciously made opinion (belief, assent, judgment) available.

Opinion is riddled with error, however. So when it comes to opinion, what is of prime importance is that we learn to conduct our understanding *rightly*. Accordingly, Locke says that after discussing the origin of ideas, the nature of knowledge, and "the bounds between opinion and knowledge," he will "examine by what measures, in things whereof we have no certain knowledge, we ought to regulate our assent, and moderate our persuasions" (1,i,3). "If we can find out those measures, whereby a rational creature put in that state, which man is in, in this world, may, and ought to govern his opinions, and actions depending thereon, we need not be troubled, that some other things escape our knowledge" (1,i,6).

The focus of our attention in what follows will be on Locke's discussion concerning the governance of opinion in Book IV of the *Essay*, and in his *Conduct of the Understanding*, originally intended as part of the *Essay*; it is in these that Locke more fully articulates and defends the thesis that we must take Reason as our guide. Moreover, as should be clear from the foregoing, we are following Locke's own estimate of importance in emphasizing this part of the *Essay*. Locke was motivated to write the *Essay* for the sake of his discussion in Book IV of the nature and scope of knowledge and the governance of opinion. And given his firm conviction that in most affairs of life we must be content with opinion, knowledge being beyond us, his own view was clearly that, within Book IV, it is the second part (from chapter xvi onwards) that is of greatest importance. As we shall see, emphasizing Book IV of the *Essay* (along with its companion *Conduct of the Understanding*) yields a rather different picture of Locke's thought from that yielded by the traditional school-book practice of emphasizing Book II of the *Essay*. The undeniable empiricist strands in his thought will be seen to be balanced, if not outweighed, by the rationalist strands.

Incidental comments along the way in the *Essay*, plus the fact that in the *Essay* the only sustained application Locke made of his general proposal for the governance of belief was to matters of revealed religion, make clear that the originating impulse of the *Essay* in a stalemated discussion on matters of morality and revealed religion continued to sustain and direct Locke's reflections.[7] It is not accidental, then, that Locke's best brief account of his conviction that we must take Reason as our guide in the governance of our belief-forming faculties should occur in the context of his discussion of faith and Reason. Locke observes that, in ordinary parlance, faith and Reason are treated as "opposed." In reality they are not opposed. For

---

[7] See Richard Ashcraft, "Faith and Knowledge in Locke's Philosophy," in John W. Yolton (ed.), *John Locke: Problems and Perspectives* (Cambridge, Cambridge University Press, 1969).

Faith is nothing but a firm assent of the mind: which if it be regulated, as is our duty, cannot be afforded to anything, but upon good reason; and so cannot be opposite to it. He that believes, without having any reason for believing, may be in love with his own fancies; but neither seeks truth as he ought, nor pays the obedience due his maker, who would have him use those discerning faculties he has given him, to keep him out of mistake and errour. He that does not this to the best of his power, however he sometimes lights on truth, is in the right but by chance; and I know not whether the luckiness of the accident will excuse the irregularity of his proceeding. This at least is certain, that he must be accountable for whatever mistakes he runs into: whereas he that makes use of the light and faculties God has given him, and seeks sincerely to discover truth, by those helps and abilities he has, may have this satisfaction in doing his duty as a rational creature, that though he should miss truth, he will not miss the reward of it. For he governs his assent right, and places it as he should, who in any case or matter whatsoever, believes or disbelieves, according as reason directs him. He that does otherwise, transgresses against his own light, and misuses those faculties, which were given him to no other end, but to search and follow the clearer evidence, and greater probability. (iv,xvii,24)

Here is the picture: God has endowed us with various faculties for the formation of beliefs. But in constructing us as God did, God had in mind not just that we *have* beliefs but that our beliefs *be true*; Locke never so much as considers the possibility that God, in designing us, might have had in mind more desiderata than truth for the beliefs produced by our belief-forming faculties. However, our faculties of belief-formation do not operate deterministically; they can be governed. Furthermore, if allowed to operate ungoverned they produce a rather high proportion of false beliefs. So God, concerned as God was with our having true beliefs, intended that we *would* govern them. The principle of governance which holds most promise for our achieving the goal God requires of us is governing our assent "according as reason directs us." It was, in good measure, for the purpose of such governance that God endowed us with the light of Reason.[8]

But what does it mean to say that we are to govern our assent according as Reason directs us? It means that belief, "if it be regulated as is our duty, cannot be afforded to any thing, but upon good reason." And what, in general, is it to believe for good reason? It is to "follow the clearer evidence, and greater probability."

---

[8] There is, of course, nothing in this paragraph that Descartes would disagree with. In Chapter 2 I shall argue, however, that the Cartesian *project*, within which these convictions find their place, is significantly different from the Lockian project. The *significance* of the shared convictions differs.

Let us follow the procedure of first explicating Locke's understanding of what it is to be a responsible believer; and then, Locke's view concerning the role of Reason in becoming such a believer. As to the first of these topics, we must follow Locke himself in speaking of knowledge before we speak of belief (and assent). Reason is a faculty which yields knowledge, and properly governed belief, on matters of maximal concernment, is *grounded on knowledge*. It is for those reasons that we must look first at Locke on knowledge – plus the fact that the situation in which Locke issued his call for the governance of belief was not only that of tradition being fractured but also that of knowledge being "short and scanty."

The distinction Locke draws between *knowledge* and *belief* (assent, opinion, *doxa*, judgment) is fundamental to his entire epistemology. We find ourselves confronted, however, with a significant difference between Locke's official account of knowledge and what one might call his unofficial account. In the course of working out the details of his views on knowledge, Locke found himself offering examples of knowledge which do not fit his official account – and aware of doing so. Yet the official account remains in the text; Locke did not blot it out and confine it to preliminary notebooks. A certain elegant and compelling "picture" of knowledge and of its difference from belief never ceased to work its spell on Locke's mind – in spite of the fact that, when immersed in working out the details, he tacitly conceded that the picture would not do. We can only understand the pattern of Locke's thought if we discern both the vision and the qualifying details; to lose sight of either would be to miss a fundamental dimension of his thinking. To dwell on the inconsistencies, to stop there, not to see the pattern behind many of them, the pattern of vision presented and vision undercut, is to be oblivious to both sides of Locke's genius. Locke was both a philosophical visionary and a philosophical craftsman. What he never managed to do was bring those two sides of his genius together.

(b) The scope of knowledge

On Locke's official doctrine, knowledge and belief, or "judgment," are fundamentally different phenomena, the difference going much deeper than just that, on Locke's explanation of the term "judgment," judgment is taking or presuming something to be true when knowledge is lacking. Locke officially rejected the thesis which has become a fundamental tenet of epistemology in our own day; namely, that knowledge is a species of belief. Knowledge and belief represent the exercise of fundamentally different faculties:

> Thus the mind has two faculties, conversant about truth and falsehood. First, knowledge, whereby it certainly perceives, and is undoubtedly satisfied of the agreement or disagreement of any ideas. Secondly, judgement, which is the putting ideas together or separating them from one another in the mind, when their certain agreement or disagreement is not perceived, but presumed to be so. (IV,xiv,4)

Though he is unemphatic about it, Locke did assume that the phenomenon of *taking to be true* typically accompanies knowledge.[9] He lacked officially sanctioned terminology for saying that, however. "Judgment" and "belief" are officially reserved for the phenomenon of *taking to be true when knowledge is absent*, as, no doubt, is "opinion"; and "assent" is officially reserved for cases when words are involved (IV,xiv,3). But Locke himself does not consistently use his terms in accordance with his official explanations (and his official explanations themselves are not consistent). So we shall both connect with contemporary modes of speech and not at all distort Locke's thought if we say that it was Locke's view that belief (and/or assent) typically accompanies knowledge – rather than being a genus of which knowledge is a species.

Knowledge for Locke is *awareness* of some *fact* – in Lockian language, awareness of some agreement or disagreement among entities. To know is to be directly acquainted with some fact, to be directly aware of it, to "perceive" it, as Locke was fond of saying. By contrast, belief (assent, judgment, opinion, and so on) on Locke's view consists fundamentally of *taking* some *proposition* to be true.[10]

---

[9] See especially the whole chapter on Maxims, *Essay* IV,vii. Here is just one example: "For that which makes the mind assent to such propositions, being nothing else but the perception it has of the agreement, or disagreement of its ideas . . ." (IV,vii,9).

[10] Michael Ayers in *Locke: Volume I: Epistemology* (London and New York, Routledge, 1991), Part II, esp. chap. 13, points out that whereas Descartes (and others) thought of propositions as entities which we can not only believe and affirm but also merely entertain, Locke's official thought prevents him from saying this. For he thinks of us as *composing* propositions by putting "ideas" together in predicative fashion; and his official explanations imply that this combinatory act involves belief (assent), or at least judgment (affirmation). Yet at various points in Book IV, Locke clearly allows for withholding belief (and affirmation) from some particular proposition. So how are we to interpret him? It appears to me that in practice Locke thought of the combinatory predicative act of composing a proposition as not necessarily involving belief or affirmation; one can, as it were, perform the act in the entertaining or withholding mode. That is how I shall interpret him. But Locke himself never recognizes the issue. As to the wavering character of Locke's distinctions between "belief," "assent," "judgment," "opinion," and so forth, see Ayers, *ibid.*, p. 312, n. 13.

The question arises: Of what sorts of facts can we human beings be directly aware? What is the potential scope of knowledge? Locke's answer to that question opens Book IV of the *Essay*. He first embraces what Thomas Reid would later call "The Way of Ideas": "the mind, in all its thoughts and reasonings, hath no other immediate object but its own ideas, which it alone does or can contemplate." From that affirmation he straightway concludes that "it is evident, that our knowledge is only conversant about" our ideas. And then he goes on at once to specify the nature and scope of knowledge: Knowledge is "nothing but the perception of the connexion and agreement, or disagreement and repugnancy of any of our ideas. In this alone it consists. Where this perception is, there is knowledge, and where it is not, there, though we may fancy, guess, or believe, yet we always come short of knowledge."

What are we to make of this? First, a brief word on the vexed topic of what Locke had in mind by ideas.[11] Two things were central in Locke's thought on the matter. For one thing, he held, as a matter of ontological principle, that the mind could be aware – *directly* aware, that is – only of *the mental*. It could be directly acquainted only with its own acts and objects – its own "modifications," as I shall call both mental acts and objects – and perhaps with itself. What I have here called "mental objects," Locke called "ideas." Locke often expressed his ontological principle in words such as those I have just cited from the opening of Book IV: "Whatsoever the mind perceives in itself, or is the immediate object of perception, thought, or understanding, that I call ideas" (II,viii,8; cf. II,i,1).[12] It seems quite clear, however, that none of Locke's formulations of the general ontological principle is fully accurate as a statement of his thought. For each of them says that the mind is never directly acquainted with anything other than its own ideas, whereas Locke rather often speaks of the mind as also being directly acquainted with its own "operations" (for example, in II,i,4 and II,i,8); and he doesn't count the mind's operations among its ideas. Possibly he also held that the mind is directly acquainted with itself; in a passage from the very last chapter of his *Essay* he says that "since the things, the mind contemplates, are none of them, *besides itself*, present to the understanding, 'tis necessary that something else,

[11] The two best recent discussions are Vere Chappell, "Locke's Theory of Ideas," in V. Chappell, *The Cambridge Companion to Locke* (Cambridge, Cambridge University Press, 1994); and Ayers, op. cit., chaps. 5 and 6.

[12] Cf., in Locke's Second Letter to Stillingfleet: "ideas are nothing but the immediate objects of our minds in thinking" (*Works* III,362).

as a sign or representation of the thing it considers, should be present to it: And these are ideas" (iv,xxi,4; my italics).

In this last passage the second important theme in Locke's thought about ideas comes to the surface: Ideas are representations, *mental* representations, of entities distinct from themselves. Locke did not hold, to be sure, that *all* ideas are representations. For one thing, not all ideas *constructed* from simple ideas are representations; he explicitly says, for example, that "archetypes" – i.e., complex ideas of non-substances, such as the idea of the triangle – are "not intended to be the copies of anything, nor referred to the existence of anything" (iv,iv,5; such ideas do have a representational *function* with respect to other ideas). But further, not even all simple ideas are representations. Presumably Locke held that such ideas as feelings of dizziness or hunger are not representations. What he emphasizes, however, is that ideas of secondary qualities are not representations, as he means "representation." In reply to an objection from Stillingfleet, he says that

I do not remember that I have any where said, of all our simple ideas, that they are none of them true representations of things without us . . . The contrary whereof appears from the words which I have set down, out of chap. 30, where I deny only the simple ideas of secondary qualities to be representations; but do everywhere affirm, that the simple ideas of primary qualities are the images or representations of what does exist without us . . . the simple ideas of secondary qualities . . . are not representations or images of anything in bodies, but only effects of certain powers in bodies to produce them in us . . . [Nonetheless] we as certainly know and distinguish things by ideas, supposing them nothing but effects produced in us by these powers, as if they were representations. (*Works* iii,75–6)

In short, what Locke wishes to insist on is simply that *some* of our ideas are representations, and that our various ways of thinking about non-mental entities all presuppose our having ideas which are representations of non-mental entities. " 'Tis evident," he says, "the mind knows not things immediately, but only by the intervention of the ideas it has of them" (iv,iv,3; "things" here is to be read as "non-mental things").[13]

[13] On whether Locke held a representational theory of perception, see Reginald Jackson, "Locke's Version of the Doctrine of Representative Perception" in C. B. Martin and D. M. Armstrong (eds.), *Locke and Berkeley* (Notre Dame, University of Notre Dame Press, 1968). In general, I go along with Chappell and Ayers (in the works just cited) in interpreting Locke as holding that ideas are mental objects; some commentators have argued that he regarded them instead as mental acts – specifically, acts of perceiving. See, for example, Douglas Greenlee, "Locke's Idea of 'Idea'" (and the ensuing discussion), in I. C. Tipton (ed.), *Locke on Human Understanding* (Oxford, Oxford University Press, 1977); and John Yolton, "Locke

The problem Locke is addressing in these passages is the problem of *reference* – mental reference in the first instance, and then, derivatively, verbal reference. How do we manage to think about some specific thing – to have it in mind? Locke's answer requires a sharp distinction between mental and non-mental reality. The only way for us to think about something non-mental is for it to be in some way "represented" in the mind. An infinite regress would ensue, however, if we said that mental reality can also be thought about only by way of representations. We think about mental objects and acts, some of them anyway, immediately, without the intervention of representations. Of some, at least, of the mind's acts and objects we have direct awareness, immediate apprehension, unmediated "perception."

The point can be made in the language of "presence," language which Locke himself does not use but which he would (I think) embrace: Reality is directly present to the mind only at that point where the individual mind thinks about itself and its own acts and objects. Mental acts and mental objects are *self-presenting*, perhaps along with the mind itself. The remainder of reality can be thought about only by the mediation of mental objects which, while themselves directly present to the mind, represent items of non-mental reality not directly present. It would distract us from our main purpose to try to puzzle out Locke's thoughts concerning the *nature* of mental representation.

Two additional points must be made about Lockian ideas. The sharp distinction we are inclined to make between concepts, on the one hand, and "intuitions," on the other, is not present in Locke. More precisely, it is not present in his theory; it might plausibly be argued that it is present in his practice. It is primarily to Kant, and secondarily to Hume, that we are indebted for this distinction. If we were to use Kant's distinction in expressing Locke's thought, the thing to say would be this: All thought about non-mental reality occurs by way of concepts and "images"; and what is

and Malebranche: Two Concepts of Ideas," in R. Brandt, (ed.), *John Locke: Symposium Wolfenbüttel 1979* (New York, Walter de Gruyter, 1981). I do not find the arguments persuasive. What emerges is that certain passages are ambiguous. All the clear ones, however, seem to me to be in favor of the interpretation of ideas as mental objects. Consider one already quoted in the text above, from IV,xxi,4: "since the things, the mind contemplates, are none of them, besides itself, present to the understanding, 'tis necessary that something else, as a sign or representation of the thing it considers, should be present to it: And these are ideas." I have argued above that such a passage as this should not be interpreted as saying that all ideas are mental representations, only that all mental representations are ideas; but it is entirely clear that this passage treats at least those ideas which are representational as mental objects.

immediately present to the mind in such thought is just those concepts and "images." There remains this large difference between Locke and Kant, however: Kant thought of concepts as incorporating, or perhaps even as *being*, rules for unifying intuitions; Locke thought of them as certain modifications of the mind whereby entities get "represented" to the mind so as to make it possible for us to have thoughts *about* those entities. For Locke, concepts are mental objects *in addition* to intuitions, not rules for *unifying* intuitions.

Secondly, though in the course of his discussion Locke often speaks as if he were a realist concerning the existence of universals, his official position is clearly nominalism. "All things, that exist, [are] particulars"(III,3,1). "Words are general . . . when used, for signs of general ideas; and so are applicable indifferently to many particular things; and ideas are general, when they are set up, as the representatives of many particular things: but universality belongs not to things themselves, which are all of them particular in their existence, even those words, and ideas, which in their signification, are general. When therefore we quit particulars, the generals that rest, are only creatures of our own making, their general nature being nothing but the capacity they are put into by the understanding, of signifying or representing many particulars" (III,3,11).

It was quite clearly Locke's thought that abstract singular terms are a species of general term. Some, such as "man," denote substances; others, such as "whiteness," denote qualia (tropes, cases, abstract particulars). "Whiteness" denotes all the whitenesses, "sweetness" all the sweetnesses (whitenesses and sweetnesses both being "powers" in the external objects). And in turn, not only do abstract singular terms multiply *denote* substances and qualia; they *express* abstract general ideas, these in turn multiply representing or signifying all the substances or qualia which the term expressing the abstract idea denotes. The abstract singular term "man" denotes all human beings and expresses the abstract idea of human being; and this abstract idea, in turn, represents all the human beings. Correspondingly, the abstract singular term "whiteness" denotes all the whitenesses and expresses the abstract idea whiteness; and this idea in turn signifies all the whitenesses. Thus not only do certain complex ideas represent concrete non-mental entities – trees, houses, ducks, God, and so on. Certain other ideas, both simple and complex, represent or signify those abstract but particular entities which are qualia – these represented or signified qualia including, but in the case of those represented or signified by complex ideas, not confined to, those to be found in our ideas of sensation and of reflection.

Using his concept of ideas, Locke, as we have seen, offers as his formula for knowledge that to know is to "perceive" some *agreement* or *disagreement* among one's ideas. Let us consider first what he meant by agreement and disagreement of ideas; and secondly, what he meant by "perceiving" an agreement or disagreement among ideas.

If I "perceive" that the three angles of a triangle are equal to two right angles, that, says Locke, is a case of "perceiving" an agreement among ideas; whereas if I "perceive" that white is not black, that is a case of perceiving disagreement. One surmises that, at least in the simplest cases, we "perceive" an agreement among ideas when we would express what we "perceive" in an affirmative sentence, and that we "perceive" a disagreement among ideas when we would express what we "perceive" in a negative sentence.

That surmise is confirmed by what Locke says about propositions. The discussion occurs in the context of his remarks about truth. We must, says Locke, distinguish two sorts of propositions, mental and verbal: "First, mental, wherein the ideas in our understandings are without the use of words put together, or separated by the mind, perceiving, or judging of their agreement or disagreement. Secondly, verbal propositions, which are words the signs of our ideas put together or separated in affirmative or negative sentences. By which way of affirming or denying, these signs, made by sounds, are as it were put together or separated one from another." Locke then goes on to remark that "every one's experience will satisfy him, that the mind, either by perceiving or supposing the agreement or disagreement of any of its ideas, does tacitly within it self put them into a kind of proposition affirmative or negative, which I have endeavoured to express by the terms *putting together* and *separating*. But this action of the mind, which is so familiar to every thinking and reasoning man, is easier to be conceived by reflecting on what passes in us, when we affirm or deny, than to be explained in words" (IV,v,6). Truth, then, can be defined as follows: "When ideas are so put together, or separated in the mind, as they, or the things they stand for do agree, or not, that is, as I may call it, mental truth. But truth of words is something more, and that is the affirming or denying of words one of another, as the ideas they stand for agree or disagree" (IV,v,6).[14]

---

[14] Earlier in the chapter Locke explained truth differently: "Truth then seems to me, in the proper import of the word, to signify nothing but the joining or separating of signs, as the

So in composing affirmative propositions, the mind puts together ideas, and in composing negative propositions, the mind separates ideas.[15] If our ideas or the things they stand for are in fact related just as we have put the ideas together in some affirmative proposition, then the ideas or things *agree* with each other, and sometimes we *perceive* that agreement (which, notice, is different from perceiving that the ideas *are* so put together in this affirmative proposition); whereas if our ideas or the things they stand for are in fact disconnected just as we have separated the ideas in some negative proposition, then the ideas or things *disagree* with each other, and sometimes we *perceive* that disagreement (which, notice, is different from perceiving that the ideas *are* separated in this negative proposition). If I affirm that sugar is sweet, then I have put together the ideas of sugar and sweetness into the affirmative proposition that sugar is sweet; and if my affirmation is about the relation of these ideas and is correct, that is to say, if it is indeed a (conceptual) truth that sugar is sweet, then the ideas of sugar and sweetness agree. Of course, Locke does rather often speak – as one would expect – not only of *perceiving agreements and disagreements among ideas*, but of *knowing the truth of propositions*; his thought, obviously, is that one knows the truth of a

things signified by them, do agree or disagree one with another. The joining or separating of signs here meant is what by another name, we call proposition" (IV,V,2). It is presupposed by this definition that the ideas joined in a mental proposition always *signify* the entities whose agreement with each other makes the proposition true – rather than, in some cases, the ideas put together in the mental proposition just being the ideas whose agreement makes the proposition true. Essentially the same formula is offered at the end of §5 of the same chapter, the only difference being that Locke speaks there of the signs as *standing for*, rather than *signifying*, the things. It is clear, however, that the formulation which accurately expresses Locke's thought is the one quoted in the text above. That sometimes the very ideas that one perceives to agree are put together into a proposition is presupposed by the sentence opening §6 of chapter V: "Every one's experience will satisfy him, that the mind, either by perceiving or supposing the agreement or disagreement of any of its ideas, does tacitly within itself put them into a kind of proposition affirmative or negative, which I have endeavoured to express by the terms putting together and separating" (IV,V,6).

15   In his discussion of these passages in Locke, Leibniz makes the correct point that if Locke regards himself as *explaining* affirmation and negation in terms of "putting together" and "separating" words or ideas, then it must be observed that not all ways of "putting together" yield affirmations and not all ways of "separating" yield negations; whereas if he regards affirmation and negation as merely a *species* of "putting together" and "separating," then nothing is said to explain the species. About the first of these possibilities, Leibniz says this: "a phrase, e.g. 'the wise man,' does not make a proposition; yet it involves a joining of two terms. Nor is negation the same as separation; for saying 'the man' and then after a pause uttering 'wise' is not making a denial." About the second possibility, Leibniz says this: "Agreement obtains between two eggs, disagreement between two enemies. What we are dealing with here is a quite special way of agreeing or disagreeing, and I do not think that your definition explains it" (G. W. Leibniz, *New Essays on Human Understanding* [tr. and ed. P. Remnant and J. Bennett (Cambridge, Cambridge University Press, 1981)], p. 396).

proposition by perceiving the corresponding fact. Thus he says: "Certainty of knowledge is, to perceive the agreement or disagreement of ideas, as expressed in any proposition. This we usually call knowing, or being certain of the truth of any proposition" (iv,vi,3).

Agreements and disagreements among ideas or other entities are *facts*, affirmative and negative facts respectively. They are relationships of a certain sort, entities-in-relation. It was Locke's official doctrine that those facts which one can "perceive" have only one's own ideas as their constituents. However, it was his actual view, as we shall see, that the facts which one can "perceive" have as their constituents not only one's own ideas but also one's mental acts, and perhaps also one's self; Locke assumes that one can "perceive" that one believes something, as indeed he assumes that one can "perceive" that one is "perceiving" something. We must be clear, though, that Locke by no means regarded facts in general as having as their constituents only the mind and its modifications. For example, the fact consisting of the moon's exerting a gravitational pull on the earth does not have as its constituents any mind, idea, or mental act. Thus it is that Locke says that "When ideas are so put together, or separated in the mind, as they, or *the things they stand for* do agree, or not, that is, as I may call it, mental truth" (iv,v,6; my italics).

Not only was it Locke's official doctrine that, from among all the facts that there are, those of which one is directly aware consist exclusively of one's own ideas-in-relation; it was also his doctrine that *propositions* consist of ideas-in-relation. More specifically, the propositions that any given person composes consist exclusively of *his or her own* ideas-in-relation. Nowhere, however, does Locke explain the ontological difference between propositions, on the one hand, and those facts whose constituents are ideas, on the other – whereby, for example, there is the true proposition that sugar is sweet, the false proposition that sugar is not sweet, plus the conceptual fact that sugar is sweet. Yet that he consistently operated with a fact/proposition distinction is indicated, among other things, by his consistently speaking of the entities *in facts* as agreeing or disagreeing, whereas he speaks of the ideas *in propositions* as put together or separated (by us): "Everyone's experience will satisfy him, that the mind, either by perceiving or supposing the agreement or disagreement of any of its ideas, does tacitly within itself put them into a kind of proposition affirmative or negative, which I have endeavoured to express by the terms *putting together* and *separating*" (iv,v,6). (This passage, incidentally, is another piece of evidence for the conclusion that Locke implicitly assumed that belief typically accompanies "perception.")

I have suggested that Locke's actual view, as distinguished from his official view, was that the facts available to one for one's "perception" have not only one's own ideas as their constituents but also one's mental acts, and perhaps one's self. A question we must consider is whether his actual view diverged even further from his official view. Might it be that the constituents of facts available to us for direct awareness are not even confined to mental entities? The question is suggested by this passage: "if our knowledge of our ideas terminate in them, and reach no farther, *where there is something farther intended*, our most serious thoughts will be of little more use, than the reveries of a crazy brain" (iv,iv,2; my italics).[16] Might Locke have been suggesting here that there are cases in which (a) the fact that we "intend" with one of our propositions consists not of an agreement or disagreement among the ideas composing the proposition, but of an agreement or disagreement among *non-mental entities which the ideas composing the proposition stand for*; and (b) that fact is known?

If Locke did indeed wish to qualify his official formula for knowledge by allowing for certain cases of knowing non-mental facts, one surmises that among such cases would be cases of what, at the opening of Book iv, he calls knowledge of real existence. In turn, if that is what he has in mind, one can understand why he would introduce the qualification at the beginning of a chapter called "Of the Reality of Our Knowledge." But let us see whether that is indeed the right interpretation of the passage quoted just above.

In a passage from that same chapter on "Real Knowledge" Locke remarks "Nor let it be wondered, that I place the certainty of our knowledge in the consideration of our ideas, with so little care and regard (as it may seem) to the real existence of things: since most of those discourses which take up the thoughts and engage the disputes of those who pretend to make it their business to enquire after truth

---

[16] Locke is responding to an objection which he formulates as follows: "If it be true, that all knowledge lies only in the perception of the agreement or disagreement of our own ideas, the visions of an enthusiast, and the reasonings of a sober man, will be equally certain. 'Tis no matter how things are: so a man observe but the agreement of his own imaginations, and talk conformably, it is all truth, all certainty. Such castles in the air, will be as strong holds of truth, as the demonstrations of Euclid. That an harpy is not a centaur, is by this way as certain knowledge, and as much a truth, as that a square is not a circle. But of what use is all this fine knowledge of men's own imaginations, to a man that enquires after the reality of things?" (iv,iv,2; cf. iv,v,7, where the point is made even more vividly – and at greater length).

and certainty will, I presume, upon examination be found to be *general propositions*, and notions in which existence is not at all concerned" (IV,iv,8). And in another passage from the same chapter he remarks that "All the knowledge we have, being only of particular or *general truths*, 'tis evident, that whatever may be done in the former of these, the latter . . . is that which with reason is most sought after" (IV,vi,2).

The thought is this: What we most want when we seek knowledge, and rightly so, is knowledge concerning general propositions – these being a species of propositions lacking existential import, i.e., propositions in which existence is not at all concerned.[17] For this reason, says Locke, he has explained knowledge in such a way as to fit our knowledge of general propositions. Nonetheless, the scope of our knowledge does go beyond such propositions, to include certain *particular* truths. And among these will certainly be those items of "real existence" that we know: the knowledge each of us has that he or she exists, the knowledge we have that God exists, the knowledge one has that there exists some external object causing one's present image, and perhaps the knowledge one has that one is entertaining this and that specific idea. (Whether or not Locke included knowledge of the last sort under knowledge of real existence, it is clear that he did in fact think that there is such knowledge; see, for example, IV,ii,14: "There can be nothing more certain, than that the idea we receive from an external object is in our minds; this is intuitive knowledge."[18]) In short, it is clear that Locke does intend a qualification to be attached to some of what he says about knowledge; for some of it is formulated so as to apply only to general or universal propositions,[19] though in

---

[17] Cf. IV,vi,16: "To conclude, general propositions, of what kind soever, are then only capable of certainty, when the terms used in them, stand for such ideas, whose agreement or disagreement, as there expressed, is capable to be discovered by us. And we are then certain of their truth or falsehood, when we perceive the ideas the terms stand for, to agree or not agree, according as they are affirmed or denied one of another. Whence we may take notice, that general certainty is never to be found but in our ideas. Whenever we go to seek it elsewhere in experiment, or observations without us, our knowledge goes not beyond particulars. 'Tis the contemplation of our own abstract ideas, that alone is able to afford us general knowledge."

[18] Cf. IV,vi,4: "Everyone finds in himself, that he knows the ideas he has; that he knows also, when any one is in his understanding . . . [H]e can never be in doubt, when any idea is in his mind, that it is there" (*ibid.*). "He knows each [idea] to be . . . in his mind, and not away when it is there" (*ibid.*).

[19] Including the following famous passage, in which Locke speaks as if all propositions which can be known to be true are either analytically necessary or synthetically necessary – which, of course, excludes our knowledge that we ourselves exist, or that something exists which is causing this present image of mine, or that we have such-and-such ideas: "We can know then

fact it is his view that there are also particular propositions of which we have knowledge.

But does he wish to qualify, in the way we are exploring, his opening official formula that the objects of knowledge are *ideas in relationship*? Is it his full view that we are capable of "perceiving" agreements and disagreements among entities other than *ideas*, and even other than the mind and its modifications? Is it his view that when we know particular propositions it is sometimes such other facts that we "perceive"?

I think not. If Locke intended this qualification, he is not only unemphatic in making it; he never undertook to explain how it can be that one can directly "perceive" agreements and disagreements among entities other than the mind's modifications, when these are the only (non-fact) entities of which we can be directly aware (plus, possibly, the mind itself). Furthermore, in his letters to Stillingfleet he over and over says that knowledge consists of the "perception" of agreements and disagreements among ideas. So let me suggest another line of interpretation. I shall approach the issue from two sides – offering first an interpretation of what he has in mind by "knowledge of real existence," and then an interpretation of what he has in mind by "the reality of knowledge."

Just two pages after he offered his formula for knowledge at the beginning of chapter i of Book IV, and long before he introduced the apparent qualification mentioned above at the beginning of chapter iv of the book, Locke, without elaboration, cited as "the fourth and last sort [of knowledge] . . . , that of actual and real

---

the truth of two sorts of propositions, with perfect certainty; the one is, of those trifling propositions, which have a certainty in them, but 'tis but a verbal certainty, but not instructive. And, secondly, we can know the truth, and so may be certain in propositions, which affirm something of another, which is a necessary consequence of its precise complex idea, but not contained in it. As that the external angle of all triangles, is bigger than either of the opposite internal angles" (IV,viii,8). Locke must here be regarded as speaking just about "general truths." He himself remarks that there is "no necessary connection of real existence, with any idea a man hath in his memory, nor of any other existence but that of God" (IV,xi,1). Thus the passage above about knowledge of two sorts of propositions has to be understood in the light of this other one which is also about two sorts of propositions which can be known: "there are two sorts of propositions. 1. There is one sort of propositions concerning the existence of any thing answerable to such an idea: as having the idea of an elephant, phoenix, motion, or an angel, in my mind, the first and natural enquiry is, whether such a thing does any where exist? And this knowledge is only of particulars. No existence of any thing without us, but only of God, can certainly be known farther than our senses inform us. 2. There is another sort of propositions, wherein is expressed the agreement, or disagreement of our abstract ideas, and their dependence one on another. Such propositions may be universal and certain" (IV,xi,13).

existence agreeing to any idea." Now, one way of construing what he meant here is this: awareness of the relationship of some existent entity E, to some concept C, of E satisfying C. But such awareness would violate in a flamboyant way the ontological principle that the mind is aware only of its own modifications; for, given that God's real existence is among the "real existences" we know, it would follow that we are aware of God. Anyone who approaches Locke from the side of twentieth-century philosophy immediately thinks of another possibility, however. It was Frege's contention that existence claims are to be understood as claims to the effect that some concept has application. Possibly Locke was thinking along those lines. Knowledge of real existence would then be this: awareness of the relationship between some concept C and the concept of *having application*, of *C satisfying* that concept.

Though it may be such facts as those which Locke had in mind when he speaks of knowledge of real existence, we remain in the dark as to why he thought that we have awareness of such facts. On this, his replies to Stillingfleet are more helpful than anything in the *Essay* as an indication of how he might have been thinking. Speaking in a manner remarkably reminiscent of Descartes about our knowledge of our own existence, Locke in one passage says that "experimenting [i.e., experiencing] thinking in myself, by the existence of thought in me, to which something that thinks is evidently and necessarily connected in my mind; I come to be certain that there exists in me something that thinks, though of that something which I call substance also, I have but a very obscure imperfect idea" (*Works* III,29).[20] So apparently each of us comes to know the fact which he or she would express with the words "I exist" by means of an argument like this: I am aware that thinking is going on; likewise I am aware that thinking cannot take place unless there exists some substance which is doing the thinking; therefore there exists something which is doing the thinking of whose occurrence I am aware; and that is myself. Hence I exist.

Fundamental objections can, of course, be raised to this argument; for one thing, it appears to beg the question in its first premise. But

---

[20] Locke's insistence that we can perceive agreements and disagreements among ideas which are not themselves entirely clear and distinct is crucial to the analysis he offers of knowledge of self-existence: "in some cases we may have certainty about obscure ideas; e.g. by the clear idea of thinking in me, I find the agreement of the clear idea of existence, and the obscure idea of a substance in me, because I perceive the necessary idea of thinking, and the relative idea of a support; which support, without having any clear and distinct idea of what it is, beyond this relative one of a support, I call substance" (*Works* III,42).

what is important for our purposes is that in clarifying his thought as to what it is that we "perceive" in that form of knowledge of real existence which is knowledge of one's own existence, Locke treats the knowledge in question as a case of *inferential* knowledge, whereas in the *Essay* he speaks of knowledge of one's own existence as a case of *intuitive* knowledge. It appears to me that by the time he set about answering Stillingfleet, Locke no longer regarded knowledge of one's own existence as intuitive; nowhere in the three Replies does he say that it is. In clarifying the nature of such knowledge, in the passage quoted above, he clearly has an argument in mind; and in one passage he himself speaks of self-knowledge as arrived at by a proof: "The idea of this action or mode of thinking is inconsistent with the idea of self-subsistence, and therefore has a necessary connection with a support or subject of inhesion: the idea of that support is what we call substance; and so from thinking experimented in us, we have a proof of a thinking substance in us, which in my sense is a spirit" (III, 33).

Locke is also more explicit in his First Letter to Stillingfleet than he is at any place in the *Essay* as to the way in which knowledge of *God's* real existence is perception of agreements among ideas:

in the present case: the proposition, of whose truth I would be certain, is this: "a knowing being has eternally existed." Here the ideas joined, are eternal existence, with a knowing being. But does my mind perceive any immediate connection or repugnancy in these ideas? No. The proposition then at first view affords me no certainty; or, as our English idiom phrases it, it is not certain, or I am not certain of it. But though I am not, yet I would be certain whether it be true or no. What then must I do? Find arguments to prove that it is true, or the contrary. And what is that, but to cast about and find out intermediate ideas which may show me the necessary connection or inconsistency of the ideas in the proposition? Either of which, when by these intervening ideas I am brought to perceive, I am then certain that the proposition is true, or I am certain that it is false. As, in the present case, I perceive in myself thought and perception; the idea of actual perception has an evident connection with an actual being, that doth perceive and think: the idea of an actual thinking being, hath a perceivable connection with the eternal existence of some knowing being, by the intervention of the negation of all being, or the idea of nothing, which has a necessary connection with no power, no operation, no casualty [*sic*], no effect, i.e. with nothing. So that the idea of once actually nothing, has a visible connection with nothing to eternity, for the future; and hence the idea of an actual being, is perceived to have a necessary connection with some actual being from eternity. And by the like way of ideas, may be perceived the actual existence of a knowing being, to have a connection with the existence of an actual knowing being from eternity. (*Works* III,62–3)

Now for the second stage of the interpretation which I am proposing: How are we to interpret that clause which initiated this part of our discussion, namely, "if our knowledge of our ideas terminate in them, and reach no farther, where there is something farther intended . . ."? I suggest that we do so in the light of what Locke says later in the chapter "Of the Reality of Our Knowledge" from which this passage comes; for later he uses the same locution. In mathematics, he says, "we intend things no farther, than as they are conformable to our ideas" (IV,iv,5). And he adds, in §6: "therefore he is certain all his knowledge concerning such ideas, is real knowledge: because intending things no farther than they agree with those his ideas, he is sure what he knows concerning those figures."

Locke opens chapter iv by considering the objection that if knowledge is nothing more than the perception of agreement or disagreement among ideas, then knowledge is only air castles having nothing to do with reality. In response, he introduces and develops his notion of *real* knowledge – which is not to be identified with *genuine* knowledge. He gives two slightly, though yet significantly, different explanations of what he has in mind by *real* knowledge. In IV,iv,3 he says that "'Tis evident, the mind knows not things immediately, but only by the intervention of the ideas it has of them. Our knowledge, therefore is *real*, only so far as there is a conformity between our ideas and the reality of things." From this passage it would appear that one's knowledge can be real without one's being sure that it is real. In IV,iv,18, however, his definition is more restrictive: "Wherever we perceive the agreement or disagreement of any of our ideas there is certain knowledge: and wherever we are sure those ideas agree with the reality of things, there is certain real knowledge." It is worth noticing that Locke here speaks of being *sure* that those ideas agree with the reality of things; he does not speak of *perceiving* that they do.

Locke then devotes the chapter to distinguishing three ways in which, when one "perceives" some agreement or disagreement among one's ideas, those ideas may conform to external reality and one may be sure that they do, so that one's knowledge is *real* knowledge. As to propositions which contain simple ideas, we can be sure that these ideas "are not fictions of our fancies, but the natural and regular productions of things without us, really operating upon us; and so carry with them all the conformity which is intended; or which our state requires: For they represent to us things under those appearances which they are fitted to produce in us" (IV,iv,4). As to propositions known which contain archetypes, i.e., complex ideas of non-substances, we can be sure that if anything in reality satisfies the archetype, it will also satisfy whatever we "perceive" as agreeing with the archetype. For example: if we "perceive" that triangles are trilateral, we can be sure that if anything in reality is triangular in shape it is also trilateral; and if we "perceive" that murder deserves death, we can be sure that if a murder occurs in reality it will deserve death.[21] Lastly, as to propositions which contain ideas of substances, we can, on the basis of experience, sometimes be sure of at least this much conformity: The simple ideas which we combine into one complex idea of a substance can coexist in reality.

Now, in all our thoughts and reasonings concerning mathematical and moral archetypes, "we intend things no farther, than as they are conformable to our ideas. [And we do intend them thus far.] So that in these, we cannot miss of a certain undoubted reality" (IV,iv,5). Though the knowledge gained in pure mathematics is gained by "perception" of agreements and disagreements among ideas, nonetheless it is not just air castles. The fact that our knowledge is only of relations among ideas is compatible with its being (in certain respects) "real" knowledge. To know a necessary truth concerning relationships among ideas is perforce to know something about "real existence."

There remains this point: Locke, as we have seen, at the beginning of *Essay* IV,iv imagines an objector protesting that if knowledge is nothing but the "perception" of agreements and disagreements among ideas, then "that an harpy is not a centaur, is by this way as

---

[21] Cf. this passage in the Second Letter to Stillingfleet: "where I examine, whether the knowledge we have of mathematical truths, be the knowledge of things as really existing: there I say (and I think I have proved) that it is, though it consists in the perception of the agreement or disagreement of ideas, that are only in the mind; because it takes in all those things, really existing, which answer those ideas. Upon which grounds it was, that I there affirmed moral knowledge also capable of certainty. And pray, my lord, what other way can your lordship proceed, in any demonstration you would make, about any other thing but figures and numbers, but the same that you do in demonstrations about figures and numbers? If you would demonstrate anything concerning man or murder, must you not first settle in your mind the idea or notion you have of that animal or that action, and then show what you would demonstrate necessarily to belong to that idea in your mind, and to those things existing only as they correspond with, and answer that idea in your mind? How else you can make any general proposition, that shall contain the knowledge of things as really existing, I that am ignorant shall be glad to know?" (*Works* III,405–6).

certain knowledge, and as much a truth, as that a square is not a circle." "To which I answer," says Locke, "that if our knowledge of our ideas terminate in them, and reach no farther, where there is something farther intended, our most serious thoughts will be of little more use, than the reveries of a crazy brain." To introduce his discussion he then says this: "But, I hope, before I have done, to make it evident, that this way of certainty, by the knowledge of our own ideas, goes a little farther than bare imagination: and, I believe it will appear, that all the certainty of general truths a man has, lies in nothing else." These last words strongly suggest that the certainty of at least some particular truths *does lie in something else*. I think, however, that in the light of the considerations we have canvassed there can be little doubt that that suggestion of the words does not fit Locke's intent. The passage should be read like this: All certainty of general truths lies in nothing else than the perception of agreements and disagreements among ideas – *as indeed, all certainty of any truths whatsoever lies in nothing else*.[22]

I conclude, in short, that Locke was consistently of the view that facts susceptible of being "perceived" have as their constituents only the mind and its modifications. His opening formula, that such facts have as their constituents only *ideas*, must indeed be qualified; they can also have mental acts and perhaps the mind itself as constituents. But he intended no qualification beyond that; in particular, he construed knowledge of real existence as a species of "perception" of agreements and disagreements among ideas.

Locke emphasized repeatedly that whatever be the nature and scope of our knowledge of real existence, it is not such as to make possible a true *scientia* of nature – nor, indeed, a true *scientia* of any

[22] Thus I do not agree with the conclusion to which R. I. Aaron comes in his *John Locke* (Oxford, Clarendon Press, 1971): "Locke left the two theories of knowledge standing side by side with little effort to make them consistent. Knowledge is the perception of relations between ideas: but we also know particular existences directly, and in this case knowledge is not the perception of relations between ideas" (p. 241). "We may conclude then that the fact of existential knowledge has caused Locke to introduce thoroughgoing alterations in his account of knowledge. He opens Book IV of the *Essay* with a theory of knowledge applicable, as it proves, merely to knowledge of relations between abstract ideas, a universal, hypothetical, and highly abstract knowledge, best typified in mathematics. Another theory became necessary for knowledge of particular existences. Consequently, Locke's whole account of knowledge is far from consistent, for he does not even try to remove this dualism or to relate the two theories" (pp. 246–7). Locke's account of knowledge is indeed not consistent, as we shall see shortly; but there is no inconsistency at the point where Aaron purports to see inconsistency. There is no second theory of knowledge in Locke which is meant for knowledge of particular existences.

substances whatsoever. There is in existence a true *scientia* of pure (not applied) mathematics, and there can in principle be a true *scientia* of pure (not applied) morality; but of substances, no *scientia* is possible. So prominent in Locke's thought was this theme of human ignorance, and so formative for the overall character of his thought, that we must take a moment to consider the grounds of his skepticism concerning the possibility of a *scientia* concerning natural substances. We must look "a little into the dark side," as Locke puts it; we must "take a view of our ignorance, which [is] infinitely larger than our knowledge" (IV,iii,22). Locke's reflections are probing; and in the light of later developments in natural science (natural philosophy, he would call it), fascinating.

The heart of Locke's argument is that a body of genuine knowledge of nature – a true *scientia* – would require a grasp of the essences of substances; however, our place in nature makes it impossible for us to attain such knowledge.[23] Though a grasp of substantial essences is *in principle* possible for an intelligent being, it is not in fact possible for us who are *human* beings. Locke has not rejected the Aristotelian vision of nature as possessing a necessary structure. He has a different view, however, as to the character of that necessary structure; and he has rejected the Aristotelian assumption that the structure of nature can be known by us. It is hidden.

What it is that Locke wished to say about essence, real and nominal, is one of the most hotly debated topics in Locke interpretation; the complexities are very thick indeed. Those who wish to enter the debates should consult the second volume of Michael Ayers' recent book, *Locke*.[24] Here all we need is the general picture, though it must be conceded that there is controversy even on some aspects of this.

Essence is properly understood, says Locke, as "the very being of anything, whereby it is, what it is" (III,iii,15). Having said this, Locke immediately enters into a polemic against the traditional "Aristotelian" understanding of essence in terms of species and genera. On that understanding, essences are thought of "as a certain number of forms or molds, wherein all natural things, that exist, are cast, and do equally partake" (III,iii,17). They are patterns, "according to which, all natural things are made, and wherein they do exactly every one of them partake, and so become of this or that species" (III,iii,17). Against this way of thinking of real essences Locke threw up a barrage

---

[23] On the role of essence in Locke's account of knowledge, see Roger Woolhouse, "Locke's Theory of Knowledge," in Chappell, *The Cambridge Companion to Locke*.

[24] *Locke: Volume II: Metaphysics* (London and New York, Routledge, 1991).

of objections, perhaps the most decisive of which was, for him, that it has "very much perplexed the knowledge of natural things" (III,iii,17). Better, he says, to think of the essence of a thing as its "inner constitution" determinative of its functioning.[25] A knowledge of the real essence of the human being would be "such a knowledge of that constitution of man, from which his faculties of moving, sensation and reasoning, and other powers flow; and on which his so regular shape depends" (III,vi,3). Such a knowledge, says Locke, "'tis possible angels have, and 'tis certain his Maker has" (III,vi,3).

As to the real essence of "corporeal" stuffs and substances, Locke held the "corpuscular hypothesis."[26] He was persuaded that the constitutions of such things consist of configurations of minute particles of some sort, and that their workings are due entirely to those configurations:

> I doubt not but if we could discover the figure, size, texture, and motion of the minute constituent parts of any two bodies, we should know without trial several of their operations one upon another, as we do now the properties of a square, or a triangle. Did we know the mechanical affections of the particles of rhubarb, hemlock, opium, and a man, as a watchmaker does those of a watch, whereby it performs its operations, and of a file which by rubbing on them will alter the figure of any of the wheels, we should be able to tell before hand, that rhubarb will purge, hemlock kill, and opium make a man sleep; as well as a watchmaker can, that a little piece of paper laid on the balance, will keep the watch from going, till it be removed; or that some small part of it, being rubbed by a file, the machine would quite lose its motion, and the watch go no more. The dissolving of silver in aqua fortis, and gold in aqua regia, and not vice versa, would be then, perhaps, no more difficult to know, than it is to a smith to understand, why the turning of one key will open a lock, and not the turning of another. (IV,iii,25)

A truly *scientific* philosophy of nature, as opposed to a merely experimental (i.e., experiential) one (IV,iii,26), would tell us how those things that have a certain real essence *must* function – not merely how they do in fact *happen* for the most part to function. It would provide us with a knowledge of *laws* (IV,iii,29), acquired in *a priori* fashion, by demonstration.[27]

---

[25] I take essences, says Locke, "but to be in everything that internal constitution, or frame, or modification of the substance, which God in his wisdom and good pleasure thinks fit to give to every particular creature, when he gives a being: and such essences I grant there are in all things that exist . . . I think the real essences of things are not so much founded on, as that they are the very real constitution of things" (First Letter to Stillingfleet; *Works* III,82–3).

[26] A fine discussion on Locke's views concerning the essence of material bodies is Edwin McCann, "Locke's Philosophy of Body," in Chappell, *The Cambridge Companion to Locke*.

[27] Mackie interprets Locke as holding that if we knew the essences of things, our knowledge of

The truth, however, is that we have very little if any such knowledge of nature. Instead of knowing laws specifying how things *must* function, given their constitution, we have only generalizations based on experience as to how for the most part they *do* function. Natural history rather than *scientia*. Discerning "no necessary dependence one on another" of the qualities of things, "we can attribute their connexion to nothing else, but the arbitrary determination of that all-wise Agent, who has made them to be, and to operate as they do, in a way wholly above our weak understandings to conceive" (iv,iii,28).[28]

Though the familiar use of things about us, take off our wonder; yet it cures not our ignorance. When we come to examine the stone we tread on; or the iron, we daily handle, we presently find, we know not their make; and can give no reason, of the different qualities we find in them. 'Tis evident the internal constitution, whereon their properties depend, is unknown to us. For to go no farther than the grossest and most obvious we can imagine amongst them, what is that texture of parts, that real essence, that makes lead, and antimony fusible; wood, and stones not? What makes lead, and iron malleable; antimony, and stones not? And yet how infinitely these come short, of the fine contrivances, and unconceivable real essences of plants and animals, every one knows. The workmanship of the all-wise, and powerful God, in the great fabric of the universe, and every part thereof, farther exceeds the capacity and comprehension of the most inquisitive and

physics would still be only "*as a priori, as* certain and demonstrative, as interpreted geometry and applied mechanics are" (J. L. Mackie, *Problems from Locke* [Oxford, Clarendon Press, 1976], p. 102). Though that is a plausible interpretation of the passage quoted above, from iv,iii,25, it's hard to see what, in his thoughts about essence, would have led Locke to such caution. And in any case, that interpretation clearly does not fit with the following passage: "Had we such ideas of substances, as to know what real constitutions produce those sensible qualities we find in them, and how those qualities flowed from thence, we could, by the specific ideas of their real essences in our own minds, more certainly find out their properties, and discover what qualities they had, or had not, than we can now by our senses: and to know the properties of gold, it would be no more necessary, that gold should exist, and that we should make experiments upon it, than it is necessary for the knowing the properties of a triangle, that a triangle should exist in any matter, the idea in our minds would serve for the one, as well as the other" (iv,vi,11).

28 There is a dispute in the literature as to what Locke meant by God's "arbitrary determination" in this passage and in others like it (for the dispute, see McCann, "Locke's Philosophy of Body"). I think it most unlikely that Locke was of the view that certain of the properties and operations of bodies have no necessary connection to their essences, and that God just arbitrarily determines the connections. I think it much more likely to have been Locke's view that "all their properties and operations flow from" their essences (iii,xvi,23); but that it was a matter of arbitrary determination on God's part *which essences He would instantiate.* Since we don't grasp the essences of material bodies, and since we certainly don't grasp how the properties and operations of bodies "flow from" their essences, and since, even if we did grasp those two things, it would still not be a matter of *knowledge* on our part which essences God instantiated, knowledge of nature is, *for those three reasons,* unavailable to us.

intelligent man, than the best contrivance of the most ingenious man, doth the conceptions of the most ignorant of rational creatures. (III,vi,9)

We "are not capable of a philosophical *knowledge* of the bodies that are about us, and make a part of us . . . [A]s to a perfect *science* of natural bodies, (not to mention spiritual beings,) . . . I conclude it lost labour to seek after it" (IV,iii,29). "[H]ow far soever human industry may advance useful and experimental philosophy in physical things, scientifical will still be out of our reach . . . Certainty and demonstration, are things we must not, in these matters, pretend to" (IV,iii,26). "[N]atural philosophy is not capable of being made a science" (IV,xii,10).

But what, we ask, is the cause of our ignorance? We do not know and cannot know the real essences, the explanatory natures, of things; we must make do without a knowledge of laws, and be content to base our science on generalizations. Why? Why can we not know the ontological *laws* of nature? Because, says Locke, we lack the requisite ideas, i.e., the requisite concepts. Perhaps we possess all or most of the simple concepts of primary qualities required; if so, the requisite complex concepts are not in principle beyond our grasp. But we have no way of knowing how to go about constructing those complex concepts. In short, our ignorance is due to

the *want of* ideas *we are capable of.* As the want of ideas which our faculties are not able to give us, shuts us wholly from those views of things, which 'tis reasonable to think other beings, perfecter than we, have, of which we know nothing; so the want of ideas, I now speak of, keeps us in ignorance of things, we conceive capable of being known to us. *Bulk, figure, and motion* we have ideas of. But though we are not without ideas of these primary qualities of bodies in general, yet not knowing what is the particular *bulk, figure, and motion* of the greatest part of the bodies of the universe, we are ignorant of the several powers, efficacies, and ways of operation whereby the effects, which we daily see, are produced. These are hid from us in some things, by being *too remote*; and in others, by being too *minute.* (IV,iii,24)

In that last sentence Locke hints at why, in turn, we find ourselves unable to arrive at the requisite concepts for a true *scientia* of nature. Partly because of the remoteness of so much of nature; but mainly because the essences of things are to be found in their microstructure, and that microstructure lies beyond the reach of our relatively gross sensory apparatus and our modest instruments.

Had we senses acute enough to discern the minute particles of bodies, and the real constitution on which their sensible qualities depend, I doubt not but they would produce quite different ideas in us; and that which is now the yellow colour of gold, would then disappear, and instead of it we should see an admirable texture of parts of a certain size and figure. This microscopes plainly discover to us: for what to our naked eyes produces a certain colour, is by thus augmenting the acuteness of our senses, discovered to be quite a different thing; and altering, as it were, the proportion of the bulk of the minute parts of a coloured object to our usual sight, produces different ideas, from what it did before . . . Blood to the naked eye appears all red; but by a good microscope, wherein its lesser parts appear, shows only some few globules of red, swimming in a pellucid liquor; and how these red globules would appear, if glasses would be found, that yet could magnify them 1000, or 10000 times more, is uncertain. (II,xxiii,11)[29]

Since we lack concepts of the microstructural natures of things, we do not (with the rarest exceptions) "perceive" which primary qualities necessarily coexist in substances; we do not even understand, in the way necessary for *scientia*, the cohesion of the minute parts of body and the communication of motion – nor, as a matter of fact, extension itself (II,xxiii,22–9). Neither do we "perceive" what effects substances of a given nature will have on other substances of the same or different natures; in particular, we do not "perceive" any connection between combinations of primary qualities in substances and the power to cause ideas of secondary qualities in us. "In vain therefore shall we endeavour to discover by our ideas (the only true way of certain and universal knowledge,) what other ideas are to be found constantly joined with that of our complex idea of any substance: since we neither know the real constitution of the minute parts, on which their qualities do depend; nor, did we know them, could we discover any necessary connection between them, and any of the secondary qualities: which is necessary to be done, before we can certainly know their necessary co-existence" (IV,iii,14).

It is of prime importance to keep in mind that Locke is speaking here of *knowledge*; we cannot *know* the microstructural natures of things. The entire argument presupposes that we do have *good reason to believe* that natural substances have a microstructural nature. Behind this presupposition there lies, in turn, Locke's realization that purely

---

[29] See also II,xxiii,12, in which Locke uses the famous metaphor of *microscopical eyes*. For a fine discussion of these matters, arguing, correctly in my view, that Locke did not regard corpuscles as in principle unobservable, nor is there anything in his system which *should have* led him so to regard them, see Lisa Downing, "Are Corpuscles Unobservable in Principle for Locke?," *Journal of the History of Philosophy* 30, 1 (January 1992), 33–52.

inductive procedures for the construction of natural philosophy are inadequate, and that such procedures must be supplemented with practices fitting what we would now call the hypothetico-deductive model.[30] The formulation of hypotheses concerning the hidden workings of nature, on analogy to its perceptible workings, and the subsequent testing of those hypotheses, is an indispensable component in the construction of natural philosophy. "Analogy in these matters is the only help we have" (IV,xvi,12); and "hypotheses, if they are well made . . . often direct us to new discoveries. But . . . we should not take up any one too hastily, (which the mind, that would always penetrate into the causes of things, and have principles to rest on, is very apt to do,) till we have very well examined particulars, and made several experiments, in that thing which we would explain by our hypothesis, and see whether it will agree to them all, whether our principles will carry us quite through, and not be as inconsistent with one phenomenon of nature, as they seem to accomodate, and explain another" (IV,xii,13).[31]

But doesn't our use of general terms show, to the contrary, that we do grasp the essences of things? Is it not, after all, essential to gold that it be malleable, fusible, and yellowish in color? Is it not essential to a human being that he or she be rational?

Such facts, says Locke, pertain to what may be called *nominal* essences, not to real essences.[32] Given the meaning of our English

---

[30] The best discussion of this matter is Laurens Laudan, "The Nature and Sources of Locke's Views on Hypotheses," in I. C. Tipton (ed.), *Locke on Human Understanding* (Oxford, Oxford University Press, 1977).

[31] Cf. IV,xvi,12: "This sort of probability, which is the best conduct of rational experiments, and the rise of hypothesis, has also its use and influence; and a wary reasoning from analogy leads us often into the discovery of truths, and useful productions, which would otherwise lie concealed."

[32] "It will, no doubt, be presently objected, Is not this an universal certain proposition, All gold is malleable? To which I answer, it is a very certain proposition, if malleableness be a part of the complex idea the word gold stands for. But then here is nothing affirmed of gold, but that that sound stands for an idea in which malleableness is contained: and such a sort of truth and certainty as this, it is to say a centaur is four-footed. But if malleableness makes not a part of the specific essence the name gold stands for, 'tis plain, all gold is malleable, is not a certain proposition. Because let the complex idea of gold, be made up of which soever of its other qualities you please, malleableness will not appear to depend on that complex idea; nor follow from any simple one contained in it. The connection that malleableness has (if it has any) with those other qualities, being only by the intervention of the real constitution of its insensible parts, which, since we know not, 'tis impossible we should perceive that connection, unless we could discover that which ties them together. The more, indeed, of those co-existing qualities we unite into one complex idea, under one name, the more precise and determinate we make the signification of that word; but yet never make it thereby more capable of universal certainty, in respect of other qualities, not contained in our complex idea; since we perceive not their connection, or dependence one on another; being ignorant

word "gold," a necessary condition of "gold" being true of something is that it be malleable, fusible, yellowish in color, and so on. If somewhere there were a community of persons who knew the real essences of things, one could imagine that community also having a language some of whose general terms expressed those real essences. Ideas of those conjunctions of primary qualities which determine the real essences of physical entities would constitute the meanings of the corresponding general terms. Our human language is not like that.[33] Ideas of the real essences of things cannot constitute the meanings of our general terms, since we do not have such ideas. And worse: There is no reason to think that the nominal essences expressed by our terms even so much as coincide in their extension with real essences. For all we know, some of the lumps of stuff that satisfy the sense of our word "gold" may differ from each other in their explanatory constitution, just as some of the lumps that do not satisfy it may share their fundamental constitution with lumps that do. Chemists especially, says Locke, "are often, by sad experience, convinced of [this], when they, sometimes in vain, seek for the same qualities in one parcel of sulphur, antimony, or vitriol, which they have found in others. For though they are bodies of the same species, having the same nominal essence, under the same name; yet they do often, upon severe ways of examination, betray qualities so different one from another, as to frustrate the expectation and labour of very wary chemists" (iii,vi,8).

In short, "our distinguishing substances into species by names, is not at all founded on their real essences; nor can we pretend to range, and determine them exactly into species, according to internal essential differences" (iii,vi,20). Yet the Aristotelian way of thinking of essence fundamentally takes our ordinary classifications for granted. Thus it is, at bottom, more a systematization of nominal essence than a theory of real essence. "All the great business of genera and species, and their essences, amounts to no more but this, that men making abstract ideas, and settling them in their minds, with names annexed to them, do thereby enable themselves to consider things, and

---

both of that real constitution in which they are all founded; and also how they flow from it" (iv,vi,9–10).

[33] Though Locke, in a fascinating passage, contends that we use many of our general terms with the *intention* that they function like that: "there is scarce anybody in the use of these words but often supposes each of those names to stand for a thing having the real essence" (iii,x,18; see §§17–19). There is an excellent discussion of Locke's distinction between real essence and nominal essence in J. L. Mackie, *Problems from Locke*, pp. 85–100.

discourse of them, as it were in bundles, for the easier and readier improvement, and communication of their knowledge" (iii,iii,20).

Locke's skepticism concerning the possibility of a true *scientia* of nature was founded, thus, on a certain model of what such a *scientia* would be like, coupled with the judgment that our position in nature makes it impossible for us to acquire the concepts necessary for such a *scientia*. With three centuries of natural philosophy between us and him, we can now see both how prescient he was and how mistaken. Our natural scientists have followed exactly the course which Locke projected as required: They have probed the microstructure of physical reality. By doing so, they have gone beyond generalizations to the discovery of laws. And though the use of the hypothetico-deductive method has been indispensable to this development, developments in technology, enabling us to perceive the remote and the minute, have likewise played an important role. Locke's intimations on this score were correct, while at the same time, his prediction that the necessary technology would remain forever unattainable has proved mistaken to an amazing degree.

It must be added, though, that even if Locke had foreseen that the new natural philosophy would succeed in discovering the microstructural natures of substances, he would still have insisted that such observation-based science does not measure up to the ideal of *scientia*. We can only believe, not know, that water, say, has the microstructural nature that our science assigns to it. This parallels Locke's insistence that it is pure and not applied mathematics which is a *scientia*, and that it is pure and not applied morality which can be brought to the point of being a *scientia*. Though we can "see" that murder deserves death, says Locke, we can only believe that this action before us is murder.

There was another point on which Locke proved prescient. Ernan McMullin, in his fine essay "The Shaping of Scientific Rationality: Construction and Constraint," observes that three ideals have weaved in and out of the history of what we now call science: the ideal of prediction, the ideal of explanation, and the ideal of high epistemic status for scientific claims; and he points out how seldom a body of learning has satisfied all three of these ideals simultaneously.[34] Locke saw the ideals as falling apart. He envisaged an explanatory science in which the claims were certain. But he thought that we human beings had to be content with something else, namely, "natural philosophy,"

[34] In Ernan McMullin (ed.), *Construction and Constraint* (Notre Dame, University of Notre Dame Press, 1988).

which consists of belief rather than knowledge. [S]peculative science,"
says Locke, "I imagine we have none, and perhaps, I may think I
have reason to say, we never shall be able to make a science of it. The
works of nature are contrived by a wisdom, and operate by ways too
far surpassing our faculties to discover, or capacities to conceive, for us
ever to be able to reduce them into a science" (*Education*, §190; *Works*,
VIII,182). Yet Locke did not confine himself to describing the new
natural philosophy coming to birth in his day as yielding generalizations;
now and then, especially when he has the role of hypotheses in mind,
he speaks of it as offering *explanations* (IV,xii,13; xvi,12). He does not
discuss what sort of explanations these might be. Since he appears to
have thought of the relevant hypotheses as hypotheses concerning the
essences of things, he may have thought of the new natural philosophy
as offering explanations only in the sense that it yields *beliefs* (not
knowledge) concerning the ontological structure of nature. Or did he
have some inkling of the fact that the explanations were of a different
sort, *causal* rather than *ontological*? Locke lived on the threshold of the
emergence of a new view of nature, according to which nature has not
just an ontological, but a causal, structure; and of the emergence of a
new view of science, according to which it is the business of science to
discover that causal structure. Did Locke have some glimpse of what
lay on the other side of that threshold? It is hard to tell.

Knowledge, then, is short and scanty; the new natural philosophy,
impressive though it be, is nothing to the contrary. Even if it should
prove to give us well-grounded beliefs concerning the essential
natures of things, it is at best *belief* that it offers us, opinion, not
knowledge. That, though, is sufficient for the life that our Creator
intended for us:

The infinite wise contriver of us, and all things about us, hath fitted our
senses, faculties, and organs, to the conveniences of life, and the business we
have to do here. We are able, by our senses, to know, and distinguish things;
and to examine them so far, as to apply them to our uses, and several ways to
accomodate the exigences of this life. We have insight enough into their
admirable contrivances, and wonderful effects, to admire, and magnify the
wisdom, power, and goodness of their Author . . . But it appears not that God
intended, we should have a perfect, clear, and adequate knowledge of them:
that perhaps is not in the comprehension of any finite being. We are
furnished with faculties (dull and weak as they are) to discover enough in the
creatures, to lead us to the knowledge of the Creator, and the knowledge of
our duty; and we are fitted well enough with abilities, to provide for the
conveniences of living: these are our business in this world. (II,xxiii,12)

(c) The nature of knowledge

We have been discussing Locke's views as to the scope of knowledge. Let us now consider its nature. Knowledge, says Locke in the formula opening Book IV, is *perception*. Obviously he is using perception metaphorically. To what does his metaphor point? Locke doesn't explicitly tell us. I propose that we try to understand what he was getting at by considering it from two different perspectives, from the perspective of the philosophical tradition, and from the perspective of ordinary speech.

Prominent in the Western philosophical tradition has been its identification of, and attention to, a certain experience which sometimes accompanies (or causes) coming to know or believe propositions of certain sorts. One may believe, say, *that one of the cups was broken* because someone one trusts tells one so. Or one may believe *that this cup is broken* because one sees that it is. Or I may believe *that I broke one of the cups* because I remember that I did. But suppose one comes to believe *that green is a color*, or *that all bachelors are unmarried*, or *that 1 + 1 = 2*, or *that either it is raining outside or it is not the case that it is*. Any one of these might be told one by someone. But even if it were, even if one did not think of it on one's own, when one fully understands it one does not believe it on the speaker's sayso. One has the experience of "just knowing it," straight-off, as soon as one grasps it. That experience is significantly different from what one has when believing something on someone's sayso, or because of perception. Again, halfway into one's highschool class on plane geometry one proves the Pythagorean Theorem. One's elder brother may earlier have mentioned the premises, and one may have believed on his sayso that the theorem follows from those. But now one has the experience of "just knowing" that it does.

I, for myself, find it difficult to imagine an adult well-formed human being who has not had this experience of "just knowing." Nonetheless, it must be acknowledged that the experience is by no means *familiar* to all, in the sense that all have isolated the experience for attention. Whole cultures, so far as one can tell, have made nothing of it. The culture of the ancient Hebrews, as it comes to expression in the Hebrew Scriptures, is an example.

The use of visual metaphors to describe this experience of "just knowing" has been standard within the philosophical tradition, and outside it as well, since the time of Greek antiquity: I just *see* that green is a color, I just *see* that the theorem follows, and so on. Whether there is some natural propriety about this metaphor, or whether we are all shaped by our cultural inheritance, is perhaps now impossible to tell. In any case, the metaphor is not innocuous. It invites us to think that in such experiences we become aware of something – rather in the way in which, when we see a cow before us, we become aware of the cow.

What might it be that one "sees" in cases of the sort I have mentioned? The classic answer is that one is aware that one and another proposition is necessarily true, and that certain relations among propositions are necessary. And the experience itself, it has been said, marks the activation of our shared human faculty for such awareness. It is to this faculty that the name *Reason* has traditionally been attached.

Assuming the propriety of the ocular metaphor, to have the "just knowing" experience is to *see that* such-and-such a proposition is true (and cannot be false) or *that* one proposition follows from another. Or sometimes the metaphor is not the metaphor of *seeing that* some proposition is true, but the metaphor of *seeing* some fact. Whether it be propositions or facts, whether it be seeing-that or seeing, sometimes it is said that the seeing occurs because Reason illumines the thing seen; Descartes was given to this way of speaking. Sometimes, on the contrary, it is said that the seeing occurs because the thing seen is itself luminous. Locke was partial to speaking in this way. Either way, whether Reason lights up what we see so that we can see it, or whether the thing itself is luminous so that by Reason we can see it, it has often been said or suggested that there is an unavoidability about believing what one "sees." When describing intuitive knowledge Locke says that "This part of knowledge is irresistible, and like the bright sunshine, forces itself immediately to be perceived, as soon as ever the mind turns its view that way; and leaves no room for hesitation, doubt, or examination, but the mind is presently filled with the clear light of it" (IV,ii,1).

In short, Locke was standing within a long – and in his own day, very much alive – philosophical tradition of thought and metaphor when he spoke of *perceiving*: "perceiving" what I have been calling "facts," what he calls "agreements and disagreements." He does not defend the propriety of this metaphor; he assumes it. The debates concerning intuitive knowledge into which he enters are not debates concerning the reality of intuition but debates concerning the necessity and utility of formal logic, specifically, syllogistic logic, for putting our faculty of intuition to work in the acquisition of knowledge. He assumes, along with the high medievals, that here and there we human beings have unobstructed openness to reality – though were a medieval to learn of Locke's view as to the ontological status of the reality to which we are open, he would feel profoundly claustrophobic. Certain facts are right there before the mind's eye. We *"perceive"* them. Such perception is knowledge. "Knowing is seeing" (*Conduct* §24; *Works* II,366); knowledge is "vision" (Fourth Letter for Toleration; *Works* V,558). Locke speaks on occasion of the faculties of knowledge. Such faculties are not productive faculties but *modes of openness* to (certain of) the facts of reality. He speaks of "the eye or the perceptive faculty of the mind" (IV,xvii,4). In the cold winter, if a man looks out at the earth "he cannot help seeing it white and hoary." So too, "our will hath no power to determine the knowledge of the mind one way or other; that is done only by the objects themselves . . . the mind cannot but receive those ideas which are presented by them"(IV,xiii,2). "[I]n bare naked perception, the mind is, for the most part, only passive; and what it perceives, it cannot avoid perceiving" (II,ix,1). In the case of belief, "that which makes me believe, is something extraneous to the thing I believe" (IV,xv,3). In the case of knowledge, it is the very fact itself. "What I see I know to be so, by the evidence of the thing itself" (IV,xix,10).[35]

This presumed capacity of ours for "perceiving" facts is of fundamental importance for Locke's vision as a whole. In his *Conduct of the Understanding* Locke asks what "a novice, an inquirer, a stranger" should do when faced with the question of what to believe. "I answer," he says, "use his eyes. There is a correspondence in

---

[35] Leibniz, in *New Essays*, p. 134, says that he "would prefer to distinguish between *perception* and *being aware*. For instance, a perception of light or colour of which we are aware is made up of many minute perceptions of which we are unaware; and a noise which we perceive but do not attend to is brought within reach of our awareness by a tiny increase or addition. If the previous noise had no effect on the soul, this minute addition would have none either, nor would the total." Locke interprets the phenomena here differently. Though awareness is not, on his view, a condition of sensory stimulation, it is a condition of perception; and in turn, it appears to be his view that there are no unperceived ideas: "A sufficient impulse there may be on the organ; but it not reaching the observation of the mind, there follows no perception . . . Want of sensation in this case, is not through any defect in the organ, or that the man's ears are less affected, than at other times, when he does hear: but that which uses to produce the idea, though conveyed in by the usual organ, not being taken notice of in the understanding, and so imprinting no idea on the mind, there follows no sensation. So that wherever there is sense, or perception, there some idea is actually produced, and present in the understanding" (II,ix,4).

things, and agreement and disagreement in ideas, discernible in very different degrees, and there are eyes in men to see them, if they please (§33; *Works* ii,379). When called to do our best in the governance of our beliefs we are to set ungrounded tradition aside and get down to the things themselves.[36] A person should pursue truth "by inquiring directly into the nature of the thing itself, without minding the opinions of others, or troubling himself with their questions or disputes about it"(*Conduct*, §35; *Works* ii,382).

A fundamental concept in the epistemological tradition which Locke inherited was that of *self-evidence*. A proposition was said to be self-evident *per se* just in case no one could grasp it without seeing it to be true and without being compelled to believe it; and a proposition was said to be self-evident *to a person S* just in case it was self-evident *per se* and was grasped by S. It was characteristically assumed that only necessarily true propositions fit the concept of self-evident *per se*. All the examples I have given thus far of things which one can "just know" to be true would be regarded by the tradition as examples of propositions which are self-evident *per se*.

Locke also speaks of self-evidence. And he says about propositions which he calls "self-evident" what the tradition said about those it called "self-evident": "all such affirmations, and negations, are made without any possibility of doubt, uncertainty, or hesitation, and must necessarily be assented to, as soon as understood" (iv,vii,4). Nonetheless, Locke is not working with the traditional concept. That is clear both from the fact that he cites as examples of self-evident propositions ones that no one from the tradition would have cited as examples – for example, *that I exist* and *that I have this idea*; and from his official

---

[36] Cf. this passage from Locke's near contemporary, John Wilkins: "It behooves everyone in the search for truth, always to preserve a philosophical liberty, not to be enslav'd to the opinion of any man as to think whatever he says to be infallible. We must labour to find out what things are in themselves, by our own experience, and a thorough examination of their natures, not what another says of them." Quoted by Barbara J. Shapiro, *Probability and Certainty in Seventeenth-Century England* (Princeton, Princeton University Press, 1983), p. 64. The following passage from Locke, *Essay* i,iv,23, makes the point by referring (rather smugly) to his own practice: "This I am certain, I have not made it my business, either to quit, or follow any authority in the ensuing discourse: truth has been my only aim; and wherever that has appeared to lead, my thoughts have impartially followed, without minding, whether the footsteps of any other lay that way, or not. Not that I want a due respect to other men's opinions; but after all, the greatest reverence is due to truth; and, I hope, it will not be thought arrogance to say, that, perhaps, we should make greater progress in the discovery of rational and contemplative knowledge, if we sought it in the fountain, in the consideration of things themselves and made use rather of our own thoughts than other men's to find it. For, I think, we may as rationally hope to see with other men's eyes, as to know by other men's understandings."

definition of "self-evidence." He officially introduces "self-evident" not to pick out certain propositions but to pick out a kind of knowledge. Officially, "self-evident" is for him a synonym of "intuitive" and "immediate";[37] its contrast is "demonstrative": "Knowledge . . . consists in the perception of the agreement or disagreement of ideas: Now where that agreement or disagreement is perceived immediately by itself, without the intervention or help of any other, there our knowledge is self-evident" (IV,vii,2).[38]

Locke's use of the locution "intuitive perception" gives one the feeling of walking out onto quicksand. The traditional notion of a self-evident proposition seems relatively clear. But if the scope of "perception" is thought of as going beyond the self-evident, how far beyond does it go? In what direction? We speak, in ordinary life, of *seeing* that it is almost twelve o'clock and of *seeing* that the leaves are beginning to turn their fall colors. Locke would never cite either of these as examples of what he has in mind by "perception." Why not? What are the limits of the proper use of the word "perception" in the metaphorical sense Locke intends? How do we discern those limits? What *is* that metaphorical sense?

Reflecting on the philosophical tradition in which Locke stands probably helps less here than attending to ordinary speech – though it is by no means irrelevant that, for example, Aquinas spoke of what is "evident to the senses," and that Descartes spoke of our faculty of intuition as enabling us to know not only certain necessary truths but propositions concerning our immediate states of consciousness. By no means did the tradition treat the scope of intuition, and of what can be evident to us, as confined to self-evident necessary truths.[39]

---

[37] This then accounts for the fact that in his Second Letter to Stillingfleet, Locke says that all knowledge (and certainty) require self-evident propositions: "that there is any knowledge, without self-evident propositions, I am . . . far from denying" (*Works* III,370); "I make self-evident propositions necessary to certainty, and found all certainty only in them" (*ibid.*, 421).

[38] There are a few passages in which it would appear that Locke is thinking of "perception" as immediate, and of propositions as self-evident, and holding that immediate "perception" of facts is the ground of assent to self-evident propositions: "Of such agreement, or disagreement as this, the mind has an immediate perception but in very few of them. And therefore in this sort, we have but very little intuitive knowledge: nor are there to be found very many propositions that are self-evident" (IV,vii,5). But he is not consistent on this.

[39] Leibniz has a very interesting discussion of intuition in *New Essays*, pp. 361–7, and 434. He says that truths known by intuition are either "truths of reason" or "truths of fact." What they have in common, he says, is that "we cannot prove them by anything more certain" (p. 367). And he adds that "the immediate awareness of our existence and of our thoughts provides us with the first a posteriori truths or truths of fact, i.e., *the first experiences*; while identical propositions embody the first *a priori* truths or truths of reason, i.e., *the first illuminations*. Neither kind admits of proof, and each can be called 'immediate' – the former

When Locke speaks of "perception," we should always hear it as coming with the adjective "direct" or "immediate": "direct perception," "immediate perception." Later we shall consider how that fits with what he says about demonstrative knowledge; but Locke wishes with the word "perception" to single out the phenomenon of *immediate* awareness. Sometimes our awareness of something is *mediated* by our awareness of something else. My awareness of what is going on in the House of Representatives in Washington is mediated by my awareness of images on my television screen; and my awareness of that in turn is mediated by my awareness of the sensations and images I am having as I look at my television screen. But what mediates my awareness of my sensations and images? It seems that nothing at all does; I am *directly* aware of them, *immediately*, *without mediation*. I suggest that it is this notion of *direct*, or *immediate*, awareness that Locke has in mind when he speaks of "perception," and when he cites examples of things that fall within the scope of "perception." He might make mistakes in citing examples; some of what he cites as falling within the scope of this phenomenon may not in fact do so. But almost always it helps to understand his moves if one thinks of this as what he is doing.[40] Of course, ever since Kant and Hegel, the claim that we human beings have direct awareness of certain facts has been rejected by a good many philosophers. Especially in recent years, the phrase of Wilfred Sellars, "the myth of the given,"[41] has been widely bandied about as if it expressed an unquestionable truth, especially by those whose official position is that there are no unquestionable truths. Such are the ironies of philosophy! But that the myth in the region is not the myth of the given but the myth that the given is a myth has recently been cogently argued by William Alston in his essay "What's Wrong with Immediate Knowledge."[42]

It is time to approach Locke's understanding of the nature of knowledge from a second angle, as he himself does. Knowledge, says Locke, is "*perception*." Just as often, and just as emphatically, he says that a hallmark of knowledge is *certainty*. For example, in speaking of

---

because nothing comes between the understanding and its object, the latter because nothing comes between the subject and the predicate" (p. 434).

[40] For a very different account of Locke's intuitionism, one which makes no use of the distinction between immediate and non-immediate awareness, see Ayers, *Locke: Volume I. Epistemology*, chap. 29.

[41] See especially Sellars' essay "Empiricism and the Philosophy of Mind," in his collection *Science, Perception, and Reality* (New York, Humanities Press, 1963).

[42] Now reprinted in Alston's collection, *Epistemic Justification: Essays in the Theory of Knowledge* (Ithaca, Cornell University Press, 1989).

our knowledge of our own existence he says that we perceive it "so plainly" but also "so certainly" that it neither needs, nor is capable of, any proof. This knowledge, he says, comes "not short of the highest degree of certainty" (iv,ix,3). And as to his general position, he remarks in his letter to Edward Stillingfleet, Bishop of Worcester, that with me to know, and to be certain, is the same thing; what I know, that I am certain of; and what I am certain of, that I know. What reaches to knowledge, I think may be called certainty; and what comes short of certainty, I think cannot be called knowledge" (*Works* iii,145).

It was not, on Locke's view, a coincidence that certainty is a sign of knowledge; "perception" *accounts for* certainty. Certainty, he says in one place, is "but the perception of the agreement, or disagreement of our ideas" (iv,iv,7). And in another, "the knowledge of the certainty of principles, as well as of all other truths, depends only upon the perception, we have, of the agreement, or disagreement of our ideas" (iv,xii,6).[43] And to the suggestion, made by Stillingfleet, that certainty requires that the ideas whose agreement or disagreement is perceived be clear and distinct, Locke insists that if one perceives some agreement or disagreement among ideas, then certainty is present *whether or not those ideas be clear and distinct*; I have not, he says, "placed certainty only in clear and distinct ideas, but in the clear and visible connection of any of our ideas, be those ideas what they will" (*Works* iii,29; Locke makes the point repeatedly, e.g., iii,42,56,123).

To explain his point, Locke observes that if ideas "are clear and distinct enough to be capable of having their agreement or disagreement with any other idea perceived, so far they are capable of affording us knowledge, though at the same time they are so obscure and confused, as that there are other ideas with which we can by no means so compare them, as to perceive their agreement or disagreement with them . . . [A]n idea, which cannot be well compared with some ideas, from which it is not clearly and sufficiently distinguishable, is yet capable of having its agreement or disagreement perceived with some other idea, with which it is not so confounded, but that it may be compared" (*Works* iii,240–1). For example: Given any idea of which one is aware, be it clear and distinct or not, one will be capable of perceiving the non-identity of that idea with certain others of one's

---

[43] The point is repeated often in Locke's discussion with Stillingfleet; for example: "For I place certainty where I think everybody will find it, and nowhere else, viz. in the perception of the agreement or disagreement of ideas" (*Works* iii,57).

ideas (III,221). In short, "an obscure or confused idea, i.e. that is not perfectly clear and distinct in all its parts, may be compared with another in that part of it, which is clear and distinct" (III,390).[44]

But what does Locke mean by certainty? Well, he speaks of "perception" as coming in *degrees* of certainty; and sometimes he clearly equates that with the objects of "perception" being more or less *evident to* the knower (for example, IV,ix,3). He also, though, speaks about an *infallible* perception (IV,ix,3); and that introduces a different note.[45] Furthermore, he speaks about beliefs as coming in degrees of probability; and he says in one place that probabilities of the highest degree "rise so near to certainty that . . . we make little or no difference between them and certain knowledge: Our belief thus grounded, rises to assurance" (IV,xvi,6). The picture which comes to mind is that of a continuum on which the highest point is the certainty (evidence) of intuitive knowledge, below that, the lesser certainty of demonstrative knowledge, below that, the yet lesser certainty of what he calls sensitive knowledge; and then probability and improbability of various degrees: "there being degrees herein, from the very neighbourhood of certainty and demonstration, quite down to improbability and unlikeliness, even to the confines of impossibility" (IV,xv,2).

In speaking of degrees of certitude and probability Locke was both reflecting and participating in the wide-ranging discussions about certainty which had been taking place in England, among theologians and scientists, for some fifty years before he wrote his *Essay*.[46] The main contributors to the discussions were members of the Royal Society and friends of members, many of them personal friends or acquaintances of Locke. There were differences in terminology among participants in the discussion, and differences in definitions

[44] To make his point yet more clear, Locke offers an interesting analogy: "there is no object which the eye sees, that can be said to be perfectly obscure, for then it would not be seen at all; nor perfectly confused, for then it could not be distinguished from any other, no not from a clearer. For example, one sees in the dusk something of that shape and size, that a man in that degree of light and distance would appear. This is not so obscure, that he sees nothing; nor so confused, that he cannot distinguish it from a steeple or a star; but is so obscure, that he cannot, though it be a statue, distinguish it from a man; and therefore in regard of a man, it can produce no clear and distinct knowledge: but yet as obscure and confused an idea as it is, this hinders not but that there may many propositions be made concerning it, as particularly that it exists, of the truth of which we may be certain" (*Works*, III,242).

[45] Cf. IV,xv,5: "intuitive evidence, which infallibly determines the understanding, and produces certain knowledge."

[46] See especially Henry G. van Leeuwen, *The Problem of Certainty in English Thought: 1630–1690* (The Hague, Martinus Nijhoff, 1963); and Shapiro, *Probability and Certainty*.

offered of common items of terminology; yet the degree of consensus in conviction was remarkable. All agreed that there are *degrees* of certainty and probability; and all attempted to pick out gamuts of those degrees. All agreed as well that a given proposition might enjoy one degree of certitude/incertitude for one person and quite a different degree for another person, or for the same person at a different time (cf. *Essay* iv,xv,1). Likewise they agreed that some propositions are such that it is impossible for anyone to assent to them with the highest degree of certitude. On this last point, they agreed with Aristotle that different subject-matters enjoy different maximal degrees of certainty, and that those working with a subject-matter whose maximal degree of certainty is less than the highest should be satisfied with that. Locke himself ringingly affirms the principle (i,i,5; and iv,xi,10). Biological propositions cannot be entertained with the same degree of certitude as mathematical ones; the wise biologist will rest content with attaining the highest degree of certitude of which his or her subject-matter is capable.

But back to Locke: *Of what* was the continuum, which he apparently had in mind, a continuum? Of certainty and probability, naturally. But what is the category of the entities which have a place on the continuum? And how are we to think of that determinable property of probability/certainty which comes in varying degrees? As we shall shortly see, Locke and his cohorts cannot be understood as equating degrees of probability/certainty with degrees of *confidence in* propositions. This latter notion was present in their thought – indeed, it was prominent there; but they needed it at a different point.

One gets the impression that the participants in the discussion were themselves not entirely clear on the matter; indeed, one gets the impression that they were *themselves of the conviction* that they were not entirely clear. Groping for something, they were never confident that they had gotten firm hold of that for which they were groping. The same is true for Locke. So let me propose an interpretation – or more strictly, a "rational reconstruction" – which, though not compelled by what he says, nonetheless develops certain clues in his text and is compatible with his thought overall.

Locke, as we have seen, insists that knowledge is an act or state of mind fundamentally different from belief or assent. Knowledge, which he connects with certitude, is perceiving some fact. Believing and assenting, which he typically connects with probability, is *taking* or *presuming* some proposition to be true. Nonetheless, Locke often speaks of the *assent* which accompanies knowledge. (See especially the chapter on Maxims, *Essay* iv,vii.) Though he resists identifying the knowing with the assenting, insisting on identifying it rather with the "perceiving," yet he acknowledges that when one "sees" a fact, one typically also assents to the corresponding proposition. This suggests that it is *assentings* and *believings* which Locke is tacitly thinking of as coming in varying degrees of certainty and probability.

I shall interpret Locke along these lines; but it is worth taking a moment to notice some mistakes and incoherences in this way of thinking. Whereas believing is an enduring mental *state*, assenting and judging are mental *acts*. (Locke says that the faculty of judgment, "when it is exercised immediately about things, is called *judgment*; when about truths delivered in words, is most commonly called *assent* or *dissent*" [iv,xiv,3]. But this distinction falls from view in the course of his discussion.) Each of us at any moment *believes* a multitude of propositions not then present before his or her mind. By contrast, to *assent to* some proposition, or *judge* it to be true, one must have it before the mind. Thus belief is not to be identified with assent. Locke's official explanation of belief as *taking to be true* seems better than his equation of belief with assent and judgment; for it does seem that each of us, at any moment, takes many things to be true which are not then present before his or her mind. On the other hand, it is plausible also to think of assent as *taking to be true*. The phrase "taking to be true" is ambiguous as between state and act.

Nowadays the distinction I have made between the state of belief and the act of assent would often be made by speaking of dispositional beliefs and occurrent beliefs. But this is a most infelicitous way of making the distinction. For one thing, it is not at all clear that the state of believing is a disposition; in any case, no one has yet succeeded in saying what it is a disposition to do or be. And secondly, there are no beliefs at all which are occurrences. Of course, one can dwell on some proposition which one believes: have it before the mind. But the *having before the mind* is not to be identified with believing it. The picture of a disposition which can be activated, with the word "belief" sometimes referring to the disposition and sometimes to what emerges from its activation, is all wrong.

Locke's thinking of knowledge as *evoking* assent, and thus of assent as the accompaniment of knowledge, will also not do. For knowledge, like belief, is a state, not an act – a point which Locke himself is forced to concede when discussing memory, as we shall shortly see. We all know a multitude of things not presently before our minds. If knowledge were an act, then of course Locke would have been right in typically picking out an act such as assent, rather than a state such as belief, as its accompaniment. But knowledge is not an act, neither the act of "perceiving" nor any other.

Whatever be the incoherences, though, I propose interpreting Locke as holding or assuming that *assentings* and *believings* are the bearers of that property which comes in varying degrees of probability and certainty. Perhaps here is the place to remark that Locke also held that propositions are bearers of probabilities; he speaks of a "proposition in itself [being] more or less probable" (IV,xv,6) and of "the probability of the thing" (IV,xv,1). Later we shall see how this recognition enters into his thought. And not only does he speak, as I have already indicated, of placing different levels of confidence in propositions; sometimes he quite clearly uses "more certain of" as a synonym of "more confident of." Thus we have the confusing situation that sometimes, in speaking of degrees of certainty and probability, Locke has in mind degrees of truth-likelihood of believings. Sometimes he has in mind degrees of confidence of believings. And sometimes he has in mind a property of propositions. Nonetheless, perhaps it is possible to penetrate beneath the confusing terminology and catch a glimpse of the pattern of his thought. Here our concern is what he meant in saying, of believings (and assentings), that they have a certain degree of *certainty* or *probability*.

The most he ever says by way of explanation is that probability is likeliness to be true (IV,xv,3). But perhaps this quick remark, when put together with his assumption that one person's believing of a certain proposition may have a different degree of probability or certainty from another person's believing of the same proposition, provides us with the clue we need to understand how he was thinking. Locke assumes – and plausibly so – that beliefs can be held in different ways. I believe one proposition on someone's sayso; another I believe because a certain perceptual experience has evoked it in me; another I believe because it is a necessary truth which I "see" to be true; yet another I believe because it ascribes a state of consciousness to me of which I am directly aware; and so on. Now add to this another conviction of Locke's; namely, that some ways of coming to believe and some ways of sustaining belief can be held in a variety of ways. I suggest that, in the light of all this, it seems not unlikely that Locke was thinking of the degree of probability

or certainty of a believing as determined by the relative reliability of
that way of forming or sustaining beliefs of which the believing in
question is an instance.[47] I emphasize, though, that this speculation
remains just that – a *speculation*.

Even this speculation does not address the fact that Locke speaks
of certainty itself as coming in degrees. What might he have had in
mind? One possibility, of course, is that he was not thinking of
certainty as a point of maximal reliability but as a gamut of
extremely high reliability. Here and there one comes across a
remark which makes one think that that was what he had in mind.
More often, though, his notion of degrees of certainty seems to have
nothing at all to do directly with truth-likelihood. It has to do
instead with the fact, as Locke sees it, that some of the things of
which we are directly aware are perceived by us more clearly than
others. For example, in his discussion of knowledge of our own
existence, Locke says that "nothing can be more evident to us"
(IV,ix,3). And in another passage he remarks that "The different
clearness of our knowledge seems to me to lie in the different way of
perception, the mind has of the agreement, or disagreement of any
of its ideas . . . 'Tis on this intuition, that depends all the certainty
and evidence of all our knowledge" (IV,ii,1). On this way of
thinking, among those believings which are certain, as determined
by the reliability of their mode of formation or sustenance, some will
be evoked by a clearer "perception" than others; they will, in that
respect, be *more* certain.

In beginning this discussion on certainty (and probability), I
remarked that Locke's thought was representative of a widespread
pattern of thought emerging in England at the time, especially among
members and friends of members of the Royal Society. Let me now
close the discussion by observing that anyone coming to the writings
of Locke and other members of the Royal Society from twentieth-
century analytic epistemology will be struck by the similarity
between their thought and that of the present-day epistemologist
Roderick Chisholm. Central to the thought of both is the endeavor to
differentiate and pick out gradations in the epistemic status of beliefs.

[47] Rather formidable difficulties will confront anyone who tries to work out this line of thought;
for example: How are modes of belief-formation and modes of belief-sustenance to be
individuated? How do we tell to which mode to assign a given believing? And what is
reliability? Exactly such difficulties have been confronted and dealt with by those who have
developed reliability theories of justification and of knowledge. See, for example, Alvin
Goldman, *Epistemology and Cognition* (Cambridge, Mass., Harvard University Press, 1986).

Indeed, much of Chisholm's terminology is even the same as theirs.[48] Using the undefined concept of *more reasonable than*, Chisholm suggests that a proposition's being *beyond reasonable doubt* for a person consists in its being more reasonable for that person to accept it than to withhold judgment on it; and he suggests that a proposition's being *certain* for someone consists in its being beyond reasonable doubt for that person and in there being nothing more reasonable for that person to accept than this. Chisholm has always found it difficult to define the *evident*; he thinks of it, though, as a degree (or range of degrees) down from the certain, and argues that evidence is enough for knowledge (provided one adds truth, and perhaps some additional minor conditions). Certitude, as he defines it, is not required for knowledge. As an example, he would say that as I write these words it is *evident* for me, though not *certain*, that there is a piece of paper before me. Since what is evident is in this case also true, he would say that I know this.

This is strikingly similar to what Locke and his associates said. It even seems likely that the range which Locke's associates (though not Locke himself) regularly called "moral certitude" is the same as that which Chisholm calls "beyond reasonable doubt." There is this difference, though: Chisholm explains his continuum as a continuum of degrees of entitlement (aptness for fulfilling one's intellectual responsibilities); Locke, on my interpretation, thinks of his as a continuum of truth-likelihood. Different ways of forming and holding beliefs differ with respect to the likelihood that the beliefs thus formed or held are true. And though Locke thought that there were degrees of certitude and degrees of probability in believings, and though he held that the highest degree of probability adjoins the lowest degree of certitude, nonetheless, unlike most of his associates, and certainly unlike Chisholm, he operated with just one major divide in the positive half of the continuum – that between certainty and probability. As to the location of knowledge on the continuum, Locke held, as we have already seen, that one knows something if and only if it is certain for one.

Our topic is the nature of knowledge, as that was understood by Locke. We have seen that Locke thinks of knowledge both as awareness of facts and as certain. But if my interpretation of Lockian certitude is correct, there is at the very least tension between Locke's official account of the nature of knowledge as "perception" and his claim that an identifying mark of knowledge is certitude. Is knowledge "perception" of facts, as Locke's official account claims; or is

[48] See Roderick Chisholm, *Theory of Knowledge*, 2nd ed. (Englewood Cliffs, Prentice-Hall, 1977), chap. 1.

knowledge a species of believings, as implied by his claim that knowledge is certain?

If awareness of facts always accompanied and was accompanied by believings which are certain, the tension would be purely verbal. Though Locke's officially stated preference would be to speak only of *awareness of facts* as knowledge, an implication of his ascription of certitude to knowledge would be that *those believings of propositions which accompany such awareness* are knowledge. But the tension proves much more than verbal; awareness and certainty acquire lives of their own, as it were. In chapter xx of Book iv of the *Essay* Locke offers examples of awarenesses of facts which are not accompanied by any corresponding believings (this is one construal of the import of his examples); and in his discussion of memory in chapter i of Book iv he offers examples of believings which, though certain, are not the accompaniments of awarenesses. Given this, Locke can no longer say that insight is what accounts for certainty. He is thus confronted with an unwelcome choice: Will he cling to his official identification of knowledge with insight, and concede that insight is not always accompanied by belief and that belief may be certain without being the accompaniment of insight; or will he cling to his claim that a hallmark of knowledge is certitude, and grant that some believings are knowledge even though they are not the accompaniment of insight? Will he conclude that certainty outstrips knowledge or that knowledge outstrips insight?

It is clear how he chooses: Knowledge outstrips insight. This is clearest in his discussion of memory in *Essay* iv,i,8. Locke there contends that some of our rememberings constitute knowledge; more specifically, certain ways of remembering a fact that one once "perceived" count as knowledge of that fact. And he tacitly concedes that those cases of remembering which count as knowledge do not fit his official account of knowledge, since they are cases of knowing a fact (at some time) without "perceiving" it (at that time). He thinks of memory as storage; and certain storages of what was once perceived, though not themselves perceptions of that, are nonetheless knowledge of it. He calls the rememberings which are knowledge, *habitual* knowledge, distinguishing that from what he calls *actual* knowledge. Actual knowledge is that which is recognized in his official account of knowledge: the present view the mind has of the agreement, or disagreement of any of its ideas, or of the relation they have one to another (iv,1,8). But habitual knowledge, that is, memory knowledge, is something quite different:

A man is said to know any proposition, which having been once laid before his thoughts, he evidently perceived the agreement, or disagreement of the ideas whereof it consists; and so lodged it in his memory, that whenever that proposition comes again to be reflected on, he, without doubt or hesitation, embraces the right side, assents to, and is certain of the truth of it. This, I think, one may call *habitual knowledge*: And thus a man may be said to know all those truths, which are lodged in his memory, by a foregoing clear and full perception, whereof the mind is assured past doubt, as often as it has occasion to reflect on them. For our finite understanding being able to think, clearly and distinctly, but on one thing at once, if men had no knowledge of any more than what they actually thought on, they would all be very ignorant: And he that knew most, would know but one truth, that being all he was able to think on at one time. (IV,1,8)

Nowhere in this or any other passage does Locke attempt to treat memory knowledge as (a type of) "perceiving."

Locke assumes that for a case of remembering to count as knowledge, what is remembered must be a fact of which at some earlier time one had actual knowledge. But he is also assuming, conversely, that not all such rememberings are cases of knowledge. For a remembering of what one once knew to count as knowledge, the following must be true: *If one would now have the proposition actively in mind, then one would without doubt or hesitation embrace the right side, assent to, and be certain of it.*

Locke intends this formula to hold both for rememberings of what one once perceived intuitively and for rememberings of what one once perceived demonstratively. Concerning rememberings of the former sort, he goes beyond the common formula and offers this more specific one: A remembering of a fact once perceived intuitively counts as knowledge just in case, *if one would now have the corresponding proposition actively in mind, one would again actually "perceive" the fact.* Concerning rememberings of the latter sort, what he says is that one must not only find the fact remembered indubitable ("cannot doubt of the truth of it") but also remember "certainly, that [one] once perceived the demonstration" (IV,i,9).

Locke remarks that he once regarded rememberings of the latter sort, in which the demonstration is forgotten, as something less than knowledge: "In his adherence to a truth, where the demonstration, by which it was at first known, is forgot, though a man may be thought rather to believe his memory, than really to know, and this way of entertaining a truth seemed formerly to me like something between opinion and knowledge, a sort of assurance which exceeds bare belief, for that relies on the testimony of another; yet upon a due examination I find it comes not short of perfect certainty, and is in effect true knowledge" (IV,i,9). What made him change his mind, he says, was the realization that though the original proof may be forgotten, nonetheless the person who remembers has an alternative proof in hand:

That which is apt to mislead our first thoughts into a mistake in this matter is, that the agreement or disagreement of the ideas in this case is not perceived, as it was at first, by an actual view of all the intermediate ideas whereby the agreement or disagreement of those in the proposition was at first perceived; but by other intermediate ideas, that show the agreement or disagreement of the ideas contained in the proposition whose certainty we remember. (IV,i,9)

What is this alternative proof which is available to us? This: Suppose that a person knowingly remembers *that he once "perceived" P demonstratively.* Suppose further that he now "perceives" *that P is either necessarily true or necessarily false* (which P will be, so Locke assumes, if it was "perceived" demonstratively; and which the person will "perceive," if he knowingly remembers that he once "perceived" it demonstratively). Then the person will now "perceive" *that P is true.* And that constitutes his now knowing P:

He remembers, *i.e.* he knows (for remembrance is but the reviving of some past knowledge) that he was once certain of the truth of this proposition, that the three angles of a triangle are equal to two right ones. The immutability of the same relations between the same immutable things, is now the idea that shows him, that if the three angles of a triangle were once equal to two right ones, they will always be equal to two right ones. And hence he comes to be certain, that what was once true in the case is always true; what ideas once agreed will always agree; and consequently what he once knew to be true he will always know to be true, as long as he can remember that he once knew it. (IV,i,9)

The argument as it stands is fallacious. The only premise in the argument which the person presently "perceives" is the premise that P is either necessarily true or necessarily false;[49] obviously from that one cannot get to the "perception" that P is true. It's true that the person also has, as a premise, that he knowingly remembers that he once "perceived" P demonstratively. But that, it must be noticed, is different from "*perceiving*" that one once "perceived" P demonstratively; nowhere does Locke argue that to knowingly remember that one once

---

[49] If I am right in my contention that what Locke has in mind by sensitive knowledge and by knowledge of one's own existence also prove, on close scrutiny, to be cases of inferential knowledge, then even this premise will not always be available.

"perceived" something is *to "perceive"* that one once "perceived" that thing.

In any case, knowingly remembering is not "perceiving," nor does Locke contend that it is. He merely contends that it is in one way or another connected with "perceiving" – in one way, if it is a case of knowingly remembering what one once "perceived" intuitively, in another way, if it is a case of knowingly remembering what one once "perceived" demonstratively. Locke's analysis of memory knowledge does not fit, nor does he in his analysis contend that it fits, his official account of knowledge as "perception."[50] Certainty becomes the hallmark of knowledge; and thereby knowledge becomes a species of belief.

Does Locke's famous category of *sensitive knowledge* similarly outstrip his official account of knowledge? Is this also belief which is certain, rather than insight? The answer requires that we get clear on what phenomenon it is that Locke intends to single out as sensitive knowledge. And that is notoriously difficult. Let me offer an interpretation.

Michael Ayers, without so much as raising a question about the matter, takes sensitive knowledge, as Locke understands it, to be a species of immediate awareness; in this he follows most commentators. Nothing much hangs on the issue, so far as I can see; but I think the evidence tilts toward the conclusion that Locke thought of it as a species of inferential knowledge. In *Essay* IV,ii,14, he poses the issue as to whether there is such knowledge in this way: "There can be nothing more certain, than that the idea we receive from an external object is in our minds; this is intuitive knowledge. But whether there be anything more than barely that idea in our minds, whether we can thence certainly infer the existence of anything without us, which corresponds to that idea, is that, whereof some men think there may

---

[50] Stillingfleet already maintained, against Locke, that memory knowledge is not a case of "perceiving" agreements or disagreements among ideas. Locke's reply deletes all the subtleties of his discussion in the *Essay*: "The third sort of propositions that your lordship excludes are those whose certainty we know by remembrance: but in these two [kinds of memory?] the agreement or disagreement of the ideas contained in them is perceived; not always indeed, as it was at first, by an actual view of the connection of all the intermediate ideas, whereby the agreement or disagreement of those in the proposition was at first perceived; but by other intermediate ideas, that show the agreement or disagreement of the ideas contained in the proposition, whose certainty we remember" (*Works* III,234). Locke then repeats, with only very minor changes, the argument from the *Essay* which, he says, led him to the view that if one knowingly remembers having demonstrated P, one might genuinely know (i.e., "perceive") P even though one has forgotten the proof.

be a question made, because men may have such ideas in their minds, when no such things exists, no such object affects their senses." If we allow this passage to be determinative in our interpretation – and I don't see any good reason why we should not – sensitive knowledge consists of knowing, by inference from a premise concerning one of one's sensory images, that there exists something or other external which is the cause of that sensory image.[51] Such knowledge, says Locke, "extends as far as the present testimony of our senses, employed about particular objects, that do then affect them, and no farther" (IV,xi,9).

The premise for such an inference is a proposition to the effect that one's image has a certain peculiar property. Locke does not attempt to describe this property. He thinks that we are all acquainted with it; and he thinks that we are typically aware of its presence when it is present. "I ask anyone," says Locke, "whether he be not invincibly conscious to himself of a different perception, when he looks on the sun by day, and thinks on it by night; when he actually tastes wormwood, or smells a rose, or only thinks on that savour, or odour? We as plainly find the difference there is between any idea revived in our minds by our own memory, and actually coming into our minds by our senses, as we do between any two distinct ideas" (IV,ii,14; cf. IV,ii,5). "[T]here is nobody who doth not perceive the difference in himself" (IV,xi,3–9).

[51] There is one passage in his Second Letter to Stillingfleet in which Locke appears to say, quite aggressively, that this is the full extent of our sensitive knowledge: "Now the two ideas, that in this case are perceived to agree, and do thereby produce knowledge, are the idea of actual sensation (which is an action whereof I have a clear and distinct idea) and the idea of actual existence of something without me that causes that sensation. And what other certainty your lordship has by your senses of the existing of anything without you, but the perceived connection of those two ideas, I would gladly know" (*Works* III,360). But there are other passages in which he clearly indicates that we can know something about the primary qualities of that which is causing our sensation – though what exactly that is, is not clear. Clearly it was his thought that one can know that something with some primary quality or other is causing one's sensation: "as to the existence of bodily substances, I know by my senses that something extended, and solid, and figured does exist; for my senses are the utmost evidence and certainty I have of the existence of extended, solid, figured things. These modes being then known to exist by our senses, the existence of them (which I cannot conceive can subsist without something to support them) makes me see the connection of those ideas with a support, or, as it is called, a subject of inhesion, and so consequently the connection of that support (which cannot be nothing) with existence. And thus I come by a certainty of the existence of that something which is a support of those sensible modes" (*ibid.*, 29). But in another passage he quite clearly indicates that we can know more than this – that we can know, to some extent, *what are* the primary qualities of the object causing our sensation: "may I not be certain that a ball of ivory that lies before my eyes is not square? And is it not my sense of seeing, that makes me perceive the disagreement of that square figure to that round matter, which are the ideas expressed in that proposition?" (*ibid.*, 232).

Locke recognizes that a sensory image's having the quality in question does not *entail* that there exists something external of which the image is the effect. And he thinks that our believing the inferred conclusion will, even in the best case, have a certainty inferior to that of intuitive and demonstrative knowledge – thus inferior, for example, to our awareness that the image has that peculiar property.

But what is it that Locke has in mind here by *certainty*? He does, in a few passages, describe sensitive knowledge as a "perception of the mind, employed about the particular existence of finite beings without us" (iv,ii,14; cf. iv,iii,2 and iv,xi,1). But he does nothing to explain or defend this description of sensitive knowledge as "*perception.*" Mainly he makes use of the *high level of confidence* concept of certainty, and contends that both this inference is ineluctable for all of us and that we all accept the conclusion with a high level of confidence. "I think nobody can, in earnest, be so sceptical, as to be uncertain of the existence of those things which he sees and feels" (iv,xi,3); "this is too evident to be doubted" (iv,xi,4); "it is an assurance that deserves the name of knowledge" (iv,xi,3).

To this, Locke adds some reflections whose import seems to be that there is good reason to think that this ineluctable inference yielding highly confident belief is maximally reliable. The beliefs are certain: "But besides the assurance we have from our senses themselves, that they do not err in the information they give us, of the existence of things without us, when they are affected by them, we are farther confirmed in this assurance, by other concurrent reasons" (iv,xi,3). Locke then offers four arguments for the reliability of sensitive knowledge (§§4–7). But he wraps up the discussion by admitting either that these arguments are not entirely decisive, or that sensitive knowledge does *not* after all have maximal certainty – it is not entirely clear which of these he intends:

the certainty of things existing *in rerum natura*, when we have the testimony of our senses for it, is not only as great as our frame can attain to, but as our condition needs. For our faculties being suited not to the full extent of being, nor to a perfect, clear, comprehensive knowledge of things free from all doubt and scruple; but to the preservation of us, in whom they are; and accommodated to the use of life: they serve to our purpose well enough, if they will but give us certain notice of those things, which are convenient or inconvenient to us. For he that sees a candle burning, and hath experimented the force of its flame, by putting his finger in it, will little doubt, that this is something existing without him, which does him harm, and puts him to

great pain: which is assurance enough, when no man requires greater
certainty to govern his actions by, than what is as certain as his actions
themselves. And if our dreamer pleases to try, whether the glowing heat of a
glass furnace, be barely a wandering imagination in a drowsy man's fancy,
by putting his hand into it, he may perhaps be wakened into a certainty
greater than he could wish, that it is something more than bare imagination.
So that this evidence is as great, as we can desire, being as certain to us, as our
pleasure or pain . . . beyond which we have no concernment, either of
knowledge or being. (iv,xi,8)

A word should be said, lastly, about Locke's doctrine of *demonstrative*
knowledge. When you and I think of demonstrations, we think of the
role of insight therein – if we are willing to concede a role for insight –
as follows: One sees that the premises are true, and one sees that the
conclusion is entailed by the premises. We do not think of claiming
that one sees that the conclusion itself is true. Locke's description of
the role of insight in demonstrations is strikingly different. One comes
to "perceive" that the ideas in the conclusion do agree or disagree as
the proposition puts those ideas together or separates them; and one
comes to do so by "perceiving" how these ideas are connected to
intermediate ideas. Presumably Locke's thinking in this way was the
consequence of his having in mind the traditional analysis of a
syllogism as containing subject term, predicate term, *and middle term* –
or perhaps of his having in mind Euclidean geometry:

the three angles of a triangle cannot be brought at once, and be compared
with any other one, or two angles; and so of this the mind has no immediate,
no intuitive knowledge. In this case the mind is fain to find out some other
angles, to which the three angles of a triangle have an equality; and finding
those equal to two right ones, comes to know their equality to two right ones.

Those intervening ideas, which serve to shew the agreement of any two
others, are called proofs; and where the agreement or disagreement is by this
means plainly and clearly perceived, it is called demonstration, it being
shewn to the understanding, and the mind made see that it is so. (iv,ii,2-3)

In the case of relatively short proofs, it seems plausible to say that
we come to see the connection of the ideas in the conclusion by way of
seeing their connection to other, mediating, ideas. But in the case of
lengthy proofs, this seems most implausible. Is the situation not rather
that we have a sequence of awarenesses, stored in memory? Locke
does not disagree:

So that to make any thing a *demonstration*, it is necessary to perceive the
immediate agreement of the intervening ideas, whereby the agreement or

disagreement of the two ideas under examination . . . is found. This intuitive perception of the agreement or disagreement of the intermediate ideas, in each step and progression of the demonstration, must also be carried exactly in the mind, and a man must be sure that no part is left out; which because in long deductions, and the use of many proofs, the memory does not always so readily and exactly retain: therefore it comes to pass, that this is more imperfect than intuitive knowledge, and men embrace often falsehoods for demonstrations. (IV,ii,7)

But if demonstrations in many cases involve a *sequence* of "perceptions" stored in memory, why does Locke nonetheless speak of *"perceiving"* the agreement or disagreement of the ideas in the conclusion? Probably it was a fashion of speech rather than a point of doctrine. We too, on our way of thinking of proofs, often speak of *seeing* that the conclusion follows, even when close scrutiny would reveal that memory was indispensably involved. (It appears, though, that we would not, for *every* proof of whose cogency we are persuaded, speak of *seeing* that the conclusion follows; apparently what is required is a rather clear image or impression of the structure of the entire proof. If that is lacking, then, even though we are persuaded of the proof's cogency, we would not speak of *seeing* that the conclusion followed.)

Locke attributes the lesser certainty of demonstrative knowledge in part to the role of memory therein (IV,ii,7, quoted above),[52] and in part to the lesser clarity with which the agreement or disagreement of the ideas in the conclusion is "perceived." The evidence he cites for the latter seems curiously irrelevant, however:

This knowledge by intervening proofs, though it be certain, yet the evidence of it is not altogether so clear and bright, nor the assent so ready, as in intuitive knowledge. For though in demonstration, the mind does at least perceive the agreement or disagreement of the ideas it considers; yet 'tis not without pains and attention: There must be more than one transient view to find it. A steady application and pursuit is required to this discovery: and there must be a progression by steps and degrees. (IV,ii,4)

Locke does not explain why the need for "pains and attention" and for a "transient view" results in less clarity of "perception." Instead he closes his discussion with a striking metaphor: "like a face reflected by several mirrors one to another, where as long as it retains the

---

[52] Cf. IV,i,9: "But because the memory is not always so clear as actual perception, and does in all men more or less decay in length of time, this amongst other differences is one, which shows, that demonstrative knowledge, is much more imperfect than intuitive." In his discussion of demonstrative knowledge in IV,xvii,15, he attributes its lesser certainty entirely to the role of memory.

similitude and agreement with the object, it produces a knowledge; but 'tis still in every successive reflection with a lessening of that perfect clearness and distinctness, which is in the first, till at last, after many removes, it has a great mixture of dimness . . . Thus it is with knowledge, made out by a long train of proofs" (iv,ii,6).

It may be asked, finally, whether Locke's doctrine of demonstrative knowledge is not simply incompatible with his thinking of "perception" as direct awareness? Is not one's awareness of the agreement or disagreement of ideas which occurs in demonstrative knowledge inherently an *indirect* awareness? That depends on what one takes direct awareness to be. Locke took direct awareness of some fact, or some entity, to be awareness of it without the mediation of something which *represents* it. In the case of our non-immediate knowledge of the conclusion of a demonstration there is, on Locke's view, no mediation by mental representations; it is, in that sense, direct awareness. In demonstrations, *direct* awareness of the relationship among certain ideas is mediated by *direct* (and unmediated) awareness of the relationship of those ideas to other ideas.

As we now leave this topic of Locke's understanding of knowledge, it may be useful to have a summary of the main lines of the interpretation I have offered. I suggest that the way to read Locke is to see him as presenting a certain elegant picture of knowledge and of its proper place in our lives to which he is deeply attracted but which, with great reluctance, he qualifies and revises. Though Locke concedes that the picture must be qualified, the unqualified picture continues to cast its spell over him. He constantly replicates the picture (especially in his replies to objectors) without mentioning the qualifications or facing up to the implications of having made them.

Essential to the picture is Locke's taking knowledge and belief/assent as fundamentally different mental states. Knowledge is awareness of facts, be they affirmative or negative – awareness of entities in relation. Belief and assent, by contrast, consist of *taking* entities to be related in certain ways. The picture which attracts Locke, then, is this: Knowledge consists of direct awareness of some fact, specifically, of some relationship among ideas. Typically, such awareness is accompanied by assent, of the highest degree of certainty, to the corresponding proposition.

Now the qualification. Locke finds himself forced to concede that knowledge goes beyond "perception." For he finds himself forced to include under knowledge what he calls sensitive knowledge;

and, even more importantly, he finds himself forced to regard some cases of remembering what one "perceived" or proved as themselves cases of knowledge. Assuming that beliefs (and assentings) are the bearers of the property which comes in varying degrees of certainty and probability, this has the consequences that knowledge in general must be for Locke not "perception" but a species of belief (assent), and that "perception" is not in all cases what accounts for certainty. It furthermore has the consequence, as we shall see, that a belief not grounded on insight may nonetheless be the result of doing one's best. The spectre of beliefs not grounded on awareness of the things themselves remains to haunt us.

(d) Belief and its governance

We have been speaking of knowledge. But Locke was convinced that for the conduct of life, if not for "speculation," something more than knowledge is needed. We cannot live by knowledge alone. Man "would be at a great loss if he had nothing to direct him but what has the certainty of true knowledge" (IV,xiv,1). We "would be often utterly in the dark, and in most of the actions of [our lives] perfectly at a stand" (IV,xiv,1) if we confined "our thoughts within the contemplation of those things, that are within the reach of our understandings" (IV,iii,22). For "our ignorance [is] infinitely larger than our knowledge"(IV,iii,22).

So what are we to do, simply "launch . . . out into that abyss of darkness (where we have not eyes to see, nor faculties to perceive anything)" (IV,iii,22)? Not at all. "The faculty, which God has given man to supply the want of clear and certain knowledge is *judgment*: whereby the mind takes its ideas to agree, or disagree; or which is the same, any proposition to be true, or false, without perceiving a demonstrative evidence in the proofs" (IV,xiv,3). Or more precisely, says Locke, "this faculty of the mind, when it is exercised immediately about things, is called *judgment*; when about truths delivered in words, is most commonly called *assent* or *dissent*" (IV,xiv,3). In short, judgment "is the putting ideas together, or separating them from one another in the mind, when their certain agreement or disagreement is not perceived, but presumed to be so"(IV,xiv,4).

In these passages Locke speaks of judgment as *a faculty* – which suggests that he thought of belief and assent as formed in us by a single mechanism. Probably his actual thought was that we all have several distinct belief- and assent-forming faculties. In any case, it is of fundamental importance for understanding Locke to realize that he regarded belief and assent as formed by some faculty or faculties and not by the will.[53] We do not *decide* to believe or assent to things – not often, anyway. Breaking decisively with almost all his philosophical predecessors, Locke repudiates one of the traditional distinctions between knowledge and opinion; namely, that in knowledge one's belief and assent are compelled by the presence of the object itself, while in opinion, they are the result of will. Though Locke obviously regards our belief- and assent-forming faculties as subject in certain ways to the control of the will – otherwise his whole picture of the responsible believer would have no application – they are not to be identified with the will.

God, to compensate for our severe shortfall of knowledge, has endowed us with assent- and belief-forming faculties. "The state we are at present in, not being that of vision, we must, in many things, content ourselves with faith and probability" (IV,iii,6). But the workings of our assent- and belief-forming faculties must be governed. We are not to let them do their work without supervision and direction. We are to monitor and intervene. It is very easily said, and nobody questions it, that giving and withholding our assent, and the degrees of it, should be regulated (*Conduct*, §33; *Works* II,379). Indeed, "In the whole conduct of the understanding there is nothing of more moment than to know when and where, and how far, to give assent" (*Conduct*, §33; *Works* II,379).[54]

---

[53] "[T]o believe this or that to be true does not depend upon our will" (*Letter Concerning Toleration; Works* v,40).

[54] James Tully, in "Governing Conduct," argues that Locke's epistemology must be seen as the repudiation of what he, Tully, calls "the dispositional account of assent." He cites some passages from *Anti-Scepticism* by Henry Lee, one of Locke's opponents, in support of this thesis. I do not find it at all clear, however, what this "dispositional account" is supposed to be. Tully's explanation runs thus: "A person assents to a proposition *because* he or she is naturally inclined towards truth and goodness, just as a stone naturally tends to its natural home, the earth. As in all forms of teleological explanation, the action, assent, is explained by its natural tendency to a certain result or end, true beliefs" (pp. 18–19). But what does such a view actually come to? Presumably it is meant to be compatible with the obvious fact that we assent to many propositions because of the workings of our perceptual capacities, to many others because of the workings of memory, etc. Is it then the thesis that our indigenous belief-forming dispositions are generally reliable? If so, Locke certainly does not disagree. He holds that we have a capacity for "perception" which gives us direct awareness of certain facts. And more generally, he held that "we fail [our faculties] a great deal more than they fail us" (*Conduct*, §34; *Works* II,380).

Tully remarks that "If the mind were not disposed in some way to the truth or the good, then it must be indifferent, and so all our knowledge is the product of custom and education" (p. 24). Accordingly he says a couple of times over that, on Locke's view, beliefs are all the

Why is that? Because there is a certain desideratum with respect to our assentings and believings which, if we allow our assent- and belief-forming faculties to do their work ungoverned, will be woefully missing. What is that desideratum? Though Locke never offers a clear and decisive formulation, I think it is pretty clear what he has in mind. It has something to do with that merit in believings which consists of the believed proposition being true, and with that demerit in believings which consists of the believed proposition being false. But to say only this is to leave open a large number of alternative views.

Alternative views, for example, as to the balance between the merit and the demerit. Are we to try our best to avoid believing falsehoods? Presumably skepticism would be the most effective policy. Are we to try our best to believe additional truths? Gullibility might be the best policy. One thinks here again of Roderick Chisholm, who also held that all of us (normal adult) human beings, just by virtue of being intellectual beings capable of believing and withholding belief from propositions, have an obligation. In his *Foundations of Knowing* Chisholm formulates this obligation as the general requirement to try to have the largest possible set of logically independent beliefs that is such that the true beliefs outnumber the false beliefs (p. 7). In his earlier *Theory of Knowledge* he suggested that the requirement is that of each person "trying his best to bring it about that for any proposition p he considers, he accepts p if and only if p is true" (p. 14).[55]

Locke, I suggest, was thinking along somewhat different lines from either of these. The obligation in question pertains not just to our believings, disbelievings, and withholdings, but to the *degree of firmness* of our believings and disbelievings – to the *levels of confidence* we place in propositions. Each of us is obligated, for certain propositions, to try to do our epistemic best – that is, to try our best to find out whether the proposition is true or false, and upon completion of the procedure required for that, to place a level of confidence in the proposition

result of custom or education (pp. 21,22). But this is just mistaken. Not only does Locke think that we possess indigenous belief-forming dispositions which *get educated* (tutored, schooled); Tully entirely overlooks the fundamental role of "perception" in Locke's thought. Locke is not Hume born out of season! Furthermore, Locke never speaks of *the mind* as indifferent; what he says, rather, is that we must *practice indifferency* – by which he means that, in the governance of our belief-forming dispositions, we must concern ourselves only with the truth and falsity of the propositions believed.

55 R. M. Chisholm, *The Foundations of Knowing* (Minneapolis, University of Minnesota Press, 1982); Chisholm, *Theory of Knowledge*.

appropriate to a certain result of the procedure. (Naturally in some cases this presupposes first doing various things to get hold of the proposition.) It will be convenient in what follows to have a name for this obligation; let me call it *the alethic obligation* (Greek *aletheia* = truth). The obligation holds for everyone, or at least for all normal adults; but it does not hold for all the propositions that come to mind. In this way too, Locke's position is different from Chisholm's in *Theory of Knowledge*. The obligation applies to a person for those propositions which are of maximal "concernment," as Locke calls it, to the person, and only for those.[56]

That speaks to the nature and scope of the obligation. But why is there an obligation in the region at all? Granted that our faculties customarily work in such a way as to dispose us, for example, to adopt "the opinions and persuasions of others, whom we know and think well of," whereas in fact "there cannot be a more dangerous thing to rely on [than the opinions of others], nor more likely to mislead one, since there is much more falsehood and errour amongst men, than truth and knowledge." Still, why the *should*, the *ought*? Might it not rather be the case that it is a *desirable* feature of our believings, disbelievings, and withholdings that our level of confidence in the proposition be proportioned to its probability, without its ever being the case that we are *obligated to try to bring about* this state? This desirable feature might be either *inherently* or *instrumentally* desirable. As to the latter: Perhaps it is the case for certain goods that the way which holds most promise for achieving those goods includes trying one's best, for certain propositions, to bring it about that one's level of confidence in those propositions is proportioned to their probability. Something like this was the position taken by H. H. Price in his book *Belief*. Price denied that there is anything morally blameworthy about assenting unreasonably (against the evidence or without regard to the evidence) or that we ought to be chastised for doing so. There is nothing wicked about such assents. It is, however, true that unreasonable assent is contrary to our long-term interest; our long-term interest lies in believing true propositions rather than false ones. And if we assent reasonably (i.e., in accordance with the evidence), it is likely that in the long run the propositions we believe

---

[56] On this fundamental point my interpretation differs from a great many commentators – for example, from, to cite one of the most recent, Peter Schouls in his *Reasoned Freedom: John Locke and Enlightenment* (Ithaca, Cornell University Press, 1992). Schouls throughout adopts a universalizing interpretation of Locke, even though he recognizes that the procedure Locke recommends takes time and that, in Locke's view, not everybody has the time or should take it.

will be more often true than false.[57] On Price's view we would be *well advised*, for certain propositions, to try our best to bring it about that we believe them if and only if they are true. Locke speaks instead of *obligation*.

Our Maker, says Locke, would have each of us "to the best of his power" keep "out of mistake and error" (IV,xvii,24). And our Maker's command for us is our moral duty (cf. II,xxviii,7–8,14). But to the best of my knowledge Locke never actually defends his view that each of us has, for certain propositions, the alethic obligation. He never, that is to say, defends his view that God commands that one adopt a certain level of confidence in those propositions, and will reward one if one makes the attempt and punish one if one does not. I presume, though, that it is to this view that he is alluding when, in the passage about religious faith quoted above from *Essay* IV,xvii,24, he says that the person who seeks sincerely to discover truth, though he may miss it, "will not miss the reward of it."

We all recognize that our believings possess a variety of merits and demerits. One merit is that of being such that the proposition believed is true; another is that of being such that the proposition believed is very probably true. But it may also be the case that one's believing that one can scale the ledge contributes crucially to one's scaling it, and that one's believing that one can play the violin passage as rapidly as the conductor wants it played contributes crucially to one's not "flubbing" it; if one has one or the other of those goals, then one will regard the causal feature of the relevant belief as a merit in it. And some beliefs, quite apart from their desirable or undesirable *consequences*, are painful or exhilarating for us – the belief that one's child has died, or that one has won the prize. Furthermore, various of these other properties of beliefs, and not just those of being such that the propositional content is true, or very probably true, are such that one can try to acquire beliefs which possess those properties. Finding one's low self-esteem unpleasant, one can undertake a regimen to acquire a better opinion of oneself.

Locke recognized all this. But he had no tolerance whatsoever for the suggestion that we also have obligations to pursue some of these other desiderata. The obligations we have for belief governance pertain only to truth and falsehood and the probability thereof. In our governance we are to practice what he calls "indifference" to all

---

[57] H. H. Price, *Belief* (London, Allen & Unwin, 1969), p. 238.

other merits and demerits in beliefs. Of course he recognized that some beliefs are more important than others – that it is more important to get things right on some matters than on others; that contributes to the fact that we have the alethic obligation with respect to some but not all propositions that come to mind. But one's only *obligation*, with respect to beliefs, is to aim at getting things right, at getting in touch with reality. And then to place the appropriate level of confidence in the proposition.

One might agree that the only thing we are *obligated to* seek for our believings is getting in touch with reality, while yet holding that it is *permissible* to aim at other things. But even that suggestion was roundly dismissed by Locke. Truth and truth alone is to be aimed at: "Right understanding consists in the discovery and adherence to truth . . . the right use and conduct of the understanding . . . is purely truth, nothing else" (*Conduct*, §42; *Works* II,391). Thus in his *Conduct of the Understanding* he repeatedly speaks of the importance of "indifference": "I have said above that we should keep a perfect indifference for all opinions, not wish any of them true, or try to make them appear so; but being indifferent, receive and embrace them according as evidence, and that alone, gives the attestation of truth. . .They that do not keep up this indifferency in themselves for all but truth, not supposed, but evidenced in themselves, put coloured spectacles before their eyes, and look on things through false glasses, and then think themselves excused in following the false appearances, which they themselves put upon them" (*Conduct*, §34; *Works* II,380).[58]

What comes through unmistakably in reading Locke is a deep horror of being out of touch with how things are. He prides himself on having followed his own exhortations. About his rewriting of the chapter in the *Essay* on the freedom of the will he says that "In what I first writ, I with an unbiassed indifferency followed truth, whither I thought she led me. But neither being so vain as to fancy infallibility, nor so disingenuous as to dissemble my mistakes for fear of blemishing my reputation, I have with the same sincere design for truth only, not been shamed to publish what a severer inquiry has suggested" (II,xxi,72).

Naturally Locke held that we have other obligations than to try to

---

[58] Cf. *Conduct*, §§11–12; *Works* II,346,348: A person "must not be in love with any opinion, or wish it to be true, till he knows it to be so, and then he will not need to wish it: for nothing that is false can deserve our good wishes, nor a desire that it should have the place and force of truth . . . To be indifferent which of two opinions is true, is the right temper of the mind that preserves it from being imposed on, and disposes it to examine with that indifferency, till it has done its best to find the truth, and this is the only direct and safe way to it."

do our epistemic best toward various propositions. Indeed, he held that doing one's epistemic best may conflict, in a given situation, with other obligations that one has, for the simple reason that it takes time and energy to do one's best. (Why that is so will become clear shortly.) Locke further held that in some cases of conflict between doing one's epistemic best and some other obligation, the other obligation may take precedence; sometimes to do one's epistemic best would require neglecting more weighty obligations. Thus Locke took for granted that only if one knows the totality of a given person's obligations can one know to which propositions that person has the alethic obligation; alethic obligation is very much a *situated* phenomenon. Nonetheless, it remains true that for each of us there are many propositions of such "concernment" – as Locke calls it – to us as to place us under the alethic obligation with respect to that proposition. Indeed, Locke was persuaded that certain central matters of morality and religion are of such "concernment" to everyone as to place everyone under obligation to try his or her best (cf. IV,xx,3).

So what does doing our epistemic best toward some proposition consist of – when we are out beyond the possibility of knowledge of that proposition? What does the implementing practice which Locke recommends look like? And incidentally, Locke assumed that the method to be applied is always the same; the method to be used for implementing one's alethic obligation in religion is no different from that to be used, say, in science. Perhaps the best brief statement Locke gives of the practice he is proposing is this:

the mind if it will proceed rationally, ought to examine all the grounds of probability, and see how they make more or less, for or against any probable proposition, before it assents to or dissents from it, and upon a due balancing the whole, reject, or receive it, with a more or less firm assent, proportionably to the preponderancy of the greater grounds of probability on one side or the other. (IV,xv,5)

I think that we can usefully unravel the practice which Locke is here proposing into three principles, to be applied in succession. The principles are meant only for *mediate* beliefs, and then only for mediate beliefs whose propositional content cannot be demonstrated. As to *immediate* beliefs: Trying to do one's epistemic best requires that one believe a proposition *immediately* only if one "perceives" the corresponding fact (alternatively, only if the immediate belief is so certain as to constitute knowledge).

One begins with evidence. But not just with whatever evidence one happens to have. The evidence must be satisfactory; when it is not that already, we must go out and acquire such evidence. "Where a truth is made out by one demonstration, there needs no farther inquiry; but in all probabilities where there wants [lacks] demonstration to establish the truth beyond doubt, there it is not enough to trace one argument to its source, and observe its strength and weakness, but all the arguments, after having been so examined on both sides, must be laid in balance one against another and upon the whole the understanding determines its assent" (*Conduct*, §7; *Works* II,339–40). Of course, we must remember that following the procedure recommended is not a *guarantee* "that men should be perfectly kept from error" (*Conduct*, §7; *Works* II,339–40). Nonetheless, this is the "measure" such that if persons "neither give nor refuse their assent but by that measure, they will be safe in the opinions they have" (*Conduct*, §34; *Works* II,380). The first of Locke's principles may then be called the "principle of evidence." It can be formulated as follows:

Principle of evidence: Acquire evidence for and against the proposition such that each item of evidence is something that one knows and such that the totality of one's evidence is satisfactory.

The evidence must consist of things one knows. Opinion is to be based on knowledge, on certitude; ideally, on insight. Otherwise it dangles loose and we drift about; or to change the metaphor, otherwise we wander in darkness. Admittedly Locke never really *says* that the evidence must be knowledge. Though the conviction that it must be is central to his vision, at least on my interpretation, he seldom makes a point of it; it functions in his writing more as unquestioned assumption than as thesis. There are a few passages, though, which at least suggest this interpretation. One occurs in *Conduct*, §21 (*Works* II,358). In the passage Locke is discussing a way of saving time in the conduct of the understanding; the foundationalist structure of his proposed practice comes through clearly:

I think it may be proposed, that for the saving the long progression of the thoughts to remote and first principles in every case, the mind should provide itself several stages; that is to say, intermediate principles, which it might have recourse to in the examining those positions that come in its way. These, though they are not self-evident principles, yet, if they have been made out from them by a wary and unquestionable deduction, may be depended on as certain and infallible truths, and serve as unquestionable truths to prove other points depending upon them.

It is because the appropriate evidence is knowledge, and because we have immediate, non-inferential knowledge, that Locke escapes the "Münchhausen Trilemma" to which Hans Albert thinks all classical Western epistemology falls prey. In his *Treatise on Critical Reason*,[59] Albert remarks about the so-called principle of sufficient reason that if "we formulate it as a methodological principle, we have gained something which we may with some justice regard as a general *postulate of the classical methodology of rational thought*, as the fundamental principle of that model of rationality that appears to dominate in classical epistemology. This principle states: always seek an adequate foundation – a sufficient justification for all your convictions" (p. 14). Albert makes the same point in another passage: "Classical methodology, as expressed in the epistemology of classical rationalism in both its intellectualist and empiricist variants . . . was based upon a methodological version of the principle of sufficient reason – on the idea, that is, that every view, every conviction, every belief must be justified through reference to positive, certain grounds, to an unshakable foundation" (p. 39).

But the demand for universal justification poses insuperable problems, says Albert:

if one demands a justification for *everything*, one must also demand a justification for the knowledge to which one has referred back the views initially requiring foundation. This leads to a situation with three alternatives, all of which appear unacceptable: in other words, to a trilemma which, in view of the analogy existing between our problem and one which that celebrated and mendacious baron once had to solve, I should like to call the *Münchhausen trilemma*. For, obviously, one must choose here between 1. an *infinite regress*, which seems to arise from the necessity to go further and further back in the search for foundations, and which, since it is in practice impossible, affords no secure basis; 2. a *logical circle* in the deduction, which arises because, in the process of justification, statements are used which were characterized before as in need of foundation, so that they can provide no secure basis; and, finally, 3. the *breaking-off of the process* at a particular point, which, admittedly, can always be done in principle, but involves an arbitrary suspension of the principle of sufficient justification. (p. 18)

Albert goes on to argue, as he already intimates in his statement of these options, that each of these is unacceptable. He concludes that

[59] Hans Albert, *Treatise on Critical Reason*, tr. M. V. Rorty (Princeton, Princeton University Press, 1985).

the acceptability of a belief cannot reside in one's having a reason for it, a justification.

Locke is as good a representative of classical epistemology as any. And it is as clear as anything can be that Locke does not commit himself to universal justificationism. Opinion is to rest on knowledge. All inferential (demonstrative and sensitive) knowledge rests on immediate knowledge; and immediate knowledge gets its "justification" not from some basis in yet other propositions but from the fact that one just sees the proposition to be true.

So the evidence must consist of things known. Which things? We are to collect evidence concerning the truth or falsehood of the proposition. How much and of what sort? In the passage quoted Locke says that the mind ought to examine all the grounds of probability. Clearly he was working with some notion of *quality* of evidence, and some notion of evidence as being *satisfactory in quality*. But what constitutes "all the grounds"? What must evidence be like to be satisfactory? Locke nowhere says. The elaborate discussions concerning rules of evidence which one finds in John Stuart Mill, for example, have no counterpart in Locke; Locke stands at the beginning. Presumably the guiding idea, though, is that of *epistemically reliable* evidence: Bodies of evidence for propositions differ with respect to how reliable they are as indicators of the truth or falsehood of the propositions. What we need is evidence which reaches up to a certain threshold of reliability. *Ceteris paribus*, a sampling of 10,000 citizens of Michigan as to how they will cast their vote for President is more reliable evidence of how a particular citizen will vote than a sampling of 100 citizens.

How reliable must the evidence be for one to have done one's best? Where is the threshold of satisfactoriness on the continuum of degrees of reliability? Locke doesn't consider the issue. In one passage there is a hint of the suggestion that the satisfactoriness-threshold may be in different places for different cases; sometimes, says Locke, we are under "the necessity of believing, without knowledge, nay, often upon very slight grounds, in this fleeting state of action and blindness we are in" (IV,xvi,4). But this is no more than a hint; I know of no passage in which Locke develops it further.

Can we *know* that our evidence is satisfactory when it is? Apparently not; at least, not always.

What we once know, we are certain is so: and we may be secure, that there are no latent proofs undiscovered, which may overturn our knowledge, or bring it in doubt. But in matters of probability, 'tis not in every case we can be sure, that we have all the particulars before us, that any way concern the question; and that there is no evidence behind, and yet unseen, which may cast the probability on the other side, and outweigh all, that at present seems to preponderate with us. Who almost is there, that hath the leisure, patience, and means, to collect together all the proofs concerning most of the opinions he has, so as safely to conclude, that he hath a clear and full view; and that there is no more to be alleged for his better information? And yet we are forced to determine our selves on the one side or other. The conduct of our lives, and the management of our great concerns, will not bear delay. (IV,xvi,3)

Locke thinks of our inability to know that our evidence is satisfactory as a practical inability. Hume will show later that it is an inability in principle.

Collecting satisfactory evidence, as Locke understands that, is often a daunting task, requiring considerable expenditure of time and energy. It is mainly for this reason that each of us has the alethic obligation with respect to only a small selection of the propositions that come to mind. Indeed, each of us, for many of the propositions that come to mind, is *obligated not to* try to do his or her best. Doing his or her best would require neglecting other more weighty obligations. Conceding that the process of collecting satisfactory evidence will have to rely crucially on memory, Locke says that

in the opinions men have, and firmly stick to, in the world, their assent is not always from an actual view of the reasons that at first prevailed with them: It being in many cases almost impossible, and in most very hard, even for those who have very admirable memories, to retain all the proofs, which upon a due examination, made them embrace that side of the question. It suffices, that they have once with care and fairness, sifted the matter as far as they could; and that they have searched into all the particulars, that they could imagine to give any light to the question; and with the best of their skill, cast up the account upon the whole evidence: and thus having once found on which side the probability appeared to them, after as full and exact an enquiry as they can make, they lay up the conclusion in their memories, as a truth they have discovered. (IV,xvi,1)

Locke adds, superfluously, one would have thought, that "This is all that the greatest part of men are capable of doing, in regulating their opinions and judgments" (IV,xvi,2).[60]

---

[60] Though to this we must add Locke's answer to the question he poses, "Who is sufficient for all this?" "I answer," he says, "more than can be imagined. Every one knows what his proper business is, and what, according to the character he makes of himself, the world may justly expect of him; and to answer that, he will find he will have time and opportunity enough to furnish himself, if he will not deprive himself, by a narrowness of spirit, of those helps that are at hand" (*Conduct* §3; *Works* II,330).

One gets the impression, upon reading passages such as the above, that Locke confused *minimally satisfactory* evidence with *ideal* evidence. But even if that confusion is eliminated, the point remains: Only toward relatively few propositions do any of us have the alethic obligation. After he has described the right conduct of the understanding, Locke says that "If it be objected that this will require every man to be a scholar, and quit all his other business, and betake himself wholly to study, I answer, I propose no more to anyone than he has time for. Some men's state and condition requires no great extent of knowledge: the necessary provision for life swallows the greatest part of it" (*Conduct*, §37; *Works* II,384). Indeed, "Who almost is there," he asks, "that hath the leisure, patience, and means, to collect together all the proofs concerning most of the opinions he has, so as safely to conclude, that he hath a clear and full view; and that there is no more to be alleged for his better information?" (IV,xvi,3; quoted above).

In this state are the greatest part of mankind, who are given up to labour, and enslaved to the necessity of their mean condition; whose lives are worn out, only in the provisions for living. These men's opportunity of knowledge and enquiry, are commonly as narrow as their fortunes; and their understandings are but little instructed, when all their whole time and pains is laid out, to still the croaking of their own bellies, or the cries of their children . . . So that a great part of mankind are, by the natural and unalterable state of things in this world, and the constitution of humane affairs, unavoidably given over to invincible ignorance of those proofs, on which others build, and which are necessary to establish those opinions: the greatest part of men, having much to do to get the means of living, are not in a condition to look after those of learned and laborious enquiries. (IV,xx,2)

Locke goes on to raise the obvious question:

What shall we say then? Are the greatest part of mankind, by the necessity of their condition, subjected to unavoidable ignorance in those things, which are of greatest importance to them? . . . Have the bulk of mankind no other guide, but accident, and blind chance, to conduct them to their happiness, or misery? Are the current opinions, and licensed guides of every country sufficient evidence and security to every man to venture his greatest concernments on; nay, his everlasting happiness, or misery? (IV,xx,3)

Locke's answer is No. For "God has furnished men with faculties sufficient to direct them in the way they should take, if they will but seriously employ them that way, when their ordinary vocations allow them the leisure." And secondly, "No man is so wholly taken up with the attendance on the means of living, as to have no spare time at all to think of his soul, and inform himself in matters of religion" (IV,xx,3).

That last sentence is an indication of Locke's thought on the matter of *which* are the propositions with respect to which one has the alethic obligation. Every person has this obligation concerning certain fundamental moral and religious matters.[61] Truth on such matters concerns everyone; and everyone, no matter how much a "beast of burden" he or she may be, has talent and time, on Sundays and holidays, for trying his or her best concerning such matters (*Conduct*, §§19,23; *Works* II,354–6,360). In addition, everyone has the alethic obligation concerning various practical matters which pertain specifically to him or her. It is for persons of "leisure" that the alethic obligation is more expansive in scope:

> Those . . . who by the industry and parts of their ancestors have been set free from a constant drudgery to their backs and their bellies, should bestow some of their spare time on their heads . . . As to men whose fortunes and time is narrower, what may suffice them is not of that vast extent as may be imagined, and so comes not within the objection. Nobody is under an obligation to know everything . . . [I]f it shall be concluded that the meaner sort of people must give themselves up to a brutish stupidity in the things of their nearest concernment, which I see no reason for, this excuses not those of a freer fortune and education if they neglect their understanding, and take no care to employ them as they ought. (*Conduct*, §§7–8; *Works* II,340–3)

Locke characteristically offers formulations of the rules he is recommending which are unqualified as to scope: Assent, "if it be regulated, as is our duty, cannot be afforded to anything but upon good reason." It is clear from the foregoing passages, however, that he wished all such universalistic statements of alethic obligation to be understood as severely limited in scope. Only toward a few propositions can we, or ought we, or even *may* we, try to do our epistemic best. And only in the light of the totality of one's obligations can one decide for which propositions one does have that obligation.[62]

---

[61] As to religious matters, this is what Locke says: "Besides his particular calling for the support of this life, everyone has a concern in a future life, which he is bound to look after. This engages his thoughts in religion; and here it mightily lies upon him to understand and reason right. Men, therefore, cannot be excused from understanding the words, and framing the general notions relating to religion, right. The one day of seven, besides other days of rest, allows in the Christian world time enough for this (had they no other idle hours) if they would but make use of these vacancies from their daily labour, and apply themselves to an improvement of knowledge with as much diligence as they often do to a great many other things that are useless" (*Conduct*, §8; *Works* II,342). See also *Conduct*, §23; *Works* II,360. A similar point concerning moral matters is made in the following section of *Conduct*, and concerning the immediately practical matters that concern a person, at the end of the preceding section.

[62] Furthermore, Locke was convinced that only the person himself or herself is in the position

The full picture, then, is this. Locke takes for granted that we human beings have a variety of innate dispositions which, when activated, yield beliefs. These dispositions can be tutored and regulated; in all of us they have in fact been tutored. All of us have learned to engage in what may be called *doxastic practices*. But further, for each of us there are some propositions of such "concernment" that we are obligated to try our best to find out whether they are true or false. Locke was profoundly convinced that in his own day and age – and no doubt in every other age of which he knew – there were many who were not trying to do their epistemic best when they should have been. His proposed method was thus a proposal for the reform of the doxastic practices of his day and of every other day to which they applied. He thought that here and there – especially in the new natural philosophy – people were trying to do their best by following the proposed method. In effect, then, his proposal was that the practice he outlined be followed much more often than it was. He thought that for everybody there are occasions on which it is one's *obligation* to follow it. Never always; that would entail violating other more weighty obligations. But for all of us there are some matters of such "concernment" as to make it obligatory for us to try to do our epistemic best; and the right method for doing that is the method he is proposing.

Let us move on. Once satisfactory evidence is in hand, what is one to do then? One is to determine the probability of the proposition in question on the satisfactory evidence in hand. Let us call this the "principle of appraisal." It may be formulated thus:

Principle of appraisal: Examine the (satisfactory) evidence one has collected so as to determine its evidential force, until one has "perceived" what is the probability of the proposition on that evidence.

How was Locke thinking of probability? In his fascinating book *The Emergence of Probability*,[63] Ian Hacking argues that our modern concept of probability was a piece of intellectual capital that became

where the judgment can be made with any reliability: It "is impossible for you, or me, or any man, to know, whether another has done his duty in examining the evidence on both sides, when he embraces that side of the question, which we, perhaps upon other views, judge false: and therefore we can have no right to punish or persecute him for it. In this, whether and how far any one is faulty, must be left to the Searcher of hearts, the great and righteous Judge of all men, who knows all their circumstances, all the powers and workings of their minds; where it is they sincerely follow, and by what default they at any time miss truth: and he, we are sure, will judge uprightly" (Third Letter for Toleration; *Works* v,299).
[63] Ian Hacking, *The Emergence of Probability* (Cambridge, Cambridge University Press, 1975).

available only around the middle of the seventeenth century. Hacking contends that the Latin word *probabilis* (and its derivatives) traditionally meant something like *worthy of approbation*, and was affirmed of those opinions held by reputable authorities – that is, by "the wise." Its sense was connected with *probity*. "Opinions are probable when they are approved by authority, when they are testified to, supported by, ancient books" (p. 30). Slowly this older notion of probability changed into our modern notion. Characteristic of our modern notion is its "Janus-faced" character. It has two aspects, an *aleatory* aspect, "connected with the tendency, displayed by some chance devices, to produce stable relative frequencies," and an *epistemic* aspect. In turn, the content of the epistemic aspect was new. Probability was now no longer connected with the testimony of authorities but "with the degree of belief warranted by evidence" (p. 1).[64]

The aleatory aspect of our modern concept played little role in Locke's thought. The notions of relative frequency and of its correlate, statistical probability, do every now and then come to the surface in Locke's writing; but what is far and away more prominent is the concept of so-called *epistemic* probability: the concept of *a proposition as more or less probable on a body of evidence*, whether or not that evidence be evidence concerning, or specifying, relative frequencies. This epistemic aspect of the new concept was made to order for Locke's preachment: Away with tradition, down to the evidence of the things themselves. Here is how Locke himself speaks, in his official voice, about probability:

Probability is likeliness to be true, the very notation of the word signifying such a proposition, for which there be argument or proofs, to make it pass or be received for true. (IV,xv,3)

The grounds of probability . . . , as they are the foundations on which our assent is built; so are they also the measure whereby its several degrees are, or ought to be, regulated. (IV,xvi,1)

Locke invites us to sort the "grounds of probability" into various types. In the first place, we can distinguish between propositions "concerning some particular existence, or as it is usually termed,

---

[64] Leibniz saw the distinction very clearly; see *New Essays*, pp. 372–3, 465–6. He calls for the "establishment of an *art of estimating likelihoods*," to supplement Aristotle's art of estimating *acceptability*.

matter of fact, which falling under observation, is capable of human testimony," and propositions "concerning things, which being beyond the discovery of our senses, are not capable of any such testimony" (IV,xvi,5). Let us begin with the former.

Evidence concerning such propositions comes in two sorts: observations one has oneself made, and testimony from others. Before one accepts some item of testimony, one must appraise that testimony itself for the probability of its being true. To conduct such appraisal, one must consider such matters as the following: "1. The number. 2. The integrity. 3. The skill of the witnesses. 4. The design of the author, where it is a testimony out of a book cited. 5. The consistency of the parts, and circumstances of the relation. 6. Contrary testimonies" (IV,xv,4).

One's own observations may differ significantly from the (reliable) testimony of someone else (and one person's testimony may differ significantly from another's). Let us first suppose that there is no significant difference; and let us distinguish such testimony into three types. The "highest degree of probability" occurs when personal observations and credible testimonies inform us of invariances – "when the general consent of all men, in all ages, as far as it can be known, concurs with a man's constant and never-failing experience in like cases, to confirm the truth of any particular matter of fact attested by fair witnesses" (IV,xvi,6). "That fire warmed a man, made lead fluid, and changed the colour or consistency in wood or charcoal . . . These and the like propositions about particular facts, being agreeable to our constant experience . . . and being generally spoke of . . . as things found constantly to be so . . . we are put past doubt, that a relation affirming any such thing to have been, or any predication that it will happen again in the same manner, is very true. These probabilities rise so near to certainty, that . . . we make little or no difference between them and certain knowledge" (IV,xvi,6).

The "next degree of probability" occurs when personal observation and reliable testimony inform one of a correlation which, though not invariant, holds for the most part. If, with this as background, reliable testimony claims that an event of the sort occurred, one has solid ground for believing that it did. For example, "History giving us such an account of men in all ages; and my own experience, as far as I had an opportunity to observe, confirming it, that most men prefer their private advantage, to the public. If all historians that write of Tiberius, say that Tiberius did so, it is extremely probable" (IV,xvi,7).

Sometimes, though, observations and testimonies concerning regularities are not in the picture; there are things that "happen indifferently, as that a bird should fly this or that way; that it should thunder on a man's right or left hand, etc." As to such matters, "when any particular matter of fact is vouched by the concurrent testimony of unsuspected witnesses, there our assent is also unavoidable" – for example, "that there is such a city in Italy as Rome: That about 1700 years ago, there lived in it a man, called Julius Caesar" (iv,xvi,8).

When the bodies of evidence, specifying correlations, which are obtained from different sources deemed reliable, do not significantly differ, then "probability upon such grounds carries so much evidence with it, that it naturally determines the judgment, and leaves us as little liberty to believe, or disbelieve, as a demonstration does" (iv,xvi,9). By contrast,

> when testimonies contradict common experience, and the reports of history and witnesses clash, with the ordinary course of nature, or with one another; there it is, where diligence, attention, and exactness is required, to form a right judgment, and to proportion the assent to the different evidence and probability of the thing; which rises and falls, according as those two foundations of credibility, *viz.* common observation in like cases, and particular testimonies in that particular instance, favour or contradict it. These are liable to so great variety of contrary observations, circumstances, reports, different qualifications, tempers, designs, oversights, etc. of the reporters, that 'tis impossible to reduce to precise rules, the various degrees wherein men give their assent. (iv,xvi,9)

Lastly, what sort of evidence are we to acquire for propositions concerning that which cannot in principle be observed by human beings – whether the propositions be about unobservable entities, such as immaterial beings or remote or minute material beings, or about imperceptible aspects of the behavior of perceptible beings? And how are we to appraise the logical force of such evidence?

"Analogy in these matters," says Locke, "is the only help we have, and 'tis from that alone we draw all our grounds of probability" (iv,xvi,12). "Thus observing that the bare rubbing of two bodies violently one upon another, produces heat, and very often fire itself, we have reason to think, that what we call heat and fire, consists in a violent agitation of the imperceptible minute parts of the burning matter" (iv,xvl,12). Such propositions, says Locke, "can appear more or less probable, only as they more or less agree to truths that are established in our minds, and as they hold proportion to other parts of our knowledge and observation" (IV,xvi,12).[65]

Obviously there is a great deal in all this that is worthy of comment and critique; between Locke and us there is a massive body of probing reflections on these matters. But let us move on. Once one has determined the probability of the proposition in question on the satisfactory evidence one has collected, then one is ready to apply the last of Locke's principles – let us call it the "principle of proportionality." For the principle to be fully intelligible, an explanation of one of the concepts used is required. I have emphasized that fundamental to Locke's proposal was the distinction between insight, on the one hand, and belief and assent, on the other. Equally fundamental was a distinction which up to this point I have used without emphasizing, that between *belief* and *assent*, on the one hand, and *firmness* of belief and assent, on the other. Locke held that a given proposition could be believed (assented to) with different degrees of firmness, and that different propositions could be believed (assented to) with the same degree of firmness.

What did he have in mind by *firmness* of belief, or assent? In recent years there has been much talk among epistemologists about *levels of confidence* in propositions – with betting situations often proposed as tests of such. Might Locke, by firmness of belief, have meant *levels of confidence*? I think not. In any case, one would hope not; for the two notions are distinct in an important way. One cannot believe P with a certain firmness without believing P; one can, though, have a certain level of confidence in P without believing P. If one believes P one will not, except through inadvertence, believe not-P at all; one will, though, have a certain level of confidence in not-P – a low one. So too, while fully aware of P, one might believe neither P nor not-P; in that situation one will, though, have a certain level of confidence in both. Thus the array of a person's believings-with-specific-firmness will not

---

[65] This last passage is used by Ernan McMullin (as it was by Laudan, "The Nature and Sources") to support his contention that Locke had some inkling of the place of the hypothetico-deductive (retroductive) method in science: "Conceptions of Science in the Scientific Revolution," in David D. Lindberg and Robert W. Westman (eds.), *Reappraisals of the Scientific Revolution* (Cambridge, Cambridge University Press), pp. 75–6. McMullin observes that Locke proved more prescient on the role of the hypothetico-deductive method than in his suggestion that we are to form hypotheses concerning imperceptible entities and processes on analogy to perceptible ones. McMullin's discussion also makes clear that Locke (along, perhaps, with Huygens) was the first significant thinker to see clearly that the new natural philosophy did not satisfy the ideals of the old *scientia*. Everyone else was trying to squeeze the new into the old, arguing that the new really did yield certainty. Not Locke.

satisfy the Pascalian calculus of probabilities: It's not true, in general, that the firmness with which one believes P varies inversely with the firmness with which one believes not-P. Whether the phenomenon of levels of confidence satisfies or should satisfy the Pascalian calculus remains, from what we have said, an open question.

The thought comes naturally to mind that to believe P with such-and-such firmness is just to have such-and-such a level of confidence in P *and* to believe P. Or might it be a mistake to think of believing a proposition as *one* thing, and having a level of confidence in it as *another* thing? Might it be that believing P just is having a level of confidence in P above a certain threshold? Does our customary trichotomy of believing/withholding/disbelieving simply pick out broad gamuts on the continuum of levels of confidence? Is talk about levels of confidence to be seen as the invitation to pick out narrower gamuts – or even, *points* – on the same continuum?

I rather doubt it; since it appears to me that one might have the same level of confidence in two different propositions while believing one and not believing the other. But I shall discuss the issues without presupposing an answer. It's worth noting, however, that even if belief is identical with levels of confidence above a certain threshold, a rule for the regulation of degrees of confidence is not automatically a rule for the regulation of belief. For the rule for degrees of confidence might tell us only that degrees of confidence are to be matched with degrees of something else; and from that we might not be able to infer how much of this something else, in absolute terms, is necessary for one to be entitled to a degree of confidence which is a case of belief – even if we knew where the line demarcating belief from non-belief fell.

Parenthetically, did Locke hold the "assimilationist" thesis, that believing P just consists of having a level of confidence in P above a certain threshold? He sometimes speaks as if he did not. Specifically, he sometimes speaks as if he believed that though belief just flows over us in certain situations, in those same situations we can, presumably by act of will, regulate the firmness of our belief – regulate the level of confidence in the proposition believed. He says, for example, that "the grounds of probability . . . as they are the foundations on which our *assent* is built; so are they also the measure whereby its several degrees are, or ought to be *regulated*" (IV,xvi,1). But if Locke held the assimilationist thesis, this would be a most surprising thing to say: that one's ability to regulate the degree of confidence one has in some proposition has this limitation on it – one cannot regulate it across the belief threshold, only within the space which lies on either side of the threshold. On the other hand, there are passages, as we shall see, in which Locke speaks of *resisting* believing; he does not always think of it as ineluctably flowing over one.

In formulating the final step of what he regards as doing one's epistemic best, Locke clearly has his eye more on the regulation of degrees of confidence than on the regulation of firmness of belief (IV,xv,2). Though he speaks often of firmness of belief, he makes no attempt whatsoever to determine a threshold for belief. Accordingly I shall formulate his principle of proportionality in terms of levels of confidence, while continuing now and then to speak, as Locke does, of firmness of assent and firmness of belief.

There are, says Locke, degrees of probability, "from the very neighbourhood of certainty and demonstration, quite down to improbability and unlikeliness, even to the confines of impossibility; and also degrees of assent from full assurance and confidence, quite down to conjecture, doubt, and distrust" (IV,xv,2). Locke's principle of proportionality is a principle specifying the proper relation of these two phenomena:

Principle of proportionality: Adopt a level of confidence in the proposition which is proportioned to its probability on one's satisfactory evidence.[66]

To understand Locke's intent we must take note of an ambiguity in the notion of proportioning levels of confidence to probability. One might mean by this simply that if the probability of P is greater than the probability of Q, then one's level of confidence in P is to be greater than one's level of confidence in Q. Such a principle would not tell us how much confidence to place in either P or Q. Of course, if the probability of R is even higher than is that of P, then, if the principle is to be satisfied, one's level of confidence in P must not be maximal. But apart from that, I see no *a priori* reason for thinking that, whatever be one's level of confidence in P, it might not have been slightly higher or slightly lower while yet the totality of one's levels of confidence satisfies the principle. The case will turn on whether there are no more discriminable degrees of probability than there are discriminable

---

[66] Now that we have all three principles before us, it is clear that contemporary Bayesian accounts of rationality bear a fascinating relationship to Locke's account of what I have called "alethic obligation." Both make crucial use of the concept of probability and the concept of levels of confidence. What is decisive in making Locke's theory come out different is his foundationalism; everything is to rest on propositions that we see to be true. Our contemporary Bayesians are coherentists.

levels of confidence. The other way of understanding the notion of proportionality is this: One might assume that, to a particular probability, a certain level of confidence has an inherent aptness (fittingness, rightness, propriety); and one might then hold that one's task is to see to it that one's level of confidence in the proposition "fits" its probability, on one's satisfactory evidence.

I know of no passage in which Locke distinguishes these interpretations and chooses between them. Nonetheless, a good deal of what he says suggests quite clearly that it is the latter interpretation he has in mind. Accordingly, that is how I shall interpret his principle. Either way, it may be noted that the principle is for the regulating of degrees of confidence and not for the regulating of degrees of belief. It is totally silent on when it is permitted for one to believe P; alternatively, it is totally silent on when the "fit" degree of confidence is above the belief threshold.

Locke says remarkably little by way of justifying his claim that we are to try to apply these principles, in succession, for propositions which are of maximal "concernment" to us. Sometimes he talks as if he finds it self-evident that we are to do so. For example, "It is very easily said, and nobody questions it, that giving and withholding our assent, and the degrees of it, should be regulated by the evidence which things carry with them" (*Conduct*, §33; *Works* ii,379).[67] There is one passage, though, in which Locke offers a defense of sorts of his method, specifically of the principle of proportionality:

There are very few lovers of truth for truths sake . . . How a man may know whether he be so in earnest is worth inquiry: and I think there is this one unerring mark of it, viz., the not entertaining any proposition with greater assurance than the proofs it is built upon will warrant. Whoever goes beyond this measure of assent, 'tis plain receives not truth in the love of it; loves not truth for truths sake, but for some other bye end. For the evidence that any proposition is true (except such as are self-evident), lying only in the proofs a man has of it, whatsoever degrees of assent he affords it beyond the degrees of that evidence, 'tis plain all that surplusage of assurance is owing to some other affection, and not to the love of truth. (iv,xix,1)

The argument lacks cogency. Locke assumes that we are obligated to be "lovers of truth for truth's sake"; and he apparently takes it as self-evident that those who do love truth for truth's sake will try to proportion their level of confidence in a proposition to its probability

---

[67] Cf. i,iv,25: "All that I shall say for the principles I proceed on, is, that I can only appeal to men's own unprejudiced experience, and observation, whether they be true, or no."

on satisfactory evidence. Accordingly, he remarks that any divergence from such fit must be due to a love of something other than truth. What is he taking *love of truth* to be? He doesn't say. But presumably love of truth (and aversion to falsehood) is to be thought of in some such way as this: If one loves truth and abhors falsehood with equal intensity, and has no other loves and aversions which inhibit or distort that love and aversion, then, for any proposition which comes within one's ken, one will do what one can, given one's other obligations, to bring it about that one believes it if and only if it is true. If, peradventure, one should succeed in that endeavor, then one's love of truth and aversion to falsehood will be requited.

But notice, now, that they have been requited no matter what level of confidence one places in what one believes. If one believes only what is true, then, no matter what the confidence with which one believes it, one's love of truth is requited; so too, if one never believes what is false, then, no matter what level of confidence one places in them, one's abhorrence of falsehood is requited. Love of truth, at least if understood along the lines suggested, gives no support at all to Locke's principles.

But if one believes some proposition with a level of confidence higher than its probability on one's evidence, won't one disregard whatever negative evidence might be forthcoming in the future? That certainly would conflict with one's love of truth.

Why would it result in such disregarding? Probably Bertrand Russell at one time believed very firmly that there is a set of all sets. That did not impede his treating the paradoxes he discovered as strong evidence against the proposition.

Or perhaps, in the passage just quoted, Locke was confusing firmness of belief with *tenacity* of belief. It is characteristic of us human beings to want to hang on to certain of our beliefs, to be reluctant to give them up, to resist giving them up, to take steps to avoid being forced to give them up. Quite clearly tenacity is different from firmness – i.e., from levels of confidence. For one thing, tenacity, unlike levels of confidence, seems to be a matter of resolution – a matter of will. But also, it seems entirely possible to be exceedingly tenacious in hanging onto beliefs in propositions about which one is not very confident, and to be entirely non-tenacious with regard to beliefs in propositions in which one has a high level of confidence. Indeed, among the beliefs which people hang onto most tenaciously are those which they hold with less than maximal firmness but which yet are of great importance to them; what gives them their importance is truth-irrelevant merits. If Locke was confusing firmness with tenacity, one can see why he offered the argument he did.

Be all this as it may, however, I think it was especially the desirable *consequences* of embracing the principle of proportionality, as they perceived those consequences, that made Locke and his cohorts in the Royal Society embrace the principle. For example, Joseph Glanville, one of the Royal Society group, argued that acting on the principle would impart a certain stability to the practice of the new natural philosophy:

if a man measures out the degrees of his assent to opinions, according to the measures of evidence, being more sparing and reserved to the more difficult, and not thoroughly examin'd theories, and assured only of those that are clearly apprehended, and have been fully thought of, he stands upon a firm basis, and his science is not moved by the gusts of phancy and humour, which blow up and down the multifarious opinionists.[68]

And many if not all of them held out the hope that accepting the principle would remove the bitterness from the controversies between Catholics and Protestants over the "rule of faith."[69] Both Protestants and Catholics were arguing that the religious life requires the highest firmness of assent: Protestants thought such assent ought to be given to the deliverances of the infallible Bible; Catholics, to the deliverances of the infallible magisterium. Bitter hostilities ensued. The Royal Society group, all of them Protestants, argued that since assent to the content of revealed religion did not have and could not have the highest degree of truth-likelihood – at best it could have "moral certainty" – we ought to hold such assent with an appropriately tempered firmness. Such tempered firmness, they insisted, is quite sufficient for the religious life; and it would stimulate such social virtues as love and toleration, thereby promoting social peace.

---

[68] Quoted in van Leeuwen, *The Problem of Certainty*, pp. 83–4. Compare this passage from Sir Geoffrey Gilbert, writing early in the next century, and making reference to Locke: "There are several degrees from perfect certainty and demonstration quite down to improbability and unlikeness, even to the confines of impossibility; and there are several acts of the mind proportioned to these degrees of evidence, which may be called degrees of assent, from full assurance and confidence, quite down to conjecture, doubt, distrust and disbelief. Now what is to be done in all trials of right, is to range all matters in the scale of probability, so as to lay most weight where the cause ought to preponderate, and thereby to make the most exact discernment that can be, in relation to the right." Quoted in Shapiro, *Probability and Certainty*, pp. 181–2.

[69] On these controversies, see Shapiro, *Probability and Certainty*, van Leeuwen, *The Problem of Certainty*, and Popkin, *The History of Scepticism*.

Naturally it was not always clear, in those who protested the application to religious beliefs of the principle of proportionality, whether their contention was that the content of these beliefs has a higher probability on the evidence than was characteristically ascribed to it by the Royal Society group, or whether, conceding that point, their contention was that not all assent to the content of revealed religion need be proportioned in its firmness to that probability; it is permissible, or even obligatory, for some to be in excess of that. But to leap forward two centuries, and from England to Denmark, Søren Kierkegaard was entirely clear on the matter: Though the probability of the Christian faith according to our evidence is distinctly less than the highest, one's assent to it ought to have as much firmness and intensity as one can muster.[70]

[70] Some time ago Alvin Plantinga published a now well-known article in which he charged classical foundationalists with self-referential incoherence: Their holding of the criterion of classical foundationalism does not satisfy the criterion they hold ("Reason and Belief in God," in Plantinga and Wolterstorff (eds.), *Faith and Rationality* [Notre Dame, Notre Dame University Press, 1983]). Was Locke in this way guilty of self-referential incoherence?

One of the ways in which classical foundationalisms differ from each other is this: They differ with respect to the sorts of beliefs to which the criterion in question is meant to apply. Not all are universalistic; and in particular, some are such that the belief that that version of classical foundationalism is true does not belong to the sorts of beliefs to which the criterion is meant to apply. For those foundationalisms, the fact that the holding of the criterion does not satisfy the criterion is not a mark of incoherence.

It should also be noticed that even though self-referential incoherence is present when one's holding of a classical foundationalist criterion for the presence of some epistemic merit falls within the intended scope of the criterion but does not satisfy the criterion, nonetheless it does not follow that one's holding of the criterion does not possess that merit. For by the correct criterion, whatever that may be, one might be holding the mistaken criterion for the possession of the merit in such a way that one's belief possesses that merit.

So once again: Was Locke self-referentially incoherent in espousing his foundationalist proposal for doing one's best? Well, does it follow from what Locke says that the criterion is to apply to epistemology? The principal issue is whether those who choose to engage in epistemology are obligated therein to try seriously to do their best. Almost certainly Locke thought so. Of course, he may have been mistaken about that; if so, no incoherence. But let us suppose that he was right about that. Then the question of self-referential incoherence is relevant.

Why did Locke hold his rules? So far as I can tell, apart from the weak argument discussed above, because he thought it was self-evident for him that one does one's best if and only if one follows these rules. Given that, does he exhibit self-referential incoherence? Yes and No.

Locke's conviction that one does one's best if and only if one satisfies his rules was not itself arrived at by following these rules. Locke's holding of the rules would satisfy the rules if they were self-evident to him – and only if they were, since he does nothing at all satisfactory by way of offering evidence for them. But they were not self-evident for him, since, as we shall see later, they are mistaken; following the rules is not always doing one's best. Hence Locke's embrace of his rules for doing one's best does not itself satisfy the rules. (Of course, since the rules are mistaken, he may nonetheless have done his best in embracing the rules!)

But Locke does not only offer a highly general criterion for doing one's best. He also has a thesis concerning obligation: For each of us there are matters concerning which we are obligated to try seriously to do our best to proportion our level of confidence in a proposition to its probability. And the fact that Locke's holding of his criterion for doing his best does not satisfy his criterion does not imply that his holding of the criterion was not the result of his

As we leave this topic of Locke's rules for the governance of belief (assent), let me summarize: When the truth or falsehood of some proposition is of maximal concernment to one, so that one is obligated to try to do one's epistemic best toward that proposition, the first thing to do is to collect satisfactory evidence concerning the truth or falsehood of the proposition. That done, one must reflect carefully on the probability of the proposition on that evidence. And finally, one is to proportion one's level of confidence in the proposition to its probability on one's (satisfactory) evidence. To accomplish all this, it is important that one be concerned solely with determining whether P is true or false, entirely "indifferent" to any other value that believing or disbelieving P might have for one. Here is one of Locke's own summaries of the whole process:

> In these two things, viz., an equal indifferency for all truth, I mean the receiving it in the love of it as truth, but not loving it for any other reason before we know it to be true; and in the examination of our principles, and not receiving any for such, nor building on them, until we are fully convinced, as rational creatures, of their solidity, truth, and certainty, consists that freedom of the understanding which is necessary to a rational creature, and without which it is not truly an understanding. It is conceit, fancy, extravagance, anything rather than understanding, if it must be under the constraint of receiving and holding opinions by the authority of anything but their own, not fancied, but perceived evidence. (*Conduct*, §12; *Works* II,347–8)

To this we may add a passage already cited:

> Probability wanting that intuitive evidence, which infallibly determines the understanding, and produces certain knowledge, the mind, if it will proceed rationally, ought to examine all the grounds of probability, and see how they make more or less, for or against any probable proposition, before it assents to or dissents from it, and upon a due balancing the whole, reject, or receive it, with a more or less firm assent, proportionably to the preponderancy of the greater grounds of probability on one side or the other. (IV,xv,5)

A picture of intense self-discipline comes to mind.[71] Max Weber thought that the most striking example of discipline in the modern

---

> *having tried seriously* to follow the criterion. And in fact, I see no reason to think that Locke's holding of the criterion was not the result of his having tried seriously to apply the criterion. Though his espousal of the criterion is not in fact the result of his doing what the criterion specifies as doing one's best, nonetheless it appears to be the result of his *having tried seriously* to do what the criterion specifies as doing one's best. And that's what Locke's account of doxastic obligation, coupled with his criterion for doing one's best, implies that he was obligated to do.

[71] A point eloquently developed by Peter Schouls in *Reasoned Freedom*.

world was the "inner-worldly asceticism" of the early Calvinists. That discipline pales when compared with the rigors of the discipline urged on all of us by John Locke. But of course Locke was reared in Puritan circles![72] We are all guilty of doxastic wrongdoing. We must repent: "Everyone is forward to complain of the prejudices that mislead other men or parties, as if he were free, and had none of his own . . . What now is the cure? No other but this, that every man should let alone other prejudices, and examine his own. Nobody is convinced of his by the accusation of another; he recriminates by the same rule, and is clear. The only way to remove this great cause of ignorance and errour out of the world, is, for every one impartially to examine himself" (*Conduct*, §10; *Works* II,344).

It is best that we not conduct this self-examination in social isolation, however; it will go better if we invite, and genuinely listen to, the challenges of our fellows:

I shall offer this one mark whereby prejudice may be known. He that is strongly of any opinion, must suppose (unless he be self-condemned) that his persuasion is built upon good grounds; and that his assent is no greater than what the evidence of the truth he holds forces him to; and that they are arguments, and not inclination, or fancy, that make him so confident and positive in his tenets. Now, if after all his profession, he cannot bear any opposition to his opinion, if he cannot so much as give a patient hearing, much less examine and weigh the arguments on the other side, does he not plainly confess it is prejudice governs him? and it is not the evidence of truth, but some lazy anticipation, some beloved presumption, that he desires to rest undisturbed in. For, if what he holds be, as he gives out, well fenced with evidence, and he sees it to be true, what need he fear to put it to the proof? (*Conduct*,§10; *Works* II,345; cf. *Conduct*, §41; *Works* II, 389)

Any program of self-mastery undertaken to cope with one's impulses to wrongdoing can be regarded in two quite different ways: One can focus on the rigors of discipline required to carry out the program, or on the liberation from the effects of the evil impulses which the implementation of the program represents. So too with the

---

[72] In Neal Wood, *The Politics of Locke's Philosophy*, there is a fine chapter (pp. 121–48) on the "Ideal of Bourgeois Man" which is implicit in Locke's *Essay*. "The ideal, almost an archetype of bourgeois man and differing markedly from the traditional conception of the aristocrat . . . A reconstruction of the ideal . . . yields a portrait of an individual who is commonsensical and pragmatic, aware of his own fallibility, sociable and tolerant. Above all, Locke's ideal man is an individualist. He is a self-directed man who labors industriously in a persevering and sober manner, is invariably moderate and self-disciplined in the pursuit of happiness, is calculating and prudent in judgment. Locke was offering his bourgeois readers a model for emulation as well as a mirror of themselves"(p. 6).

practice Locke urges on all of us. I have just now emphasized the discipline. But to succeed in doxastic self-mastery would be to free oneself from the evil effects, if not the dynamics, of all those faculties and impulses and desires which so regularly lead us into doxastic wrongdoing. This theme of liberation will become prominent in the writers of the Enlightenment; it is by no means absent in Locke: The freedom to examine what one believes is "a freedom which few men have the notion of in themselves, and fewer are allowed the practice of by others; it being the great art and business of the teachers and guides in most sects to suppress, as much as they can, this fundamental duty which every man owes himself" (*Conduct*, §41; *Works* II,389).[73]

(e) Reason's role

Almost nothing has been said about Reason in our discussion thus far. That so much of Locke's vision could be described without speaking of Reason is significant. Yet Locke himself, in the presentation of his vision, over and over gave Reason central place. We must follow the dictates of Reason, obey Reason's voice, respond to Reason's deliverances, "own no other guide but Reason" (IV,xvi,4). Either we obey Reason's voice or we continue to wander in darkness. Many, of course, are content blindly to believe things on sayso. Others, such as the religious enthusiasts, think it permissible to follow strong inner persuasion. But "if Reason must not examine their truth by something extrinsical to the persuasions themselves; inspirations and delusions, truth and falsehood will have the same measure, and will not be possible to be distinguished" (IV,xix,14).

So Reason it must be. "Reason must be our last judge and guide in everything" (IV,xix,14). Let it be carefully noted: The injunction is not to make Reason the *source* of all our beliefs, not even to make it the

---

[73] Cf. *Conduct*, §12; *Works* II,347: "In these two things, viz. an equal indifferency for all truth; I mean the receiving it, the love of it, as truth, but not loving it for any other reason, before we know it to be true; and in the examination of our principles, and not receiving any for such, nor building on them, till we are fully convinced, as rational creatures, of their solidity, truth, and certainty; consists that freedom of the understanding which is necessary to a rational creature, and without which it is not truly an understanding. It is conceit, fancy, extravagance, anything rather than understanding, if it must be under the constraint of receiving and holding opinions by the authority of anything but their own, not fancied, but perceived, evidence. This was rightly called imposition, and is of all other the worst and most dangerous sort of it. For we impose upon ourselves, which is the strongest imposition of all others; and we impose upon ourselves in that part which ought with the greatest care to be kept free from all imposition."

source of the *basis* of all our beliefs. The intuitive knowledge that one exists is not a product of the faculty of Reason, nor is the knowledge that one has such-and-such ideas. Yet these can serve in the evidential base, when we are trying our best. Reason is to be our *guide*.

God has endowed each of us with Reason. The Reason lodged within each of us offers deliverances, makes pronouncements; to be human is to have Reason speaking within one. It is this that sets us off from the "brutes" – and what sets us off even more is listening to Reason, conducting ourselves rationally, *being* rational. To disregard Reason is to violate the very ground of one's dignity. It is to degrade oneself.

Further, the Reason within each is for each his or her authority. Locke's picture of the community of responsible believers is the picture of a democracy in which each listens to his or her own inner voice of Reason and no one treats any voice outside himself or herself as authoritative – unless his or her Reason tells him or her to do so. "Every man carries about him a touchstone if he will make use of it, to distinguish substantial gold from superficial glittering, truth from appearances . . . [T]his touchstone . . . is natural reason" (*Conduct*, §3; *Works* II,329). Listening to the voice of Reason does not guarantee truth. Nonetheless, Reason is the best guide we have, as we leave behind the "broad daylight" of knowledge and enter the "twilight" of properly governed belief (IV,xiv,2).

But what is Reason? In the babble of competing voices, what do we listen for so as to hear Reason's voice? Fundamental in human life is inference, which, says Locke, "is nothing but by virtue of one proposition laid down as true, to draw in another as true" (IV,xvii,4). But obviously some inferences are good and some are bad. And one of the central functions of Reason is to assist us in making and evaluating inferences. "The question now is to know, whether the mind has made this inference right or not" – whether "it has proceeded rationally, and made a right inference." If not, "it has not so much made . . . an inference of right Reason, as shewn a willingness to have it . . . be taken for such" (IV,xvii,4).

Reason is a faculty, specifically, that faculty whereby we discover arguments and "perceive" their logical force, thereby also forming beliefs as to the cogency of the inferences of which those arguments are the content (IV,xvii,2). I use the word "perceive" advisedly; for Locke uses it in this connection, repeatedly and emphatically. Reason is a faculty whose yield is knowledge, not opinion. And Locke makes it clear that, on his view, it is the same faculty at work when we perceive that a proposition is *entailed* by certain premises as when we perceive that it has such-and-such a degree of probability with respect to those premises. Reason, he says,

consists in nothing but the perception of the connexion there is between the ideas, in each step of the deduction, whereby the mind comes to see, either the certain agreement or disagreement of any two ideas, as in demonstration, in which it arrives at knowledge, or their probable connexion, on which it gives or withholds its assent, as in opinion ... For as Reason perceives the necessary, and indubitable connexion of all the ideas or proofs one to another, in each step of any demonstration that produces knowledge: so it likewise perceives the probable connexion of all the ideas or proofs one to another, in every step of a discourse, to which it will think assent due. This is the lowest degree of that, which can be truly called reason. (IV,xvii,2)[74]

More briefly: Reason is "the discovery of the certainty or probability of such propositions or truths, which the mind arrives at by deductions made from such ideas, which it has got by the use of its natural faculties, viz., by sensation or reflection" (IV,xviii,2).[75]

---

[74] Ayers remarks, in the light of passages such as this, that "it is worth noting that ... it is the connection between subject and predicate which we are said to perceive, not (as any modern notion of 'perceiving probabilities' would surely presume) the connection between a hypothesis and the evidence for it" (*Locke: Volume I: Epistemology*, pp. 105–6). The point, is of course, correct; but it's a point that pertains to Locke's view in general of our knowledge of arguments. In explicating Locke, I have been speaking, and shall continue to speak, of "perceiving" the relation of a conclusion to premises and of a proposition to evidence; Locke thought that the proper analysis of that was in terms of "perceiving" the relation between a subject-idea and a predicate-idea by way of "perceiving" relationships among intermediate ideas.

[75] What I have presented in the text above is part of Locke's official definition of "Reason" in the *Essay*. However, just before saying that Reason "consists in nothing but the perception ...," Locke said that Reason "contains" two "other intellectual faculties, viz., sagacity and illation" (inference). Obviously there is confusion here; but it is purely verbal, and relatively harmless. I shall follow what appears to me to be Locke's dominant practice, of taking Reason to be a faculty of "perception." Essentially the same explanation which I quote in the text above is offered in Locke's early *Essays on the Law of Nature* (p. 125), and is repeated in his Second Letter to Stillingfleet thus: "the agreement or disagreement of two ideas ... perceived by the intervention of a third, which I, and as I guess other people, call reasoning, or knowing by reason" (*Works* III,232). In another passage from the same letter, however, he speaks of all cases of "perception," whether immediate or non-immediate, as the result of the exercise of Reason: "the perception of the agreement or disagreement of ideas, is either by an immediate comparison of two ideas, as in self-evident propositions; which way of knowledge of truth, is the way of reason; or by the intervention of intermediate ideas, i.e. by the deduction of one thing from another, which is also the way of reason" (III, p. 353). In a passage from his First Letter to Stillingfleet, Locke includes yet more capacities under what he calls Reason, namely, the capacity to form general, relative, and complex ideas out of simple ones: "mere ideas are the objects of the understanding, and reason is one of the faculties of the understanding employed about them; and ... the understanding, or reason, whichever your lordship pleases to call it, makes or forms, out of the simple ones that come in by sensation and

Believing that the premises of an argument support its conclusion is different from believing the conclusion on the basis of the argument. The former is that assent which accompanies the insight yielded by the faculty of Reason. The latter, when the argument is probabilistic rather than demonstrative, is an example of mere *opinion*. The faculty which accounts for this opinion is something else than Reason, understood as a faculty of "perception." Locke sometimes calls it, or appears to call it, "inference" and "illation." Reason produces the "perception" that some proposition P is highly probable on some evidence (and that in turn evokes firm and certain *assent* to the proposition that P is highly probable on that evidence); the faculty of inference, under certain conditions (including the condition of believing the premises), produces assent to P itself. My believing the proposition, upon "perceiving" the fact, *that P is highly probable on this evidence,* is certain; my believing the proposition P itself is merely probable.

In thus associating Reason with the perception of the validity or invalidity of arguments Locke stands in a long tradition; he departs from that tradition only in seeing Reason as being as much at work in the determination of probabilities as in the determination of entailments – though this, of course, is an extremely important departure. It is interesting to note that Locke also accepts the traditional view that reasoning (inference), in distinction from Reason, is an inferior mode of coming to knowledge and belief just because of its inherent discursiveness.

In the discovery of, and assent to [self-evident] truths, there is no use of the discursive faculty, no need of reasoning, but they are known by a superior, and higher degree of evidence. And such, if I may guess at things unknown, I am apt to think, that angels have now, and the spirits of just men made perfect, shall have, in a future state, of thousands of things, which now, either wholly escape our apprehensions, or which, our short-sighted Reason having got some faint glimpse of, we, in the dark, grope after. (IV,xvii,14)

reflection, all the other ideas, whether general, relative, or complex, by abstracting, comparing, and compounding its positive simple ideas. . . And therefore I never denied that reason was employed about our particular simple ideas, to make out of them ideas general, relative, and complex; nor about all our ideas, whether simple or complex, positive or relative, general or particular: it being the proper business of reason, in the search after truth and knowledge, to find out the relations between all these sorts of ideas, in the perception whereof knowledge and certainty of truth consists" (III, 70–1). Lastly, in a passage from the Second Letter, Locke says that though in the *Essay* he treated Reason "no otherwise than as a faculty," yet "reason" may also be used "as standing for true and clear principles, and also as standing for clear and fair deductions from those principles" (III, 424).

Though reasoning may be inferior to intuitive understanding in its discursiveness as well as in its dependence on memory, nonetheless Reason, for Locke, yields acquaintance with reality which is as direct as that yielded by intuition. It is, in fact, a species of intuitive knowledge. By virtue of the faculty of Reason we are directly acquainted with facts consisting of propositions standing in entailment and probability relationships with each other. We notice them, "perceive" them, see them. We have unobstructed insight, vision. Or to put it the other way round, by virtue of this faculty, reality is directly present to us.

The deep structure of Locke's thought begins to emerge. Some propositions we just see to be true. The fact presents itself to us directly. Others, though we cannot see them to be true, are still such that we can see that they are probable with respect to those that we see to be true. These phenomena of insight are the fundamental phenomena to be used as we set about trying our best to proportion our level of confidence in propositions to their probability. Their fundamental role in the practice Locke recommends is what accounts for the foundationalist character of that practice, as it accounts (in part) for the prominent place he gives to Reason in his summations of the proposed practice. Reason is a mode of *insight*. Locke thinks that for our non-immediate beliefs we must have *reasons*, *good* reasons, evidence. Reason tells us which reasons are good reasons; Reason yields *insight*.

Since Locke there have been many who have denied that there is a faculty of Reason yielding insight into the reality of logical relationships among propositions, as well as many who have denied that probability is a logical relation among propositions, and many who have denied that all good reasons are such that the conclusion is either entailed by, or probable on, the premises. But it is important to see that even if we grant to Locke these controversial theses, that is to say, even if we grant to him his contested understanding of the nature of Reason, his injunction "Listen to the voice of Reason" is most inadequate as a summary of his vision. That is true in various ways.

In the first place, Reason, as already remarked, is never understood by Locke as the sole source of those insights/beliefs which are the evidential base for trying our best. The evidential base, when we are trying our best, consists of immediate beliefs which count as knowledge. But most immediate beliefs are not evoked by Reason's insight. Reason yields immediate "perception" of certain sorts of facts, including facts of the form: *P is entailed by (probable with respect to) propositions P_1 . . . P_n* . . . But the immediate knowledge which constitutes the evidential base for a given implementation of the Lockian practice is certainly not limited to knowledge of facts of the latter sort. For one thing, the basis includes our knowledge of self-evident necessary truths which are not of this logical-relationship-among-propositions form. Admittedly there is a deep similarity between self-evident propositions of this logical-relationship-among-propositions sort and other sorts of self-evident necessary truths, so much so that most thinkers of the Western tradition have thought that it was the same faculty at work and have called it Reason in both cases. But then what has to be added is that Locke regards immediate knowledge as also going beyond knowledge of self-evident necessary truths; it includes various contingent truths. In short, we have to listen to more of our faculties than just Reason if we are to try to do our epistemic best.

Secondly, the injunction "Listen to the voice of Reason" is woefully incomplete as a formulation of the injunction Locke had in mind. Locke did not think that one should listen to what Reason says about *all* arguments which come to mind for *any* proposition. It was only for arguments of certain sorts – those whose premises constitute satisfactory evidence – and for propositions satisfying certain conditions that he proposed listening to what Reason says about the argument for the proposition.

And then there is the question: What am I to do with what I hear Reason saying about those arguments for those propositions? Locke's own view was that we are to apply the principle of proportionality to what we hear Reason saying. But there are other possible answers than this to the question. Karl Popper, for example, proposed something quite different from Locke's principle, a falsificationist rather than a justificationist principle. In addition, one can imagine justificationist principles quite different from Locke's. The imperative "Listen to the voice of Reason" is useless until fleshed out with answers to questions in two directions: Listen to it with respect to which body of evidence for which propositions? and, Do what with that which I hear it saying?

Lastly, there are many more injunctions in Locke's proposal concerning the "conduct of the understanding" than just the injunction, "Listen to the voice of Reason." In the course of our discussion we have uncovered many of those other injunctions. The central injunctions, at least in my presentation, are the injunctions to obey the principles of evidence, of appraisal, and of proportionality. But those principles presuppose, and are supplemented by, a number of others – the principle of indifference, for example, which says that we are to be concerned only with the truth and falsehood of our beliefs.

There is, thus, a strange misperception – or misrepresentation – in Locke, and in very much epistemology since Locke. Listen to the voice of Reason, says Locke, as if, on the one hand, that captured what he was saying, and as if, on the other, it was advice that would be contested – by traditionalists and enthusiasts, for example. But nobody who grants that there is a faculty of Reason thinks that we should ignore what Reason says. Our disputes are over whether there is such a faculty; and among those who believe that there is, over what it says, and with respect to which arguments for which propositions one ought to listen to what it says, and what one ought to do with what one hears it saying. Some in recent years have accused Reason of tyranny. Reason is no tyrant. The tyranny lies in what is done with Reason.

Perhaps there was something else at work. Perhaps what was coming to the surface was Locke's conviction that *the theory itself*, in all its complexity, is a deliverance of Reason – that the theory was self-evident to him. Perhaps it was not only Locke's conviction that to fail to conduct one's understanding as he recommends is to fail to use one's Reason properly, but also his conviction that *one's Reason tells one* that this is to fail to use one's Reason properly. Reason itself tells us how Reason is to be used. To fail to accept the theory that we ought to listen to the voice of Reason is itself to fail to listen to the voice of Reason. We have already seen, however – and shall see in more detail later – that Reason says nothing of the sort.

A new question must now be raised, a question whose answer as developed by Locke is not only fascinating in its own right but serves to undercut his entire vision. The question is this: Can one be mistaken in one's appraisal of probabilities? Locke says in one passage that

Those who want skill to use those evidences they have of probabilities; who cannot carry a train of consequences in their heads, nor weigh exactly the preponderancy of contrary proofs and testimonies, making every circumstance its due allowance, may be easily misled to assent to positions that are not probable. There are some men of one, some but of two syllogisms, and no more; and others that can but advance one step farther. These cannot always discern that side on which the strongest proofs lie; cannot constantly follow that which in itself is the more probable opinion. (iv,xx,5)

Locke teeters on the edge of saying that our Reason itself may sometimes be in error. But he stops short of saying that, both here and elsewhere. A man's being of one syllogism does not, on Locke's view, take the form of his Reason telling him that a proposition is entailed by some evidence when it is not. It takes the form of his Reason not telling him anything at all about entailments except for "one syllogism"; and on that one syllogism, it tells him the truth.[76] Of course, the man of "one syllogism" may have *beliefs* about other arguments; but then it is some faculty other than his Reason which is producing those beliefs. Perhaps he holds those beliefs on sayso.

What would Reason's being in error consist of?[77] Presumably it would consist of Reason, with respect to some falsehood, producing in one an experience which is phenomenologically no different from the "just knowing" experience – this in turn producing a belief. Locke, so far as I can see, held firmly to the conviction that that never happens; as indeed he rejected the possibility that we have in us some other faculty which, with respect to falsehood, perfectly mimics the "just knowing" experience. Mistaken beliefs about entailment and prob-ability-on-evidence are not the result of misleading phenomenology, whether produced by Reason or some other faculty; but of failure to attend with sufficient care to the presence or absence of the phenomenology in us. It is sometimes this failure of close attention which has the consequence that we believe some proposition to be entailed by, or more probable than not on, some evidence when it is not. On Locke's view, it never *genuinely appears* to us that we are "perceiving" some fact when we are not; what happens rather is that sometimes we *believe* we are when we are not. In intuitive knowledge, he says, "there is barely one simple intuition, wherein there is no room for any the least mistake or doubt: the truth is seen all perfectly at once. In demonstration, 'tis true, there is intuition too, but not altogether at once; for there must be a remembrance of the intuition

---

[76] Cf. Third Letter for Toleration; *Works* v,537: "That which hath evidence enough to make one man certain, has not enough to make another so much as guess it to be true; though he has spared no endeavour or application in examining it."

[77] Though the theme of the infallibility of Reason plays an exceedingly dominant role in Schouls' book on Locke, *Reasoned Freedom*, Schouls, oddly, never considers what the infallibility of Reason consists in, other than to suggest, in one passage, that it consists in the infallible ability to pick out episodes of Reason "perceiving" something. If we take it to consist in this, then, as I shall argue, Locke does not hold that Reason is infallible.

of the agreement of the medium, or intermediate idea, with what we compared it before, when we compare it with the other: and where there be many mediums, there the danger of the mistake is the greater" (IV,xvii,15). To this passage may be added the following: "whatever grounds of probability there may be, they yet operate no farther on the mind, which searches after truth, and endeavours to judge right, than they appear" (IV,xvi,1).

Nonetheless, in chapter xx of Book IV of the *Essay* Locke discusses what he calls "wrong measures of probability"; so we must look at what he says about these. How, while affirming the infallibility of Reason, can Locke admit that we make mistakes about the probability of a proposition on a body of evidence?

The discussion is fascinating, even brilliant. Locke calls attention to certain *wounds of the mind*, as I shall call them,[78] which have the consequence that, in the face of evidence which would lead a person to assent to P if his mind were functioning properly, he in his woundedness does not assent. Sometimes so grievous are the wounds that one despairs: "What probabilities . . . are sufficient in such a case? . . . All the arguments can be used, will be as little able to govern, as the wind did with the traveller, to part with his cloak, which he held only the faster" (IV,xx,11). Wounds of the mind are not wounds of Reason. Reason itself is invulnerable. Nonetheless, the admission that there are such wounds proves to have a devastating effect on Locke's vision.

The first sort of example Locke cites is this: "propositions that are not in themselves certain and evident, but doubtful and false," may be inculcated in us from youth up as (self-evident) *principles*. And "these have so great an influence upon our opinions, that 'tis usually by them we judge of truth, and measure probability, to that degree, that what is inconsistent with our *principles*, is so far from passing for probable with us, that it will not be allowed possible. The reverence is born to these principles is so great, and their authority so paramount to all others, that the testimony not only of other men, but the evidence of our own senses are often rejected, when they offer to

---

[78] Though the phrase is mine, Locke himself regularly uses the medical metaphor of disease. He speaks of "the variety of distempers in men's minds" (*Conduct*, §38; *Works* II,384); and he says that there are perhaps as many "weaknesses and defects in the understanding, either from the natural temper of the mind, or ill habits taken up . . . as there are diseases of the body, each whereof clogs and disables the understanding to some degree, and therefore deserves to be looked after and cured" (*Conduct*, §38; *Works* II, 349). As one would expect, he also regularly speaks, as in that last passage, of "cures" and "remedies" (e.g., *Conduct*, §41; *Works* II, 388-9).

vouch any thing contrary to these established rules . . . For he hath a strong bias put into his understanding which will unavoidably misguide his assent, who hath imbibed wrong principles, and has blindly given himself up to the authority of any opinion in itself not evidently true" (iv,xx,8). Locke offers, as an example of wounding by the inculcation of a principle, the inculcation from youth up in the mind of a "Romanist" of the doctrine of transubstantiation.[79]

Locke does not recommend, as a cure for the wounds of inculcated principles, anything like the radical therapy of Cartesian doubt; the recommended cure is this much more genial regimen: "every one ought very carefully to beware what he admits for a principle, to examine it carefully, and see whether he certainly knows it to be true of itself by its own evidence, or whether he does only with assurance believe it to be so, upon the authority of others" (iv,xx,8).[80] Locke's discussion of the wounds of inculcated principles makes clear that the experience of "perceiving" a self-evident truth is susceptible to mimicry so cunning that only the most careful self-scrutiny can tell the real article from the fake.

Another sort of wound is inflicted by what Locke calls "received hypotheses." A person may over the years have become so attached to a certain explanation of various phenomena that evidence which would sway him if he did not have this attachment has no effect on his assent. "Would it not be an insufferable thing for a learned professor, and that which his scarlet would blush at, to have his authority of forty years standing wrought out of hard rock Greek and Latin, with no small expence of time and candle, and confirmed by general tradition, and a reverend beard, in an instant overturned by an upstart novelist [i.e., deviser of novelties]? Can any one expect that he should be made to confess, that what he taught his scholars thirty years ago, was all errour and mistake; and that he sold them hard words and ignorance at a very dear rate?" (iv,xx,11) Locke does not

---

[79] On inculcated principles, see also *Essay* i,iii,22–7.

[80] By no means, however, does Locke think that even careful examination will always result in getting things right. "The tempers of men's minds; the principles settled there by time and education, beyond the power of the man himself to alter them; the different capacities of men's understandings, and the strange ideas they are often filled with; are so various and uncertain, that it is impossible to find that evidence . . . which one can confidently say will be sufficient for all men" (Third Letter for Toleration; *Works* v,297). Furthermore, "Who is there almost that has not prejudices, that he does not know to be so . . . ? It is not everyone knows, or can bring himself to DesCartes's way of doubting, and strip his thoughts of all opinions, till he brings them to self-evident principles, and then upon them builds all his future tenets" (*ibid.*, 297–8).

explicitly say what regimen we should undertake so as to cure ourselves of such a wound as this.

Before proceeding to Locke's other two types of "wrong measures of probability," let us pause for a moment to reflect on the structure of the examples he has offered thus far. In the first case, a belief which a person already has, for example, the doctrine of transubstantiation, inhibits his assent to some self-evident or testified proposition (or to some proposition about what is sensed); if he did not have that belief, he would assent. Errors of all sorts follow in the train of this one. Perhaps also the second-order belief, that the doctrine of transubstantiation is self-evident for one, plays a role in the inhibition of assent which in the healthy person would be forthcoming. In the second case, a belief which a person already has inhibits his assent to the proposition that such-and-such is a good argument, i.e., that the evidence is satisfactory and that it supports the proposition; if he did not have that belief, he would agree that it is a good argument. In the last sort of case to be considered, a belief which a person already has inhibits his assent to *the conclusion* of an argument; if he did not have that belief, he would assent.

Obviously the same issue arises in each of these three types of cases. A prior belief serves to inhibit assent to a self-evident or obvious truth, or to the fact that some argument is a good one, or to the conclusion of what is in fact a good argument.[81] How might such inhibition work? One possibility is that the person actually does "perceive" the fact, that is, the self-evident truth or the force of the argument; but his coming with the belief that he does come with serves to inhibit the normal causal efficacy of that "perception," so that he neither believes the proposition corresponding to that fact, nor believes the second-order proposition that he is "perceiving" that fact. The other possibility is that his coming with the belief he does come with serves to inhibit the "perception" itself – and hence, also, both the first-order and second-order beliefs.

What must be noted is that, either way, the consequences for Locke's vision are disastrous. It was his conviction that trying our best to get in touch with reality requires that our beliefs be grounded on what we "perceive." "To the facts themselves" was his motto. Now it

---

[81] A somewhat similar point played a very large role in Descartes's thought, as all of Locke's readers, then and now, would recognize. Descartes's precise point, as I shall argue, is that *praejudicia* inhibit a person's ability to distinguish between propositions of which he or she is certain and propositions of which he or she is not certain.

turns out that false beliefs we already have inhibit either "perception" itself or its efficacy in producing the relevant first-order and second-order beliefs. The beliefs we already have either obstruct our direct access to the facts or render that access irrelevant for our purposes, since the corresponding beliefs are not evoked.[82] And Locke was not so naïve and unrealistic as to propose that we cope with this difficulty by emptying our head of beliefs before we set about using his proposed doxastic practice. In iv,xiii,2 he had remarked that "what a man sees he cannot but see; and what he perceives, he cannot but know that he perceives." If by that last clause Locke not only means, *cannot but "perceive" that he "perceives,"* but means also to suggest, *cannot but believe with certitude that he "perceives,"* then his own analysis in chapter xx shows why he has to retract this.

There is no better example of "deconstruction" in the history of Western philosophy. If those convictions "that pass for principles, are not certain," says Locke, "(which we must have some way to know, that we may be able to distinguish them from those that are doubtful,) but are only made so to us by our blind assent, we are liable to be misled by them; and instead of being guided into truth, we shall, by principles, be only confirmed in mistake and errour." And how shall we discern the error of principles? By "barely considering" ideas, "without any other principles," "finding their agreement and disagreement" (iv,xii,5–6). But Locke himself darkens the vision: Principles "being once established in any one's mind, it is easy to be imagined, what reception any proposition shall find, how clearly soever proved, that shall invalidate their authority" (iv,xx,10). To use the doxastic practice which Locke recommends, we must be able to pick out episodes of "perceiving" some fact. To do that, we must have beliefs of the form, "I believe that I am 'perceiving' fact F." It turns out that the beliefs one already has will often inhibit the formation of exactly such beliefs, perhaps even, sometimes, when they would be true.

But let us not follow C. S. Peirce and his host of twentieth-century imitators in supposing that the possibility of misidentifying episodes of direct awareness is a reason for concluding that there are no such

---

[82] A similar point was made by Locke already in ii,ix,8 and 10, where he observed that the object judgments we are habitually disposed to make, upon having certain sensory input, *alter* our perceptions. "We are farther to consider concerning perception, that the ideas we receive by sensation, are often in grown people altered by the judgment, without our taking notice of it."

episodes.[83] If there were episodes of direct awareness, says Peirce – or of "intuition," to use his terminology – then it would be plausible to suppose that among the facts one intuits are facts consisting of one's intuiting some fact. In Peirce's words, it would be plausible to suppose that we have the "power of intuitively distinguishing intuitions from other cognitions,"[84] the "intuitive faculty of distinguishing intuitive from mediate cognition,"[85] "the faculty of distinguishing, by simple contemplation, between an intuition and a cognition determined by others."[86] Peirce tacitly assumes that if one did intuit that one was intuiting some fact, one would believe that one was; likewise he assumes that from this it would be a simple non-controversial inference to the conclusion that one had the faculty of intuition. He then argues that we do "not possess the faculty of distinguishing, by simple contemplation, between an intuition and a cognition determined by others."[87] If we did have such a faculty, none of us would be unsure as to whether a particular cognition was or was not an intuition, for our convictions on the matter would be infallible; neither would there be any controversy among us as to the existence of this faculty. But in fact those who assume the existence of intuitions often find themselves unsure, and presumably not at all infallible, in their identification of them; by analogy, "every lawyer knows how difficult it is for witnesses to distinguish between what they have seen and what they have inferred."[88] And those who assume the existence of intuitions discover that their claim is much contested. Thus – by *reductio ad absurdum* – it follows that we do not have intuitions, that is, direct awarenesses.

The argument is scarcely compelling. It is indeed plausible to assume that if we can be directly aware of certain facts, then among the facts of which we can be directly aware will be facts consisting of our being directly aware of some fact. It would be naïve to assume that such awareness would follow the simple rule that if S intuits F, then S also intuits the fact that he or she intuits F. But that some (at least) of the facts consisting of one's intuiting some fact are *accessible to* one's direct awareness is a plausible assumption for those who hold that there is direct awareness.

But why assume that if we have intuitions, we shall always be confident that we have correctly identified them; and why assume

[83] See C. S. Peirce, "Questions Concerning Certain Faculties Claimed for Man," in *Collected Papers of Charles Sanders Peirce*, ed. P. Weiss and A. Burke (8 vols., Cambridge, Mass., Harvard University Press, 1931–58), vol. v (1934).   [84] *Ibid.*, p. 136.
[85] *Ibid.*, p. 143.   [86] *Ibid.*, p. 139.   [87] *Ibid.*   [88] *Ibid.*, p. 138.

that our identifications will always be correct? Consider *literal seeing*: One can see a tree without being confident that one has done so and without always being correct in one's belief that one has done so. Lawyers do indeed know that it is difficult for witnesses to distinguish what they saw from what they inferred; but most of them do not draw the conclusion that there is only inferring, no seeing.

At the basis of Peirce's argument is a confusion which has spread like a virus throughout contemporary philosophy – the confusion between the *ontological* issue of whether we can have direct awareness of facts and the *epistemological* issue of whether beliefs to the effect that such-and-such is an example of direct awareness are incorrigible. Why should it not be the case that though we have direct awarenesses of certain facts, our attempt to identify such acts of awareness is a fallible enterprise?

Of course, the role in one's philosophy of the phenomenon of direct awareness may well become problematic if one grants that attempts to pick out episodes of the phenomenon are fallible. I have observed that that is true for Locke. But that then is the point to emphasize. Locke's admission that the attempt to identify episodes of direct awareness is fallible introduces deep tensions into his overall picture. But contrary to Peirce's argument, that admission poses no problems for the thesis itself that we do have direct awareness of certain facts.

Peirce, after concluding to his own satisfaction that "it is not self-evident that we have such an intuitive faculty, for it has just been shown that we have no intuitive power of distinguishing an intuition from a cognition determined by others," addresses himself to another possibility; namely, that "the existence or non-existence of this power [of intuition] is to be determined upon evidence."[89] He considers a number of cases which had been cited as examples of intuition, and shows that in each case other cognitions enter into the "determination" of the cognition in question. His observations seem to me in the main correct. Once again, however, they do not tell against the existence of direct awareness.

For one thing, many of the cases in which Peirce spies inference are cases in which Locke would also happily spy inference. But secondly and more importantly, assembling evidence for the conclusion that all cognitions are determined by other cognitions – that is, that prior cognitions enter into the causal conditions of every cognition – is

---

[89] *Ibid.*, p. 144.

irrelevant to the issue. The partisan of direct awareness (and of immediate belief and assent) need not deny such causal conditioning; he or she would, in fact, be well advised not to do so. The question is not whether the causal conditions for the occurrence of awarenesses always include other states of mind. The question is whether we can only be aware of something *by way of* being aware of something else – and in turn, of that something else by way of being aware of something else, etc. Nothing Peirce says constitutes any reason whatsoever for thinking that the answer to this latter question should be Yes. Peircean coherentism is fully compatible with the existence of direct awareness and immediate belief.

A third type of wrong measure of probability, the fourth in Locke's own listing, is *allegiance to authority*. It is not entirely clear whether Locke understood this too as a wounding of the mind, the wound working in the way I have just described; or whether it is a straightforward voluntary failure, either to apply the principles of evidence and appraisal, or to apply the principle of proportionality. In any case, nothing so effectively stirs up eloquence in Locke as this subject of assent to authority:

> The fourth and last wrong measure of probability I shall take notice of, and which keeps in ignorance, or errour, more people than all the other together, is that which I have mentioned in the fore-going chapter, I mean, the giving up our assent to the common received opinions, either of our friends, or party; neighbourhood, or country. How many men have no other ground for their tenets, than the supposed honesty, or learning, or number of those of the same profession? As if honest, or bookish men could not err; or truth were to be established by the vote of the multitude: yet this with most men serves the turn. The tenet has had the attestation of reverend antiquity, it comes to me with the passport of former ages, and therefore I am secure in the reception I give it: other men have been, and are of the same opinion, (for that is all is said,) and therefore it is reasonable for me to embrace it. A man may more justifiably throw up cross and pile for his opinions, than take them up by such measure. (IV,xx,17)

Locke cites one more source of "wrong measures of probability," actually the third in his own listing. This is by far the most interesting and complex of the four. Consideration of what he says will plunge us into a topic which thus far we have broached without entering – the topic, namely, of belief and the will. The issue is fundamental to Locke's entire recommendation. If I *ought* to proportion the level of confidence I place in a proposition to its probability on satisfactory evidence, then presumably I can do so. But *can* I? If so, how?[90]

Here is part of Locke's statement of his third source of "wrong measures of probability":

> Probabilities, which cross men's appetites, and prevailing passions, run the same fate. Let never so much probability hang on one side of a covetous man's reasoning, and money on the other; and it is easy to foresee which will outweigh. Earthly minds, like mud walls, resist the strongest batteries: and though, perhaps, sometimes the force of a clear argument may make some impression, yet they nevertheless stand firm, keep out the enemy truth, that would captivate, or disturb them. Tell a man, passionately in love, that he is jilted; bring a score of witnesses of the falsehood of his mistress, 'tis ten to one but three kind words of hers, shall invalidate all their testimonies . . . What suits our wishes is forwardly believed, is, I suppose, what every one hath more than once experimented [experienced]: and though men cannot always openly gainsay, or resist the force of manifest probabilities, that make against them; yet yield they not to the argument. (IV,xx,12)

Locke is pointing here to some defect of will – and behind that, to some defect of motivation; close scrutiny will reveal, however, that a wounding of the belief-forming faculties of the mind is also involved.

We find within ourselves not only love of truth but other loves as well – love of gain, love of members of the opposite sex, and so on. These loves sometimes motivate us to undertake the act of *resisting* believing in accord with what appears to be strong evidence. We discern that to believe in accord with the apparently strong evidence would amount to admitting that our love of gain or person was disappointed. But acknowledging disappointed love is painful. So we resist.

Why is resistance in the picture? Is it not in our power freely to decide to what to give our assent and with what degree of firmness? Let us step back a bit to gain a broader view of the situation. As we noted earlier, Locke thinks that just as there are faculties in us which produce insight, so too there are faculties which produce assent and belief. He assumes that there is a faculty which produces assent

---

[90] An excellent exposition of Locke's account of the power of the will is to be found in Part B of Schouls' *Reasoned Freedom*. It is worth quoting Schouls' summary: "A person avoids being incorporated into the mechanism of nature through the complex act that includes suspension of natural desires, examination of these desires and their potential consequences, contemplation of true good, judgment of the suspended desires in terms of the good contemplated, and submission to the outcome of that judgment" (p. 145). This is Locke's own summary: "This at least I think evident, that we find in ourselves a power to begin or forbear, continue or end several actions of our minds . . . barely by a thought or preference of the mind ordering, or as it were commanding the doing or not doing such or such a particular action. This power which the mind has, thus to order the consideration of any idea, or the forbearing to consider it . . . in any particular instance is that which we call the will" (II,xxi,5).

corresponding to the "perceptions" which constitute knowledge. And he notes the presence in us of the faculty called *inference*, whose workings he describes, in a passage already quoted, thus: "To infer is nothing but by virtue of one proposition laid down as true, to draw in another as true, i.e., to see or suppose such a connexion of the two ideas, of the inferred proposition" (IV,xvii,4). As Locke indicates here, our inference may or may not be grounded on "seeing" that the premises provide evidential support for the conclusion.

It is not clear whether Locke thought that we have assent-forming faculties in addition to these. He regularly cites testimony as something that produces assent in us; and he often cites, as examples of beliefs, generalizations from experience. It appears, however, that he thought that believing something on sayso proves, on scrutiny, to be a case of inference (IV,xv,1). And it may well be that he thought the same for all cases of assent which do not accompany "perception." If so, then it was his view that all assent, except for that which accompanies immediate "perception," is *mediate* – if we define "mediate assent" as assent produced by the faculty of inference.

But whether or not that was his view, what is directly relevant to our purposes here is Locke's assumption that our assent-forming and belief-forming faculties produce not only assent and belief in us but also, sometimes, the *inclination* to assent or believe without actually doing so. It is this inclination that can be resisted – sometimes successfully. Though Locke held that only rarely are the circumstances such that one can *decide to believe*, he clearly held that we are commonly in circumstances in which we can *decide to withhold belief*, or *decide to resist believing*, or *decide to believe with a particular firmness*.

The scope which Locke assigned to the influence of will on belief is most easily grasped by focusing on the sorts of cases in which choice and successful resistance are not possible.[91] What Locke himself says, by way of generalization, is that "It is not in our choice to take which side we please, if manifest odds appear on either. The greater probability, I think, in that case, will determine the assent: and a man can no more avoid assenting, or taking it to be true, where he perceives the greater probability, than he can avoid knowing it to be true, where he perceives the agreement or disagreement of any two ideas" (IV,xx,16). If one believes that the probability of some

---

[91] The only ample discussion of these matters of which I am aware is J. A. Passmore, "Locke and the Ethics of Belief," in A. Kenny (ed.), *Rationalism, Empiricism, and Idealism* (Oxford, Clarendon Press, 1986).

proposition on evidence which one takes to be satisfactory is ·5, or just barely above that, or if one "perceives" that the probability on what one believes to be such evidence is ·5 and one does not believe that it is substantially higher, then perhaps one has it in one's power to decide to believe as well as to decide to refrain from believing (IV,xvi,9; xx,15–16). But where the probability on what one believes to be satisfactory evidence is believed or "perceived" (without countervailing belief) to be high, "Probability upon such grounds carries so much evidence with it, that it naturally determines the judgment, and leaves us as little liberty to believe, or disbelieve, as a demonstration does" (IV,xvi,9; cf. xvii,16; xx,15).

However, it is already clear from Locke's discussion of "received hypotheses" that this generalization does not fully capture his thought; its inadequacy becomes even clearer in his discussion of the role of passions in the formation of belief, which we shall consider shortly. A "rational reconstruction" of his thought would instead look something like this: First, if one *"perceives"* some proposition P and does not *believe* that one is not "perceiving" it, then one cannot refrain from believing P. Secondly, if one "perceives" that P is highly probable on evidence that one believes is satisfactory and one does not *believe* that P is not highly probable on that evidence, then one cannot refrain from believing P. And thirdly, if one *believes* that one is "perceiving" P, whether or not one is, or believes that one is "perceiving" that P is highly probable on evidence which one believes is satisfactory, whether or not one is, then one cannot refrain from believing P.

It is especially in his discussion of his third type of wrong estimates of probability that Locke makes clear that even if as a matter of fact one has clearly in view the logical force of one's evidence for P, and even if as a matter of fact that evidence is satisfactory and strongly supports P, nonetheless it may well be that one does not assent to P. In many such situations one's belief-forming faculties may produce in one a strong *inclination* to believe P, so that believing P has to be resisted; but resistance is possible. To understand how this can be, we must once again bring into the picture the beliefs one has when entering the situation.

If a person *believes* that she does not "perceive" the relation of premises to conclusion, whether or not in fact she does, that may inhibit either her "perception" of the relation or the evocation of the corresponding assent (it is not clear which of these options Locke would choose), with the result that she also does not assent to the conclusion. So also, if a person *believes* that the evidence is not satisfactory, whether or not in fact it is, that may well inhibit her assent to the conclusion.

So that, I think, we may conclude, that in propositions, where though the proofs in view are of most moment, yet there are sufficient grounds, to suspect that there is either fallacy in words, or certain proofs, as considerable, to be produced on the contrary side, there assent, suspense, or dissent, are often voluntary actions: but where the proofs are such as make it highly probable and there is not sufficient ground to suspect, that there is either fallacy of words, (which sober and serious considerations may discover,) nor equally valid proofs yet undiscovered latent on the other side, (which also the nature of the thing, may, in some cases, make plain to a considerate man,) there, I think, a man who has weighed them, can scarce refuse his assent to the side, on which the greater probability appears. (IV,xx,15)

And what accounts for the emergence and non-emergence of beliefs to the effect that one has or has not acquired satisfactory evidence, or to the effect that one has or has not apprehended the probability of the proposition on the evidence? Locke never gives a general account. But what he does suggest is that if one has some love of something other than truth, that may keep alive in one, longer than would otherwise be the case, the belief that the present evidence is not satisfactory or that its evidential force is not fully apprehended. Thus again a wounding of the mind takes place.

We now at last see why Locke insists so adamantly on "indifference." Indifference is exactly what is needed to cure those wounds of the mind which have been inflicted on it by passion. Presumably a wounding might also have the opposite effect: We might believe too quickly that we have acquired satisfactory evidence, or that we "perceive" its evidential force. There are presumably wounds of gullibility as well as wounds of skepticism:

a man hath a power to suspend and restrain [the understanding's] inquiries, and not permit a full and satisfactory examination, as far as the matter in question is capable, and will bear it to be made. Until that be done, there will be always these two ways left of evading the most apparent probabilities. First, that the arguments being (as for the most part they are) brought in words, there may be a fallacy latent in them: and the consequences being, perhaps, many in train, they may be some of them incoherent. There be very few discourses, are so short, clear and consistent, to which most men may not, with satisfaction enough to themselves, raise this doubt; and from whose conviction they may not, without reproach of disingenuity or unreasonableness, set themselves free with the old reply . . . though I cannot answer, I will not yield. Secondly, manifest probabilities may be evaded, and the assent withheld upon this suggestion, that I know not yet all that may be said on the contrary side. And therefore though I be beaten, 'tis not necessary I should yield, not knowing what forces there are in reserve behind. (IV,xx,12–14)

A strategy for resisting unwelcome beliefs is naturally suggested by these observations: Keep saying to oneself that perhaps the evidence presently available is not satisfactory, or that its evidential force may not really be what it presently appears to be. This *saying to oneself* won't work always, or forever; but often it will work for a while.

It should be remarked, finally, that even when assent to some conclusion is compelled by evidence, a role will have been played by one's will in the formation of one's assent. Indeed, even knowledge is in certain ways a consequence of what we will; it "is neither wholly necessary nor wholly voluntary" (IV,xiii,1). "If it were not so," says Locke, "ignorance, error, or infidelity could not in any case be a fault" (IV,xx,16).

There are two ways in which our knowledge and our ignorance are a consequence of what we will, with the result that ignorance is sometimes blamable. "He that has eyes, if he will open them by day, cannot but see some objects, and perceive a difference in them" (IV,xiii,1). In *that* we have no choice. What we *can* do is decide whether or not to look at something. "Though a man with his eyes open in the light cannot but see; yet there be certain objects, which he may choose whether he will turn his eyes to" (IV,xiii,1). Thus someone can be blamed for not knowing the speed limit in a certain village. He should have taken notice of the signs; if he had, he would have known.

Secondly, says Locke (IV,xiii,2), we have it in our power not only to look at something but to look carefully, not only to listen, but to listen carefully; and sometimes a culpable lack of knowledge is due not to failure to look or listen but failure to look or listen carefully. A person may sometimes be blamed for not knowing that the last movement of the symphony was in rondo form. He should have listened more carefully; if he had, he would have known. Or again, "he that has got the idea of numbers," says Locke, "and hath taken the pains to compare one, two, and three, to six, cannot choose but know that they are equal" (IV,xiii,3). What he *can* choose to do or not do is take the pains to compare them.

In short, says Locke, "all that is voluntary in our knowledge, is the *employing*, or withholding any of our faculties from this or that sort of objects, and a more, or less accurate survey of them. But they, being employed, our will hath no power to determine the knowledge of the mind one way or another; that is done only by the objects themselves, as far as they are clearly discovered" (IV,xiii,2). Later he draws out the analogy to assent:

> As knowledge, is no more arbitrary than perception: so, I think, assent is no more in our power than knowledge. When the agreement of any two ideas appears to our minds whether immediately, or by the assistance of Reason, I can no more refuse to perceive, no more avoid knowing it, than I can avoid seeing those objects, which I turn my eyes to, and look on in daylight: And what upon full examination I find the most probable, I cannot deny my assent to. But though we cannot hinder our knowledge, where the agreement is once perceived; nor our assent, where the probability manifestly appears upon due consideration of all the measures of it: Yet *we can hinder both knowledge and assent, by stopping our enquiry*, and not employing our faculties in the search of any truth. (IV,xx,16)[92]

I entered this somewhat lengthy discussion on "wrong measures of probability" by asking whether, on Locke's view, one could be mistaken in one's appraisal of probabilities. We first found him saying that *Reason itself* cannot make mistakes. Confronted with a body of evidence for a proposition, Reason might well produce *no* belief as to the probability of the proposition on that evidence; but it will not produce a false belief. Nonetheless, there can be mistaken estimates of such probability. We went on to discuss the four types which Locke singles out – observing along the way the destructive effects of his analysis on his vision as a whole. The way to put the various pieces of Locke's view together is this: Reason will not yield mistaken beliefs about the probability of a proposition on specified evidence. Nonetheless, some other faculty may produce mistaken beliefs on such matters. The effect of inculcated principles is that we have false beliefs about the evidence, including about what we know immediately. The effect of received hypotheses is that we have false beliefs about the probability of propositions on evidence. The effects of truth-irrelevant

---

[92] It appears to me that Leibniz, in the *New Essays*, was entirely in agreement with Locke on the power of the will with respect to belief. Beliefs, he says, "are inherently involuntary" (p. 520); "nevertheless we can bring it about indirectly that we believe what we want to believe" (p. 517). He then gives examples of the Lockian sort. Accordingly, "a man is not responsible for having this or that opinion at the present time, but . . . he is responsible for taking steps to have it or not have it later on. So that opinions are voluntary only in an indirect way" (p. 456).

passions is that we have false beliefs about the quality of our evidence and false beliefs (or no beliefs) about the probability of a proposition on evidence.

These admissions force one to raise a fundamental question about Locke's principle of proportionality. Doing our best to fulfill our alethic obligation requires, on Locke's view, proportioning the level of confidence we place in the proposition in question to its probability on satisfactory evidence. That is what we ought to *try* to do, when some proposition is of sufficient "concernment" to us. But we often fail in this attempt. We believe that what we are taking as evidence consists of what we know, when it doesn't. We believe it is satisfactory, when it is not. We believe that we have correctly determined the probability of the proposition on our evidence, when we have gotten it wrong somehow. And those failings raise this question: When we get one of these determinations wrong, what is it that we ought to do by way of proportioning assent?

Locke almost always talks in thoroughly *externalist* fashion about the criteria we are to use in the governance of our beliefs.[93] He does not say that we are to proportion our level of confidence in a proposition to what we *believe* to be its probability on what we *believe* to be satisfactory evidence consisting of what we *believe* ourselves to know. He says instead that we are to proportion our level of confidence in a proposition to its actual probability on a set of propositions which are actually known and which actually constitute satisfactory evidence.[94]

But surely this is not correct. Suppose that some proposition P is of such "concernment" to me that I am obligated to try to do my epistemic best toward it. Suppose further that I try to apply the method Locke proposes. And suppose that I emerge believing that P has a probability of ·6 on my evidence, this consisting of propositions each of which I believe myself to know and the totality of which I believe to constitute satisfactory evidence for P. Add, if you will, that I have reflected as carefully on each of these points as I think that I should have; my beliefs have not been formed in what I regard as

[93] On the distinction between internalist and externalist criteria for the presence of doxastic merits, see Wm. Alston, "Internalism and Externalism in Epistemology," in Alston, *Epistemic Justification: Essays in the Theory of Knowledge* (Ithaca, Cornell University Press, 1989).

[94] Here is one exception, from his Third Letter for Toleration: "the equality that is here the question, depends not upon the truth of the opinion embraced; but on this, that the light and persuasion a man has at present, is the guide which he ought to follow, and which in his judgment of truth he cannot avoid to be governed by" (*Works* v,334).

mindless haste. But suppose that as a matter of fact I am mistaken in one or the other of these beliefs. Locke thinks, implausibly so it seems to me, that a proposition will never phenomenologically appear to have a certain probability on certain propositions when it does not. But we have seen that Locke nonetheless admits the possibility of error at all three of these points. What now *ought* I to do? What am I epistemically culpable for not doing?

Suppose, in the first place, that I am mistaken about the character of the evidence. Locke's answer is apparently that I ought to continue collecting evidence until it is in fact satisfactory; I am doxastically culpable unless I do this. Suppose, alternatively, that I am right about the character of the evidence but wrong about the probability. Locke's answer is that I ought to proportion my level of confidence in the proposition to what is in fact its probability on the evidence; if I do not do that, I am doxastically guilty, doxastically culpable, a doxastic wrongdoer. But surely both answers are mistaken. For suppose that I embraced Locke's criterion. Then I would, according to the criterion, be doxastically guilty if I did not do what I did not on careful reflection believe that I should do. And if I applied the criterion in accordance with my beliefs, I would be doxastically guilty for doing what on careful reflection I believed that I should do.

That is one approach to the situation: from the side of where my guilt would lie. But we can also approach it from the side of *guidance*. If I offer you a suggestion as to the best procedure for achieving a certain goal, if you accept it as such, and if the procedure comes in stages, then in trying to implement later stages you have to go by your *beliefs* as to the results of trying to implement earlier stages. What else could you go by?

So whether we approach a proposed rule for the determination of one's doxastic responsibilities from the side of responsibilities, or from the side of guidance, we get the same result: In one's attempt to follow later stages of the rule, one has to go by what one believes to be the result of having attempted to follow earlier stages. One can attach conditions to these beliefs – for example, that the beliefs be formed reflectively. But still, one must go by what one believes.[95]

---

[95] A final question. In formulating Locke's principle of proportionality, I have said nothing about believing the proposition in question *on the basis* of the evidence – or more broadly, about *basing* one's level of confidence *on* the evidence. I have not done so because Locke (with rare exceptions) does not do so. But is this another deficiency in his principle, as it stands? What if I follow all the principles but then believe the proposition in question not *on* the evidence but on untested sayso? Would that count as doing my best?

One last question calls out for reflection: Do we in fact have the voluntary control over belief and levels of confidence which Locke's principles presuppose? No doubt we can by acts of will implement the first two principles of evidence and appraisal. Or rather, any doubts on this score will arise not from doubts as to whether we have it in our power to decide to collect evidence and to decide to determine its evidential force but from doubts as to the clarity of the notions of satisfactory evidence and conditional probability. It is when we arrive at the principle of proportionality that doubts arise. Is it in our power to do what the principle of proportionality presupposes that we are able to do?

What does the principle actually presuppose? To answer this question it will be useful to have a taxonomy distinguishing different types of control by the will of belief. In his article "The Deontological Conception of Epistemic Justification,"[96] William P. Alston constructs exactly such a taxonomy. I propose borrowing it. In constructing his taxonomy, Alston explicitly considers not just belief but the three propositional attitudes of believing, rejecting, and withholding; in this respect his discussion, unlike most recent discussions on belief and the will, proves directly relevant to Locke's claims. His taxonomy fails us, though, in not at all considering the relation of the will to levels of confidence.

One preliminary matter must be considered before we look at Alston's distinctions and arguments. In the course of his discussion Alston announces and argues for a certain principle as follows:

one has control over a given type of state only if one also has control over some field of incompatible alternatives. To have control over believing that *p* is to have control over whether one believes that *p* or not, that is, over whether one believes that *p* or engenders instead some incompatible alternative. The power to choose A at will *is* the power to determine at will whether it shall be A or (some form of) not-A ... If the sphere of my effective voluntary control does not extend both to A and to not-A, then it attaches to neither. If I don't have the power to choose between A and not-A, then we

---

It may have been Locke's view that as a matter of psychological fact this could not be; if one follows the principles, then one just will, as a matter of psychological fact, base one's level of confidence on the evidence. But even if he did not hold this, it's not clear that Locke need have added this additional stipulation. For if in fact one's belief is in accord with the principle of proportionality, then what difference does it make, for Locke's purposes, on what basis one holds the proposition in question?

[96] In *Epistemic Justification: Essays in the Theory of Knowledge* (Ithaca, Cornell University Press, 1989), pp.115–52.

are without sufficient reason to say that I did A *at will*, rather than just doing A, accompanied by a volition.[97]

I find Alston's formulations here ambiguous as between two different principles:

(1) To be able to choose A at will, I must be able to choose A at will and be able to choose not-A at will.

(2) To be able to choose A at will, I must be able to choose at will whether A or not-A.

The difference between these two principles is relevant to interpreting Locke, since, when it comes to belief, Locke apparently held that, in some cases, we have the power specified in the latter but not that specified in the former. Locke apparently held that one is frequently able to choose at will to withhold believing P, thus able to choose at will whether one will believe P or not believe P; but one is (almost) never able to believe propositions at will, thus (almost) never able to choose at will to believe P and choose at will to withhold belief from P. Though some of Alston's formulations seem to me more apt as expressions of principle (1) and some more apt as expressions of principle (2), the reason he offers for the principle would seem to justify only the weaker principle (2), which Locke may have assumed, and not the stronger principle (1), which he clearly denies.

Alston distinguishes three modes of voluntary control: direct control, long-range control, and indirect influence. In turn, he distinguishes two kinds of direct control: basic and non-basic. An agent has direct control over some act or state when "the agent is able to carry out the intention 'right away,' in one uninterrupted intentional act, without having to return to the attempt a number of times after having been occupied with other matters."[98] Agents have *basic* (direct) control over some act or state if their doing it does not require their doing it by way of doing something else voluntarily; intentionally raising one's arm and turning one's thought to the prospects of one's favorite soccer team, are examples. By contrast, agents have *non-basic* (direct) control over some act or state if they are able to do it only by doing something else voluntarily. Turning on a light would be an example. We human beings are able to do this only by flipping or turning or pressing a switch, or something of that sort.

Alston argues that believing, rejecting, and withholding are rarely

[97] *Ibid.*, pp. 120, 123.   [98] *Ibid.*, p. 129.

if ever within the *direct* control of human agents – either within their *basic* direct control or within their *non-basic* direct control. He notes that his "argument for this, if it can be called that, simply consists in asking you to consider whether you have any such powers."[99] As for himself, he finds that he does not; and he very much doubts that other people are different from him in this regard. For example, asks Alston, do I have effective, direct, basic or non-basic "voluntary control over whether I do or do not believe that the tree has leaves on it when I see a tree with leaves on it just before me in broad daylight with my eyes working perfectly?"[100] His answer is that "it is perfectly clear that in this situation I have no power at all to refrain from that belief." In other situations, one would not have it in one's power to *come* to believe.

But suppose that I have a motive of a roughly Lockian sort. Suppose that I am firmly persuaded that if I am not entitled to believe some proposition, I ought to give up believing it – then and there; and that I believe, in addition, that I am not entitled to this belief. Could I then give it up? Might it be that the reason we cannot retract assent from an immediate perceptual belief in the sort of case Alston envisages is that we lack an adequate motive? Alston does not consider this possibility. It seems clear to me, however, that even if I had this persuasion and this belief, I would not be able to withhold belief from the proposition in question in the situation envisaged. And so, correspondingly, for cases of *coming* to believe.

We must not draw the conclusion that everyone in the sort of situation envisaged will *ineluctably* believe that there is a leafy tree before him or her. If for some reason one believes falsely that one is looking at a painting of a tree rather than at a tree, then, though one is in fact seeing a leafy tree, one will not believe that the tree before one has leaves on it. Whether or not the perceptual experience of seeing a tree produces in one the belief that there is a tree before one depends, among other things, on the beliefs one brings to the situation. But in the case envisaged, what one comes to believe depends on one's sensory experience *plus one's other beliefs*; it does not depend on whether one decides to believe, or on whether one decides or does not decide to withhold belief. When I see a tree while believing that I am looking at a painting, I do not *decide* not to believe that I am seeing a tree. The disposition to believe that there is a tree before me is simply not

---

[99] *Ibid.*, p. 122.   [100] *Ibid.*, p. 123.

activated. Though the requisite sensory experience is present, the belief that I am looking at a painting functions to inhibit the activation of the disposition.

Let us take a moment to consider an example of the sort which occupied so much of Locke's attention: Believing what someone says on his or her sayso. Suppose a man tells me that he has just seen a car accident on the corner a block away. Usually those who have discussed belief and the will would put the following question to this situation: Is it then in my power to believe at will and also in my power to not believe at will? But we must divide the question. For we have seen that someone might hold that it is not in our power to believe at will, though it is in our power to *refrain* from believing. Let it be noticed that we do sometimes say, "I decided not to believe him." (Though we also say, "I decided *to* believe him.")

It seems to me clear that if I do believe him, that will never be because I *decided* to do so; and if I don't, that will never be because I decided not to. It is true that a good deal of deciding typically goes into such a situation; and perhaps it is this which leads us in ordinary speech to speak of deciding not to believe someone. I can decide to attend closely to the facial expressions of the reporter, to his agitation or lack thereof, to the fact that I heard nothing though I was outdoors a block away, to the fact that everybody in view seems to be going about their ordinary business in their ordinary way, and so on. All this and more I can, by act of will, take note of. It may be that after initially believing the person and then doing such things I no longer believe him. But then I *find* myself not believing him. I don't *decide* not to believe him. And now in general: I think it is as decisively clear as anything ever is in philosophy that when we find ourselves believing something, we cannot by act of will give up that belief; nor, when we find ourselves not believing something, can we by act of will begin believing. Such actions are simply not within our power.

Perhaps it will help to take note of two sorts of mental acts which are (in good measure) under the direct control of the will and which are so closely related to believing as to be easily confused with it. There is, for one thing, the phenomenon of *admitting* or *not admitting* that one believes or does not believe – admitting to others, but perhaps more importantly, to oneself. Often we human beings find the phenomenon of believing such-and-such, or of not believing such-and-such, painful. So we determine not to acknowledge our situation – not to admit that we do believe or not admit that we do not believe. When someone else assumes that we believe, we passionately repudiate the assumption. We go out of our way to avoid acting and speaking as believers would normally act and speak. When the belief comes to mind, we immediately think of something else. And so forth. The ways of the heart are devious. Very much – though perhaps not all – of what goes into not admitting one's belief or disbelief is under the direct control of the will.

Believing must also be distinguished from what one might call *accepting*. Paradigmatic examples of what I have in mind by accepting occur in religious revival meetings. The evangelist urges those in the audience who have not "accepted Jesus" to come forward and make their decision. Some do come forward; they speak of having decided to accept Jesus. A striking feature of conversion literature is that though the language is sometimes that of being overwhelmed, of resisting but then no longer being able to resist, at other times it is that of deciding. I suggest that these two ways of speaking fit two closely related, yet distinct phenomena: believing versus accepting. One *finds* oneself believing; one *decides* to accept.

Deciding to accept some proposition consists, roughly, of deciding to say "Yes" to that proposition and then as much as possible letting that Yes-saying play the role in one's emotional, motivational, and intellectual life that believing it would play. Deciding to accept is, if you will, deciding to engage in, and to let oneself be engaged in, a certain role – the role of believer. There need be nothing insincere or deceptive in such role-playing; any such connotation which the phrase "role-playing" carries must be discarded. My own experience is that often it is difficult, and sometimes impossible, for me to determine whether my stance toward a certain proposition is that of accepting or that of believing.

The phenomenon I have been calling *accepting* is different from that to which some philosophers have called attention as important in science, and which is best called *accepting-as*. A scientist might *accept* a certain theory *as* a working hypothesis. Similarly, a general might *accept* the guess of one of his lieutenants concerning the enemy's deployment of forces *as* having the least calamitous consequences if it proves mistaken. In cases of *accepting-as*, the phenomenon of playing the role of believer, which I have identified with accepting, may be missing. The researcher might believe that the hypothesis is false and yet accept it *as* a working hypothesis – to see where it goes.

Believing versus admitting one's belief. Believing versus accepting.

Accepting versus accepting-as. These are subtle distinctions within a fascinating terrain. A whole field for investigation opens up before us. But this is not the occasion to step into it. My aim is not to explore the phenomena but only to make the necessary distinctions. Some of what goes into not admitting that one believes such-and-such is within one's direct voluntary control. So too accepting is within one's direct voluntary control, as is accepting-as. But believing and withholding are not. Any rule or principle or method which presupposes that they are must be rejected as presupposing something false.

But what about Alston's category of *long-range* control over propositional attitudes? Surely we can often take steps designed to bring it about that we shall wind up with some propositional attitude toward some proposition. That is to say, some *specific* propositional attitude toward some *specific* proposition. I can read the encyclopedia with the aim of coming to believe some proposition or other concerning the land area of Pakistan. Or, if I already have a particular proposition on the matter in mind, I can read the encyclopedia with the aim of taking up some propositional attitude or other toward that proposition – belief, disbelief, withholding. But given a specific proposition and a specific attitude, I can sometimes also take steps to bring it about that I have *that* attitude toward *that* proposition. Something said by Pascal is frequently cited in the literature as an example: If one wants to believe Catholic dogma but finds oneself not doing so, one thing which has a chance of securing one's desire is attendance at Catholic mass. Other strategies might work as well – for example, reading Catholic polemics against Orthodoxy, Protestantism, other religions, and atheism, while not reading what the other side has to say in response.

But I agree with Alston's assessment of all this: The results are too unpredictable to ground obligations to believe, reject, and withhold. The reason one can have an obligation to turn on the light, even though that is not within one's basic control, is that there is a stable and well-known causal connection between flipping the switch and the light going on. In this matter of taking steps to bring about a specific propositional attitude toward a specific proposition, there are rarely if ever such stable and wellknown causal connections. In Alston's words:

It is very dubious that we have reliable long-range control over any of our beliefs, even in the most favorable cases, such as beliefs about religious and philosophical matters and about personal relationships. *Sometimes* people succeed in getting themselves to believe (disbelieve) something. But I doubt that the success rate is substantial. To my knowledge there are no statistics on this, but I would be very much surprised if attempts of this sort bore fruit in more than a very small proportion of the cases . . . Thus a long-range control thesis does not provide much grounding for deontologism, even for the sorts of propositions people do sometimes try to get themselves to believe or disbelieve. Much less is there any such grounding for those propositions with respect to which people don't normally even try to manipulate their attitudes.[101]

This leaves us, lastly, with the category of *indirect* voluntary control over assent. Undoubtedly we do often have such control. Though I now have no belief whatsoever as to the land area of Pakistan, it is within my power by act of will to do things which will result in my having a belief on the matter. And perhaps sometimes I ought to. Thus an ethic of belief which assumes indirect voluntary control over believing and withholding and nothing more will, so far forth, be acceptable; and *only* those ethics which assume such control and nothing more will be acceptable.

With this map in hand, let us consider whether we human beings do in fact have the powers of will necessary for applying Locke's principle of proportionality. Pretty clearly Locke ascribed to the will powers which, in the light of the foregoing, it does not have. His overall view seems to have been that though *deciding to believe* is a rare event – in his first *Letter Concerning Toleration* he said that "to believe this or that to be true does not depend upon our will" – nonetheless one can decide *not to believe* some proposition just so long as one does not judge it to have a rather high probability on what one judges to be satisfactory evidence. That view, in the light of the foregoing, is untenable. But our concern here is not to appraise the tenability of Locke's own expressed views as to the powers of the will, but rather, to appraise the tenability of his *proposed doxastic practice* in the light of the foregoing conclusions concerning human nature. And it is much less obvious that Locke's proposed practice presupposes powers of the will over belief which it does not have than that he himself in the course of his discussion ascribed such powers to the will.

Suppose that one has made a suitably serious attempt to apply the principles of evidence and appraisal in a given case; and that the result is that one now believes that one has a satisfactory body of evidence concerning P, and that the probability of P on that evidence is high – say, $\cdot 9$. It was clearly Locke's view that one would then just

[101] *Ibid.*, pp. 135–6.

find oneself believing P; no act of will is involved. It was also his view that if one doesn't believe the evidence is satisfactory, or if one doesn't believe that one has discerned the probability of the proposition on one's evidence, then one can resist whatever inclinations one might have to believe or disbelieve P. Perhaps now and then one can even, in such cases, *decide* to believe P. But these are cases in which one judges that one's attempt to apply one of the earlier principles in the sequence of evidence, appraisal, and proportionality has not proved successful. And one is to move on to a later principle only if one's serious attempt to implement the earlier principles has proved successful, in one's judgment.

Incidentally, one point Locke leaves obscure is what obligations we have, if any, concerning belief for those cases of maximal concernment where we haven't yet, in our judgment, successfully applied the first two principles. If it was his view that, in cases of maximal concernment, we are to *suspend belief* until such time as we judge ourselves successfully to have applied the principles, then our discussion above leads us to doubt that this is possible. But his proposal does not require him to say this.

Back, then, to our example: Suppose one finds oneself believing P, in the situation described. What, then, about the principle of proportionality; how does it enter the picture? Apparently it was Locke's view that though belief is compelled in such a situation, some particular degree of firmness of belief is not compelled. For if that were also compelled, we would need no third principle; everything that one could do would already have been done by applying the first two principles of evidence and appraisal. But this view is most implausible. The firmness with which we believe things is no more under the direct control of the will than believing is. In particular: if, in the case described, I believe that P is highly probable on satisfactory evidence, I shall also find myself believing P with considerable firmness.

Could Locke have conceded this point and revised his proposal accordingly? Yes, he could have. The proposal would then be that in cases of maximal concernment we are obligated to apply the two principles of evidence and appraisal. Locke's proposal is not rendered incoherent by removing from it the principle of proportionality. Yet I judge that Locke would be acutely unhappy to remove it; in his various statements of his proposal it is often the principle of proportionality which occupies the center of attention. One of his reasons for thinking the principle important was his conviction that social tranquility will be promoted if we all follow the principle of proportionality; people will then no longer fight to the death for propositions whose probability is well short of maximal.

So far, then, we have found no decisive conflict between Locke's proposal, on the one hand, and the facts, on the other hand, concerning belief and the will. But now consider a case of the sort which fills the pages of Hume and Reid: a case of a belief being formed in one immediately and ineluctably in a situation in which evidence, of the sort Locke allows, for the truth of the proposition is weak. Suppose that in good daylight and with my eyes working properly I see a leafy tree before me, and find myself believing immediately that there is a leafy tree before me. That is to say, suppose that some process of belief-formation other than the process of believing on the basis of other beliefs produces this belief in me. Suppose further that this case is, and that I judge it to be, a matter of maximal concernment to me. And suppose lastly that on the evidence of the totality of facts which (on Locke's view) I directly "perceive" this proposition has low probability – and that I judge it to have low probability. Hume and Reid relentlessly argue that, as a matter of fact, the proposition that there is a leafy tree before me will have very low probability on that evidence; I judge them to be right about that.

Locke tells us two things about this situation: that we will, in such a case, just find ourselves disbelieving P; and that we *ought to* disbelieve it with considerable firmness. But surely he is mistaken on both counts; Hume and Reid are right. Our judgment, that arguments from facts of direct awareness to the existence of external objects are weak arguments, has no effect whatsoever on the formation of immediate perceptual beliefs; such beliefs are formed in us ineluctably. And since we cannot disbelieve them with any firmness whatsoever, it is not the case that we *ought* to.

But notice: We have still not turned up any point at which Locke's proposal decisively conflicts with the facts concerning belief *and the will*. It turns out that on this issue, Locke emerges triumphant – provided he surrenders the principle of proportionality! What we have found instead is that Locke was mistaken in an assumption he made about *the dispositions* which form our beliefs. He assumed that one will ineluctably believe or disbelieve a proposition according as one judges it probable or improbable on what one judges to be satisfactory evidence consisting of facts of which one is directly aware. It was the great merit of Hume and Reid, in the generation following

Locke, to have discerned that Locke was mistaken about this, to have argued the point with power, and to have pursued the implications of its acknowledgment. Our perceptual beliefs, our inductive beliefs, our memory beliefs have at best low probability on the facts of which we are (on Locke's view) directly aware. Discerning that serves neither to dislodge those beliefs from our mind nor to place us in a situation where we can by direct act of will dislodge them. Even when we have the time, our nature often prevents us from doing that which Locke praises as doing our epistemic best.

II APPLICATIONS OF THE VISION

(a) Religion

I remarked at the beginning of my exposition that the genesis of the *Essay* was a resolution Locke formed after perplexities arose in a discussion among some friends and himself "about the principles of morality and revealed religion." Having described the doxastic practice he recommends, Locke did not neglect to go back and indicate how it applied in these two areas; it was these areas which Locke always regarded as properly of the greatest "concernment" for every human being. So let us consider these two applications. And let us begin with Locke's discussion of revealed religion; what he says about the application of the proposed practice to this is both the presupposition of, and more ample than, what he says about its application to morality – not to mention having been vastly more influential.[102]

In the first edition of the *Essay*, Locke devoted one rather long chapter to the topic of faith and reason. However, so vexed was he by the *enthusiasts* – people claiming private revelations from God without (to his mind) having any good evidence thereof – that in the fourth edition he inserted an entire chapter devoted to these people who "flattered themselves with a persuasion of an immediate intercourse with the Deity, and frequent communications from the Divine Spirit" (IV,xix,5). To the beliefs of these people, that they had received private revelations from God, Locke issued what might be called the *evidentialist challenge*. Religious and moral matters are of such "concernment" to all of us who are intelligent adults that we are all

---

[102] The best extant discussion is Ashcraft, "Faith and Knowledge in Locke's Philosophy."

obligated to try our best to get in touch with reality on these matters. Accordingly, unless these people proportion the firmness of their belief to probability on satisfactory evidence, they are acting irresponsibly. Since Locke was convinced that the enthusiasts were not doing this, his evidentialist challenge became an *evidentialist objection*. He had written his *Letter Concerning Toleration*; though he viewed enthusiasm as a social danger, he would not recommend the forcible suppression of such people. Instead he preached that they were violating their doxastic obligations. Sometimes, of course, inducing guilt feelings in people, or social disapproval in their neighbors, is as effective in suppressing their behavior as dragging them before the law. The doxastic practice Locke was proposing could serve as effectively as an instrument of social power as those practices he was opposing!

Locke's attack on the enthusiasts provides a good entrance into his reflections on faith and reason. He did not deny – indeed he affirmed – that God can and sometimes still does "enlighten men's minds in the apprehending of certain truths, or excite them to good actions by the immediate influence and assistance of the Holy Spirit" (iv,xix,16). "God . . . cannot be denied to be able to enlighten the understanding by a ray darted into the mind immediately from the fountain of lights" (iv,xix,5). But Locke was confident that in the case of the enthusiasts it was not God's enlightenment that accounted for their convictions but a disordered psyche, a "warmed or overweening brain" (iv,xix,7). The people susceptible to enthusiasm are those "in whom melancholy has mixed with devotion," along with those "whose conceit of themselves has raised them into an opinion of a greater familiarity with God, and a nearer admittance to his favor, than is afforded to others" (iv,xix,5). "Their minds being thus prepared, whatever groundless opinion comes to settle itself strongly upon their fancies, is an illumination from the Spirit of God, and presently of divine authority: and whatsoever odd action they find in themselves a strong inclination to do, that impulse is concluded to be a call or direction from heaven, and must be obeyed" (iv,xix,6). So Locke charged the enthusiasts with irresponsibility. If one is to believe responsibly that God revealed so-and-so on such-and-such an occasion, one's believing must be in accord with the "dictates of Reason."

But is it clear that the enthusiasts were violating Locke's principles? Did not their religious experience supply them with the evidence required? Locke thought not. For when we interpret their metaphors, we see that to the question why they believe that God has spoken to them, their answer is just that they believe it strongly. "If they say they know it to be true, because it is a revelation from God, the reason is good: but then it will be demanded, how they know it to be a revelation from God. If they say by the light it brings with it, which shines bright in their minds, and they cannot resist; I beseech them to consider, whether this be any more than what we have taken notice of already, viz., that it is a revelation because they strongly believe it to be true. For all the light they speak of is but a strong, though ungrounded persuasion of their minds that it is a truth" (IV,xix,11). In short, "their confidence is mere presumption: and this light, they are so dazzled with, is nothing, but an *ignis fatuus* that leads them continually round in this circle. It is a revelation, because they firmly believe it, and they believe it, because it is a revelation" (IV,xix,10).

Locke's analysis will leave even those believers sympathetic to his approach uneasy at a certain point. Is not God's power and freedom such that God might well reveal something to some person without providing to that person satisfactory evidence on which it is probable that God has revealed that? Might God not simply effect in a person the firm conviction that God has revealed such-and-such to the person? But if we agree that God could and might do this, and also agree with Locke that his proposed practice ought to be applied to all such cases, we are then in the curious position of admitting that God may reveal something in the absence of a certain kind of evidence that God has done so, while yet resolving never in the absence of such evidence to *believe* that God has done so. Does not following Locke's practice put us in risk of sometimes not believing what God has revealed? True, there is, in general, nothing paradoxical about a thesis which implies that there are states of affairs of a sort such that it is both causally possible that they occur and not causally possible that one be in a situation where one is permitted to believe that they occur. But the case before us seems special: Why would God reveal something to us if God did not want us to *believe* that God revealed it? And if God wants us to believe, are we not at least *permitted* to believe?

Locke never explicitly considers the matter. He just assumes without argument that God would not reveal in an evidential void. "God, when he makes the prophet, does not unmake the man," says Locke:

He leaves all his faculties in their natural state, to enable him to judge of his inspirations, whether they be of divine original or no. When he illuminates the mind with supernatural light, he does not extinguish that which is natural. If he would have us assent to the truth of any proposition, he either evidences that truth by the usual methods of natural reason, or else makes it known to be a truth, which he would have us assent to, by his authority, and convinces us that it is from him, by some marks which reason cannot be mistaken in. Reason must be our last judge and guide in everything. I do not mean, that we must consult reason, and examine whether a proposition revealed from God can be made out by natural principles, and if it cannot, that then we may reject it: but consult it we must, and by it examine, whether it be a revelation from God or not. (IV,xix,14)[103]

Locke is confident that God will play by the rules of evidence. The creating Ground of our existence may indeed break through the crust of that existence to reveal things to us. But we must insist that if It wants us to *believe* that It has done so, It provide us with satisfactory evidence.

Locke adds that our demanding of God that God authenticate God's revelation is something that God demands of us. Locke regards it as *God's* will that we govern our assent by the principle of proportionality in accord with the verdicts of Reason. Presumably, then, God will oblige us, by offering us evidence that God has revealed so-and-so when God has. Any revelation of God unaccompanied by evidence would be idle chatter on God's part, to which God does not require us to pay attention.

But why does Locke think anything at all has to be done about the enthusiasts? Why not leave them alone, on the ground that religion is a matter of individual taste? Because the enthusiasts weren't leaving others alone. Civil war had been raging in England. England had been torn apart by religious strife; and in this strife, the enthusiasts

---

[103] Leibniz was both more subtle and more traditional in his understanding of the relation between faith and Reason. Commenting on Locke's view, he says that "If you take faith to be only what rests on *rational grounds for belief*, and separate it from the inward grace which immediately endows the mind with faith, everything you say, sir, is beyond dispute. For it must be acknowledged that many judgments are more evident than the ones which depend on these rational grounds. Some people have advanced further towards the latter than others have; and indeed plenty of people, far from having weighed up such reasons, have never known them and consequently do not even have what could count as *grounds for probability*. But the inward grace of the Holy Spirit makes up for this immediately and supernaturally, and it is this that creates what theologians strictly call 'divine faith.' God, it is true, never bestows this faith unless what he is making one believe is grounded in reason – otherwise he would subvert our capacity to recognize truth, and open the door to enthusiasm – but it is not necessary that all who possess this divine faith should know those reasons, and still less that they should have them perpetually before their eyes. Otherwise none of the unsophisticated or of the feeble-minded – now at least – would have the true faith, and the most enlightened people might not have it when they most needed it, since no one can always remember his reasons for believing" (*New Essays*, p. 497).

were participants. Enthusiasm is socially pernicious; that's why
something has to be done about it. Convictions such as those the
enthusiasts display have as their "constant concomitant" the arbitrary
exercise of "an authority of dictating to others, and a forwardness to
prescribe to their opinion." Dogmatism in religion has authoritarianism
in society as its companion. "How almost can it be otherwise," says
Locke, "but that he should be ready to impose on others' belief who
has already imposed on his own? Who can reasonably expect
arguments and conviction from him in dealing with others whose
understanding is not accustomed to them in his dealing with himself"
(iv,xix,2)? We have already come across Locke's claim that failing to
apply the Lockian practice, when one ought to, amounts to "imposing"
on oneself; his claim now is that the person who imposes on himself is
likely to impose on others as well.

To this it may be added that to act as the enthusiasts act is to violate
one's dignity as a human being, and to do so in that very domain of
life which ought especially to manifest our dignity – namely, in
religion. "To this crying up of faith in opposition to reason, we may, I
think, in good measure, ascribe those absurdities that fill almost all
the religions which possess and divide mankind . . . religion, which
should most distinguish us from beasts, and ought most peculiarly to
elevate us as rational creatures above brutes, is that where in men
often appear most irrational, and more senseless than beasts themselves"
(iv,xviii,11).

And the enthusiasts are failing in their duty. Faith, says Locke, "is
nothing but a firm assent of the mind: which if it be regulated, as is our
duty, cannot be afforded to anything but upon good reason"
(iv,xvii,24). And to the objection that no one can follow the Lockian
practice for all of his beliefs, Locke replies, as we have seen, that
everyone can and ought to do so for religious belief: "everyone has a
concern in a future life, which he is bound to look after. This engages
his thoughts in religion; and here it mightily lies upon him to
understand and reason right" (*Conduct*, §8; *Works* ii,342). Everybody
in England has the time it takes on Sundays and holidays (*Conduct*,§8;
Works ii,342)!

For Locke, the decisive consideration establishing that faith is
belief (opinion) rather than knowledge is that faith lacks the kind or
ground of certitude requisite for knowledge. In his Second Letter to
Edward Stillingfleet, Bishop of Worcester, Locke says that "the
certainty of faith, if your lordship thinks fit to call it so, has nothing to

do with the certainty of knowledge. And to talk of the certainty of faith, seems all one to me as to talk of the knowledge of believing – a way of speaking not easy to me to understand . . . Faith stands by itself, and upon grounds of its own; nor can be removed from them, and placed on those of knowledge. Their grounds are so far from being the same, or having anything common, that when it is brought to certainty, faith is destroyed; it is knowledge then, and faith no longer" (*Works* III,146).

Locke is willing to speak of the "assurance of faith"; he regards the New Testament as calling for that (III, 274–5). But the assurance of faith, he insists, is to be distinguished from knowledge: "With what assurance soever of believing, I assent to any article of faith, so that I steadfastly venture my all upon it, it is still but believing. Bring it to certainty, and it ceases to be faith" (III, 146–7). More specifically, the "assurance" of faith, as Locke understands it, is the *steadiness* of faith; an assured faith may be as steady and unwavering as knowledge: "the full assurance of their faith as steadily determines their assent to the embracing of that truth, as if they actually knew it" (III, 281). "[T]his assurance of faith may approach very near to certainty, and not come short of it in a sure and steady influence on the mind" (III, 276). What Locke denies, however, is that faith either can or should be held with the *firmness* which characterizes or accompanies knowledge.[104] Maximal steadiness does not require maximal firmness: "But though bare belief always includes some degrees of uncertainty, yet it does not therefore necessarily include any degree of wavering; the evidently strong probability may as steadily determine the man to assent to the truth, or make him take the proposition for true, and act accordingly, as knowledge makes him see or be certain that it is true. And he that doth so, as to truths revealed in the scripture, will show his faith by his works; and has, for aught I can see, all the faith necessary to a Christian, and required to salvation" (III, 299).[105]

---

[104] Though he says, perplexingly, "I know not what greater pledge a man can give of a full persuasion of the truth of anything, than his venturing his soul upon it, as he does, who sincerely embraces any religion, and receives it for true. But to what degree soever of assurance [persuasion?] his faith may rise, it still comes short of knowledge" (Third Letter for Toleration; *Works* V,145).

[105] In his Fourth Letter for Toleration, Locke finds felicitious phrases for the two aspects of faith that he is distinguishing, namely "firm persuasion" and "full assurance." He furthermore suggests that the firmness of a person's belief will have behavioral manifestations: "Men act by the strength of their persuasion, though they do not always place their persuasion and assent on that side on which, in reality, the strength of truth lies" (*Works* V,564). All of this raises an interesting question when combined with what he says about martyrdom: "Nor is

The assumption underlying these points is that faith, *in its very nature*, is something different from knowledge. Though its *assurance* can and ought to be as high as that of (the beliefs which accompany or constitute) knowledge, and though its *firmness* may approach that of (those beliefs which accompany or constitute) knowledge, yet faith is not knowledge. Locke stands in that long line of Christian reflection which regards faith as a species of *believing on the basis of revelation.* Specifically, faith is believing something on (what one takes to be) *God's* revelation of it. And this is inherently different from the"perception" which Locke (officially) identifies with knowledge; "a definition of knowledge, which [is] one act of the mind, [does] not at all concern faith, which [is] another act of the mind quite distinct from it" (Second Letter to Stillingfleet; *Works* III,282). For "*faith* . . . is the assent to any proposition . . . upon the credit of the proposer, as coming from God in some extraordinary way of communication" (IV,xviii,2).

It is important to realize that Locke – once again in accordance with the tradition – did not regard the holding of theistic beliefs in general as a matter of faith. A three-fold distinction must be made in how human beings hold beliefs about God. Sometimes they hold them as mere matters of *opinion*, on the basis of tradition or whatever. Sometimes they hold them as that special form of opinion which is *faith*. And sometimes they *know* them – demonstratively, however, not intuitively (IV,iii,21; IV,x).[106] To establish and implement this last

there among the many absurd religions of the world, almost any one that does not find votaries to lay down their lives for it: and if that be not firm persuasion and full assurance that is stronger than the love of life, and has force enough to make a man throw himself into the arms of death, it is hard to know what is firm persuasion and full assurance . . . The persuasion they have of the truth of their own religion, is visibly strong enough to make them venture themselves" (*ibid.*, 563–4). Was it Locke's view that it is inappropriate to hold one's faith with so much firmness (confidence) that one is willing to give one's life for it? Consider this passage: "I know not what greater pledge a man can give of a full persuasion of the truth of anything, than his venturing his soul upon it, as he does, who sincerely embraces any religion and receives it for true. But to what degree soever of assurance his faith may rise, it [faith?] still comes short of knowledge" (Third Letter for Toleration; *Works* V,145).

[106] In his own way, then, Locke follows the practice developing in his time of distinguishing between natural religion and revealed religion. We must not suppose, however, that on his view, one *must* first come to a natural *knowledge* of God and then come to faith. In his Second Letter to Stillingfleet he says, for example: "If your lordship means, that to suppose a divine revelation, it is necessary to know, that there is simply an intelligent being; this also I deny. For to suppose a divine revelation, it is not necessary that a man should know that there is such an intelligent being in the world: I say, know, i.e. from things that he does know, demonstratively deduce the proof of such a being: it is enough for the receiving divine revelation, to believe, that there is such a being, without having by demonstration attained to the knowledge that there is a God . . . if nobody can believe the Bible to be of divine

conviction, Locke offers a version of the cosmological argument, concluding thus: "from the consideration of ourselves, and what we infallibly find in our own constitution, our Reason leads us to the knowledge of this certain and evident truth, that *there is an eternal, most powerful, and most knowing being*; which, whether any one will please to call *God*, it matters not. The thing is evident, and from this *idea* duly considered, will easily be deduced all those other attributes, which we ought to ascribe to this eternal being" (iv,x,6).

"The thing is evident," says Locke. In another passage he says that "'Tis as certain, that there is a God, as that the opposite angles, made by the intersection of two straight lines, are equal" (i,iv,16), adding that "There was never any rational creature, that set himself sincerely to examine the truth of these propositions, that could fail to assent to them" (i,iv,16). Locke readily acknowledged that not all human beings have set themselves sincerely to examine the argument in question. Yet he found the suggestion implausible that a whole people might fail to have knowledge of God's existence: "the visible marks of extraordinary wisdom and power, appear so plainly in all the works of the creation, that a rational creature, who will but seriously reflect on them, cannot miss the discovery of a Deity . . . it seems stranger to me, that a whole nation of men should be anywhere found so brutish, as to want the notion of a God; than they should be without any notion of numbers, or fire" (i,iv,9).

Once again, then: Faith is a species of belief, not a species of knowledge.[107] Faith is the correlate of revelation. Faith consists of believing things on the ground that they have been revealed by God, rather than knowing them on the ground of some demonstration (the assumption being that it cannot be *demonstrated* that God has revealed

revelation, but he that clearly comprehends the whole deduction, and sees the evidence of the demonstration, wherein the existence of an intelligent being . . . is scientifically proved; there are, I fear, but few Christians among illiterate people, to look no farther" (*Works* iii,290–1).

[107] In his Second Vindication of the Reasonableness of Christianity, Locke says that "To prevent this calumny, I, in more places than one, distinguished between faith, in a strict sense, as it is a bare assent to any proposition, and that which is called evangelical faith, in a larger sense of the word; which comprehends under it something more than a bare simple assent." Then, after citing some passages from *Reasonableness*, he adds: "By these, and more, the like passages in my book, my meaning is so evident, that nobody, but an unmasker, would have said, that when I spoke of believing, as a bare speculative assent to any proposition, as true, I affirmed that was all that was required of a Christian for justification: though that in the strict sense of the word, is all that is done in believing." What is needed for justification is "not a bare idle speculation, a bare notional persuasion of any truth whatsoever, floating in our brains; but an active principle of life, a faith working by love and obedience" (*Works* vi,286).

so-and-so). Let us be clear that it is not the proposition *that God has revealed P* which is the object of faith (unless one believes it to have been revealed *that P has been revealed* – see iv,xviii,6). Rather it is P itself, the proposition one believes to have been revealed by God, that is the object of faith. On the other hand, one cannot identify faith by picking out propositions of a certain sort and then saying that faith is simply the acceptance of those propositions; for the very same proposition may be both known and taken on faith. (Not, however, simultaneously by the same person. A person cannot simultaneously know something and believe it on the basis of revelation; awareness will overwhelm faith.[108])

We must distinguish two types of revelation. In *original revelation* an impression "is made immediately by God, on the mind of" the person (iv,xviii,3).[109] *Traditional revelation*, by contrast, occurs when someone communicates to another what has been originally revealed to himself or herself or someone else. Faith, in response to this latter type of revelation, consists of accepting, as revealed by God, what that person communicates as having been (originally) revealed to someone.[110]

We can know intuitively that whatever God reveals is true; we can "perceive" it. "Whatever God hath revealed is certainly true; no doubt can be made of it" (iv,xviii,10). Locke never considers the possibility that God might offer to us for our belief things which, though strictly speaking not true, nonetheless serve to guide us well on the paths of life. He just takes it as necessarily true that if God reveals P, then P is true.[111] But that God did in fact reveal something on some

---

108 "But however it be called light and seeing; I suppose, it is at most but belief, and assurance: and the proposition taken for a revelation is not such, as they know, to be true, but take to be true. For where a proposition is known to be true, revelation is needless: and it is hard to conceive how there can be a revelation to any one of what he knows already. If therefore it be a proposition which they are persuaded but do not know, to be true, whatever they may call it, it is not seeing, but believing. For there are two ways, whereby truth comes into the mind, wholly distinct, so that one is not the other. What I see I know to be so by the evidence of the thing itself: what I believe I take to be so upon the testimony of another" (*Essay* iv,xix,10).

109 In his paraphrases of St. Paul's epistles, Locke several times over says that Paul, for example, was a recipient of original revelation – *Works* vii,30–1,34,432.

110 The "impression" of which Locke speaks in explaining original revelation is presumably the belief. But if the belief is produced *immediately* in one by God, then, so it would seem, one is not accepting it *on the ground* that it has been revealed by God. Thus it appears that Locke's definition of "faith," when combined with his account of original revelation, yields the result that the believer's *response* to original revelation is not a case of faith.

111 In An Answer to Remarks upon an Essay concerning Human Understanding, Locke angrily remarks that "anyone who appears among Christians, may be well ashamed of his name, when he raises such a doubt as this, viz. whether an infinitely powerful and wise being be veracious or no; unless falsehood be in such reputation with this gentleman, that he concludes lying to be no mark of weakness and folly" (*Works* iii,187). But of course the

occasion cannot be known; nor can it be known what God revealed if God did reveal something. We can only *believe* that an occurrence of revelation has occurred, and can only *believe* that we have correctly interpreted the content of some purported occurrence of revelation. *That God revealed P* can never be something known. Speaking of Christianity, Locke says to one of his opponents that if you mean, in speaking of faith as knowledge,

> that the true religion may be known with the certainty of knowledge properly so called; I ask you farther, whether that true religion be to be known by the light of nature, or needed a divine revelation to discover it? If you say, as I suppose you will, the latter; then I ask whether the making out of that to be a divine revelation, depends not upon particular matters of fact, whereof you were no eye-witness but were done many ages before you were born? and if so, by what principles of science they can be known to any man now living." (A Third Letter for Toleration; *Works* v,424)[112]

It is because we can never know *that God has revealed P* that our acceptance of P itself, on the ground that it has been revealed by God, is never knowledge (or the accompaniment of knowledge). "Whatsoever truth we come to the clear discovery of, from the knowledge and contemplation of our own ideas, will always be certainer for us, than those which are conveyed to us by traditional revelation. For the knowledge, we have, that this revelation came at first from God, can never be so sure, as the knowledge we have from the clear and distinct perception of the agreement, or disagreement of our own ideas" (IV,xviii,4).[113] What Locke says here concerning traditional revelation, he meant for revelation in general.

In deciding whether to accept P, on the ground of its having been

---

parent who gives the child advice which, though not "strictly speaking true," is nonetheless helpful, is not *lying!*

[112] The passage continues: "we neither think that God requires, nor has given us faculties capable of knowing in this world several of those truths, which are to be believed to salvation."

[113] In this passage, Locke speaks of the *knowledge* that God revealed something, as he does in two other passages in *Essay* IV,xviii,4–5: "our assurance can be no greater, than our knowledge is, that it is a revelation from God." "Since the whole strength of the certainty depends upon our knowledge, that God revealed it . . ." Possibly these are just slips of the pen. I think it more likely, however, that they are to be read in the light of this comment in one of the letters to Stillingfleet: "I think it is possible to be certain upon the testimony of God . . . where I know that it is the testimony of God; because in such a case, that testimony is capable not only to make me believe, but, if I consider it right, to make me know the things to be so; and so I may be certain. For the veracity of God is as capable of making me know a proposition to be true, as any other way of proof can be; and therefore I do not in such a case barely believe, but know such a proposition to be true, and attain certainty" (*Works* III,281). I think that we are to read this passage as if it continued thus: *However, though anyone who knows that something is the testimony of God knows also that it is true, one can never* know *that something is the testimony of God.*

revealed by God, we must appraise the probability on satisfactory evidence of the proposition *that God has revealed P*. Only if this is more probable than not on such evidence are we entitled to believe P itself – unless, of course, we have independent reason for accepting P. Locke makes clear that he is not insisting that we need independent evidence in favor of P – in favor of the content of the purported revelation – to be justified in accepting it. Quite to the contrary: The very genius of revelation is that, by this means, God can present to us for our belief things which the unaided use of our faculties has not entitled us to believe. What is required is not satisfactory independent evidence in favor of P, but satisfactory evidence in favor of the proposition *that God has revealed P*.

It should not be overlooked, however, that on Locke's view a good deal of the content of revelation lies within the reach of our unaided natural faculties. In *The Reasonableness of Christianity* he tries to show that this is the case for Christian revelation, not only for what it teaches us concerning our moral duties, but even for what it teaches us concerning what is required for salvation. The book, says Locke, was addressed mainly to deists,[114] "designed ... chiefly for those who were not yet thoroughly, or firmly, Christians, proposing to work on those, who either wholly disbelieved, or doubted of the truth of the Christian religion" (A Vindication of the Reasonableness; *Works* VI,164). His goal in writing it was to "convince ... men of the mission of Jesus Christ, make them ... see the truth, simplicity, and reasonableness, of what he himself taught, and required to be believed by his followers." If this were accomplished, one "need not doubt ... such converts will not lay by the scriptures, but by a constant reading and study of them get all the light they can from this divine revelation, and nourish themselves up in the words of faith" (VI, 164–5).[115]

The strategy Locke adopted for accomplishing his goal had two parts: to display what "natural reason" *is capable of* telling us to be

---

[114] Second Vindication; *Works* VI,188–9, 264–5.

[115] "But when I had gone through the whole [of the gospels], and saw what a plain, simple, reasonable thing Christianity was, suited to all conditions and capacities; and in the morality of it now, with divine authority, established into a legible law, so far surpassing all that philosophy and human reason had attained to, or could possibly make effectual to all degrees of mankind; I was flattered to think it might be of some use in the world; especially to those, who thought either that there was no need of revelation at all, or that the revelation of our Saviour required the belief of such articles for salvation which the settled notions, and their way of reasoning in some, and want of understanding in others, made impossible to them. Upon these two topics the objections seemed to turn, which were with most assurance made by deists, against Christianity; but against Christianity misunderstood" (*Works* VI,188).

necessary for salvation, and to display what the revelation found in the teachings of Jesus *does in fact* tell us to be necessary for salvation.[116] (Locke seems never to have questioned that the gospels give us an accurate record of the teachings of Jesus.[117]) The two, as Locke presents them, coincide. Or rather, they *almost* coincide. The person who is acquainted with Jesus must, for his salvation, not only believe and do that which "natural reason" is capable of telling us is necessary for salvation; he must, in addition, believe *that Jesus is the Messiah*. The words "is capable of telling us," used of natural reason, are important. It was Locke's view that natural reason has never even *approached* telling anybody the totality of that which it *is capable in principle* of telling us – either concerning the full extent of our moral

---

[116] Locke states in the *Reasonableness*, and emphasizes repeatedly in the several Vindications, that he is discussing what Jesus (and the New Testament writers) teach as necessary for being a Christian; he is not discussing what Christians ought to believe. As to the latter: they ought to believe whatever they, on reflection, believe that God has revealed. "Though all divine revelation requires the obedience of faith, yet every truth of inspired scriptures is not one of those that by the law of faith is required to be explicitly believed to justification . . . Those are fundamentals which it is not enough not to disbelieve; everyone is required actually to assent to them. But any other proposition contained in the Scripture, which God has not thus made a necessary part of the law of faith (without an actual assent to which, he will not allow anyone to be a believer) a man may be ignorant of without hazarding his salvation by a defect in his faith" (*Reasonableness*; *Works* VI,156). Cf., in the various Vindications, *Works* VI,176,227–36,306–7,320–1, 355–7,407–8.

[117] He holds, in fact, that they are *infallible*: "All that is contained in the inspired writings, is all of divine authority, must all be allowed for such, and received for divine and infallible truth, by every subject of Christ's kingdom, i.e. every Christian" (*Works*,VI,356). For infallibility, see also *ibid.*, 313; and *Essay* III,ix,23. As suggested by the passage just quoted, it was because Locke viewed the Scripture writers as *inspired by God* that he viewed their writings as infallibly true. It is much less clear what he regarded as the connection between inspiration and revelation. It appears to me, however, that he regarded the content of any *writing* inspired by God as *revealed* by God. Thus he seems to have regarded the New Testament throughout as the inspiredly infallible record of original revelation (i.e., revelation to the writer), with some of this inspiredly infallible record being, in turn, a report of traditional revelation (i.e., a report of revelation to someone other than the writer, e.g., to Jesus). Locke seems to assume that Christians do, or should, agree with him on this. And thus he draws the conclusion that Christians are obligated to believe all the claims of the New Testament writers – or rather, everything that they on reflection *believe* those writers to have claimed. To do otherwise would be to dishonor God: ". . . the inspired writings of the holy scriptures. Every part of it is [God's] word, and ought, every part of it, to be believed by every christian man" (*Works* VI,351). The New Testament is all "of divine authority, one part as much as another. And, in this sense, all the divine truths in the inspired writings are fundamental, and necessary to be believed" (VI, 349). "And thus all the scripture of the New Testament, given by divine inspiration, is matter of faith, and necessary to be believed by all Christians, to whom it is proposed" (VI, 321). As to its being the obligation of Christians to believe all that they, on serious reflection, *believe* that the New Testament writers claimed, rather than all that they did in fact claim, see especially A Second Vindication, in *Works* VI, 390–3, where Locke's example of the general point is this: Whatever a Christian on serious reflection takes to be the import of Christ's words, "this is my body" and "this is my blood," *that* is what he ought to believe.

duties, or concerning what is required for salvation. He added that even if it had told someone these things, its nature is such that it would not have done so with the effectiveness that characterizes the Messiah's way of telling us these things.[118]

Let us return to the topic of faith. Though it is not the case that P must be more probable than not, on satisfactory independent evidence, to entitle one to believe *that God revealed P*, nonetheless, the epistemic status of the content of a purported revelation, judged independently of any evidence that it has been revealed, does have a bearing on the epistemic status of the proposition concerning the occurrence. If any proposition (self-evidently) contradicts something of which one judges oneself to have intuitive (or demonstrative) knowledge, one must reject the proposal that God has revealed that proposition. "Since no evidence of our faculties by which we receive such revelations can exceed, if equal, the certainty of our intuitive knowledge, we can never receive for a truth anything that is directly contrary to our clear and distinct knowledge . . . no proposition can be received for divine revelation, or obtain the assent due to all such, if it be contradictory to our clear intuitive knowledge, because this would be to subvert the principles and foundations of all knowledge, evidence, and assent whatsoever" (IV,xviii,5).

What, then, about the case in which, though the content of the purported revelation does not contradict what one judges oneself to know, nonetheless it is *improbable* on evidence which one judges to be satisfactory? More specifically, suppose that one judges the proposition *that God has revealed P* to be probable on satisfactory evidence, whereas

---

[118] This is the content: God, "by the light of reason, revealed to all mankind, who would make use of that light, that he was good and merciful. The same spark of the divine nature and knowledge in man, which making him a man, showed him the law he was under, as a man; showed him also the way of atoning the merciful, kind, compassionate Author and Father of him and his being, when he had transgressed that law. He that made use of this candle of the Lord, so far as to find what was his duty, could not miss to find also the way to reconciliation and forgiveness, when he had failed of his duty . . . The law is the eternal, immutable standard of right. And a part of that law is, that a man should forgive, not only his children, but his enemies, upon their repentance, asking pardon, and amendment. And therefore he could not doubt that the author of this law, and God of patience and consolation, who is rich in mercy, would forgive his frail offspring, if they acknowledged their faults, disapproved the iniquity of their transgressions, begged his pardon, and resolved in earnest, for the future, to conform their actions to this rule, which they owned to be just and right. This way of reconciliation, this hope of atonement, the light of nature revealed to them: and the revelation of the gospel, having said nothing to the contrary" (*Reasonableness*; *Works* VI, 133). The "new covenant" simply adds to this "old covenant": "These two, faith and repentance, i.e. believing Jesus to be the Messiah, and a good life, are the indispensable conditions of the new covenant" (*ibid.*, 105).

one judges P itself to be improbable on satisfactory independent evidence. Is one then somehow to weigh up the probability of the proposition *that God has revealed P* against the improbability of P itself, and go with the stronger (remembering that to determine the former, one must consider both the evidence for the proposition that one is confronted with an occurrence of revelation, and the evidence for the proposition that one is correctly interpreting the content of that purported occurrence)? Though Locke is far from lucid on this matter, I think his answer is Yes – as indeed, in his system, it should have been. He says that "since God in giving us the light of Reason has not thereby tied up his own hands from affording us, when he thinks fit, the light of revelation in any of those matters, wherein our natural faculties are able to give a probable determination, revelation, where God has been pleased to give it, must carry it, against the probable conjectures of Reason" (IV,xviii,8; cf. IV,xviii,9).

There is one more connection between content and presentation: One is not to believe P with a firmness in excess of that with which one is entitled to believe *that God has revealed P*.[119] In the case of faith, "our assent can be rationally no higher than the evidence of its being a revelation, and that this is the meaning of the expressions it is delivered in. If the evidence of its being a revelation, or that this is its true sense be only on probable proofs, our assent can reach no higher than an assurance or diffidence, arising from the more, or less apparent probability of the proofs" (IV,xvi,14).[120]

And what, finally, is Locke willing to accept as evidence for the occurrence of revelation? The inner experience of the enthusiasts will not do. What will? Locke gives the matter lamentably short shrift; nonetheless, his answer is clear: miracles.

---

[119] And that, says Locke, is sufficient for salvation: "though bare belief always includes some degrees of uncertainty, yet it does not therefore necessarily include any degree of wavering; the evidently strong probability may as steadily determine the man to assent to the truth, or make him take the proposition for true, and act accordingly, as knowledge makes them see or be certain that it is true. And he that doth so, as to truths revealed in the scripture, will show his faith by his works; and has, for aught I can see, all the faith necessary to a Christian, and required to salvation" (Second Reply to the Bishop of Worcester; *Works* III,299).

[120] And as for biblical revelation, Locke insisted that there is no special "biblical hermeneutic." He says to Stillingfleet that he reads "the holy scripture with a full assurance, that all it delivers is true: and though this be a submission to the writings of those inspired authors, which I neither have nor can have, for those of any other men; yet I use the same way to interpret to myself the sense of that book, that I do of any other" (*Works* III,341). In the Preface to his paraphrases of the epistles of St. Paul, Locke spells out his interpretative principles. A very helpful discussion of the role of Locke's thought in the origins of modern biblical criticism is H. G. Reventlow, *The Authority of the Bible and the Rise of the Modern World* (Philadelphia, Fortress Press, 1985).

We see the holy men of old, who had revelation from God, had something else besides that internal light of assurance in their own minds, to testify to them, that it was from God. They were not left to their own persuasions alone, that those persuasions were from God; but had outward signs to convince them of the author of those revelations. And when they were to convince others, they had a power given them to justify the truth of their commission from heaven; and by visible signs to assert the divine authority of the message they were sent with. (IV,xix,15)[121]

Sprinkled about in Locke's writings are references to a number of biblically reported miracles;[122] invariably he takes it as obvious that the miracle reported confirms that the person performing the miracle, or in one way or another the subject of the miracle, is the recipient of divine revelation. For example, "The evidence of our Savior's *mission* from heaven is so great, in the multitude of miracles he did before all sorts of people, that what he delivered cannot but be received as the oracles of God, and unquestionable verity; for the miracles he did were so ordered by the divine providence and wisdom, that they never were, nor could be, denied by any of the enemies or opposers of Christianity" (*Reasonableness*; *Works* VI,135).

This view, traditional though it be, that miracles are evidence for divine revelation, bristles with problems. To mention just one: How much of what a person believes has been divinely revealed to him is *confirmed* as having been divinely revealed to him by the miraculous sign of which he is the recipient? Correspondingly, how much of what a person *claims* to have been divinely revealed to him is *confirmed* as having been divinely revealed to him by his performance of a miracle? To these problems, Locke never addressed himself.

Neither did he address with care the question Hume raised: Under what circumstances, if any, are we permitted to accept testimony to the effect that a miracle has occurred? He remarks that "the credibility and attestation of the report is all that is of moment, when miracles done by others in other places are the argument that prevails" (Third Letter for Toleration; *Works* V,524); it is not necessary that miracles accompany the present-day presentation of a report of revelation. But Locke was of the view that the biblical reports of miracles are more than reliable: they are *infallible*. Attestation will accordingly have to be unusual; in fact, it will have to be evidence

---

[121] Locke's discussion of the nature of miracles, which does not here concern us, is to be found in his posthumously published "A Discourse of Miracles."

[122] Apparently he believed that the occurrence of miracles continued into, at least, the early church; see his Third Letter for Toleration; *Works* V,448ff.

that these writings were *inspired by God*. And that evidence will itself have to consist of miracles performed by these writers. Thus Locke speaks of "an undoubted testimony that miracles were done by the first publishers of [the gospel]" (v, 443); and he says not only that the gospel is still accompanied by this testimony, but that this is all that most readers of it have ever had: "all those, who were not eye-witnesses of miracles done in their presence, it is plain had no other miracles than we have; that is, upon report; and it is probable not so many, nor so well attested as we have" (v,443).

Is Locke suggesting that it is probable, on *extra-biblical* evidence, that those who wrote the biblical books worked miracles; and is he suggesting that we are to believe on this basis, and with a certain tempered level of confidence, that they were inspired, and hence infallible? I think not. Instead his thought appears to be that the relevant evidence for the inspired status of their writings is offered by the biblical writers *in their books*; in their books they report the miraculous evidence which confirms that they were recipients of revelation. Of course, that invites the question whether, say, Moses was the author of those books which report revelations received by Moses along with their miraculous confirmations – as indeed it invites the question whether, if these books were written by Moses, he correctly reported his experience. Locke, in one passage, himself recognizes the relevance of these questions:

the history of the deluge is conveyed to us by writings, which had their original from revelation: and yet nobody, I think, will say, he has as certain and clear a knowledge of the flood, as Noah that saw it; or that he himself would have had, had he then been alive, and seen it. For he has no greater an assurance than that of his senses, that it is writ in the book supposed writ by Moses inspired: But he has not so great an assurance, that Moses writ that book, as if he had seen Moses write it. So that the assurance of its being a revelation, is less still than the assurance of his senses. (iv,xviii,4)

One final point: Locke mentions one circumstance in which it is, if not exactly permissible, nonetheless harmless, to believe that God has revealed something to one, even though one lacks the evidence of miracles; namely, the circumstance of the content of the purported personal revelation already having been revealed in Scripture. In that circumstance, one can be assured that, whether or not one has received a revelation, the content of the purported revelation belongs to what God has revealed (iv,xix,16)!

(b) Morality

Locke's presentation of his thoughts on moral obligation is considerably more scattered than that of his thoughts on "revealed" and "natural" religion. Nonetheless, the structure of his thought is relatively clear.[123] And as to the importance of the topic, he never wavered: "since our faculties are not fitted to penetrate into the internal fabric and real essences of bodies; but yet plainly discover to us the being of a God, and the knowledge of our selves, enough to lead us into a full and clear discovery of our duty, and great concernment, it will become us, as rational creatures, to employ those faculties we have about what they are most adapted to, and follow the direction of nature, where it seems to point us out the way. For 'tis rational to conclude, that our proper employment lies in those enquiries, and in that sort of knowledge, which is most suited to our natural capacities, and carries in it our greatest interest, *i.e.*, the condition of our eternal estate. Hence I think I may conclude, that *morality is the proper science, and business of mankind in general*; (who are both concerned, and fitted to search out their *Summum Bonum*)" (IV,xii,11).

"Amongst the simple ideas, which we receive both from sensation and reflection, pain and pleasure are two very considerable ones," says Locke (II,xx,1). He goes on to say that things "are good or evil, only in reference to pleasure or pain. That we call good, which is apt to cause or increase pleasure, or diminish pain in us; or else to procure, or preserve us the possession of any other good, or absence of any evil. And on the contrary, we name that evil, which is apt to produce or increase any pain or diminish any pleasure in us; or else to procure us any evil, or deprive us of any good" (II,xx,2). Locke's subsequent discussion makes clear that the words "pain" and "pleasure" are misleading as names for the phenomena he has in mind. He is taking note of the fundamental fact that much of our experience is "phenomenologically valorized" – some of what we experience, we like; some, we dislike. That this is different from the pleasure/pain contrast is easily seen by observing, for example, that persons sometimes like pain. Locke himself says that "By *pleasure* and *pain* . . . I

---

[123] An excellent discussion of Locke's ethical theory is John Colman, *Locke's Moral Philosophy* (Edinburgh, Edinburgh University Press, 1983). See also Hans Aarsleff, "The State of Nature and the Nature of Man in Locke," in John W. Yolton (ed.), *John Locke: Problems and Perspectives* (Cambridge, Cambridge University Press, 1969); J. B. Schneewind, "Locke's Moral Philosophy," in Chappell, *The Cambridge Companion to Locke*; and chap. 8 of Ian Harris, *The Mind of John Locke* (Cambridge, Cambridge University Press, 1994).

must all along be understood . . . to mean, not only bodily pain and pleasure, but whatsoever delight or uneasiness is felt by us, whether arising from any grateful, or unacceptable sensation or reflection" (II,xx,15). Though commentators often speak of Locke's *hedonism*, he is better thought of as standing in the long classical tradition of *eudaimonism*. He himself, on a number of occasions, uses "happiness" to express what he has in mind.[124]

Having given his account of good and evil, Locke then takes note of what he calls "uneasiness": the state of lacking something that one believes would be pleasant, when that state itself is unpleasant (II,xx,6). This, he says, is the same as *desire* (II,xxi,31).[125] And uneasiness, or desire, is what causes the passions (II,xx,3–18) and determines the will (II,xxi,29–39) – though, as Locke sees clearly, one may desire something without choosing it, even when free to do so (II,xxi.40,46ff.).

Though the concepts of good and evil enter into Locke's analysis of moral obligation, nonetheless the concept of moral obligation is understood by him as fundamentally different from that of good. Obligation is what is required by divine law. A law in general is a certain sort of rule for voluntary action (II,xxviii,4–5); specifically, a rule for voluntary action is a law if someone who wills that the rule be followed and has the right to command that it be followed attaches sanctions – rewards and punishments – to its observance and breach.[126] Three sorts of laws may be distinguished: "1.The *divine* law. 2.The *civil* law. 3.The law of *opinion* or *reputation*, if I may so call it. By the relation they bear to the first of these, men judge whether their actions are sins, or duties; by the second, whether they be criminal, or innocent; and by the third, whether they be virtues or vices" (II,xxviii,7).[127]

---

[124] See, for example, *Essay* I,iii,3; I,iii,5; II,xxi,55; II,xxi,65; *Reasonableness; Works* VI,149.

[125] "The uneasiness a man finds in himself upon the absence of anything, whose present enjoyment carries the idea of delight with it, is that we call desire" (II,xx,6).

[126] II,xviii,6; *Essays on the Law of Nature*, pp. 151 and 183.

[127] In II,xxviii,12, Locke considers the objection that he is forgetting his own concept of a law when he says that social customs may have the status of law. His reply is interesting: "If anyone shall imagine, that I have forgot my own notion of a law, when I make the law, whereby men judge of virtue and vice to be nothing else, but the consent of private men, who have not authority enough to make a law: Especially wanting that, which is so necessary, and essential to a law, a power to enforce it: I think, I may say, that he, who imagines commendation and disgrace, not to be strong motives on men to accomodate themselves to the opinions and rules of those, with whom they converse seems little skilled in the nature, or history of mankind: the greatest part whereof he shall find to govern themselves chiefly, if not solely, by the law of fashion." What then follows is an impressive discussion of the force of social approval and disapproval.

Thus "what duty is, cannot be understood without a law; nor a law be known, or supposed without a lawmaker, or without reward and punishment" (I,iii,12). Specifically, duty is what is required by divine law. Locke's theory of moral obligation is a divine command theory – though it is important to add that the commands are those of a necessarily loving God whose goal is the happiness of all his human creatures.[128] "That God has given a rule whereby men should govern themselves, I think there is nobody so brutish as to deny," says Locke. "He has a right to do it, we are his creatures: He has goodness and wisdom to direct our actions to that which is best: and he has power to enforce it by rewards and punishments, of infinite weight and duration, in another life: for nobody can take us out of his hands. This is the only true touchstone of moral rectitude" (II,xxviii,8).

The sanctions attached to divine law are of course goods and evils, "pleasures" and "pains." And since divine law is the determinant of moral obligation, we can call those goods and evils, *moral* goods and *moral* evils – without, however, identifying moral good with obligation.[129] "[Divine law] is the only true touchstone of *moral rectitude*; and by comparing them to this law, it is, that men judge of the most considerable *moral good* or *evil* of their actions; that is, whether as *duties, or sins*, they are like to procure them happiness, or misery, from the hands of the Almighty" (II,xxviii,8). "*Morally good and evil* then, is only the conformity or disagreement of our voluntary actions to some law, whereby good or evil is drawn on us, from the will and power of the lawmaker; which good and evil, pleasure or pain, attending our observance, or breach of the law, by the decree of the lawmaker, is that we call *reward* and *punishment*" (II,xxviii,5).

It may well be that sometimes the mere prospect of not doing what

---

[128] For a contemporary analogue, developed with a much more sophisticated attention to the nature of meaning than one finds in Locke, see Robert M. Adams, *The Virtue of Faith and Other Essays in Philosophical Theology* (Oxford, Oxford University Press, 1987), esp. the chapters entitled "A Modified Divine Command Theory of Ethical Wrongness" and "Divine Command Metaethics Modified Again."

[129] "That which has very much confounded men about the will and its determinations has been the confounding of the notion of moral rectitude and giving it the name of moral good. The pleasure that a man takes in any action or expects as a consequence of it is indeed a good in itself able and proper to move the will, but the moral rectitude of it considered barely in itself is not good or evil nor in any way moves the will but as pleasure and pain either accompanies the action itself or is looked on to be a consequence of it. Which is evident from the punishments and rewards which God has annexed to moral rectitude or pravity as proper motives by the will which would be needless if moral rectitude were itself good and moral pravity evil." Quoted from Locke's Commonplace Book of 1693 in Colman, *Locke's Moral Philosophy*, pp. 48–9.

one recognizes to be one's duty stirs up in one a motivating "uneasiness." Our human condition, however, is such that that is by no means always the case; it is for that reason, then, that God has attached sanctions to God's law. But though the prospect of securing happiness or avoiding unhappiness is always what motivates us, it remains the case that what determines our obligations is divine law, not utility: "if the source and origin of all this law is the care and preservation of oneself, virtue would seem to be not so much man's duty as his convenience, nor will anything be good except what is useful to him; and the observance of this law would be not so much our duty and obligation, to which we are bound by nature, as a privilege and an advantage, to which we are led by expediency."[130]

It seems clear that a law is a determinant of obligation only if the person laying down the law has the *right* to command obedience of those to whom the law applies; otherwise the issuance of the command is simply an exercise of power. In his early (unpublished) work *Essays on the Law of Nature*, Locke repeatedly and emphatically acknowledges the point; and argues that God has such a right. To understand whence some "bond of law takes its origin," says Locke, "we must understand that no one can oblige or bind us to do anything, unless he has right and power over us; and indeed, when he commands what he wishes should be done and what should not be done, he only makes use of his right. Hence that bond derives from the lordship and command which any superior has over us and our actions, and in so far as we are subject to another we are so far under an obligation. But that bond constrains us to discharge our liability, and the liability is twofold: First, a liability to pay dutiful obedience ... Secondly, a liability to punishment, which arises from a failure to pay dutiful obedience."[131] That God, in particular, has the right to lay down commands for our actions follows, says Locke, from the fact that we are God's creatures. In the *Essays* Locke states the point brutally: "for who will deny that the clay is subject to the potter's will, and that a piece of pottery can be shattered by the same hand by which it has been formed?"(p.155). In the *Second Treatise of Government* he states it somewhat more delicately: "men being all the workmanship of one omnipotent, and infinitely wise maker; all the servants of one sovereign master, sent into the world by his order, and about his business; they are his property, whose workmanship they are, made to

---

[130] *Essays on the Law of Nature*, p. 181.   [131] *Ibid.*, pp. 181–3.

last during his, not one another's pleasure" (§6; *Works* IV,341).

The right to which Locke is here appealing appears to be the right to dispose of one's property as one wishes; we are God's property. But how, in Locke's system, are we to understand the status of such a right? Earlier in the *Essays* Locke had remarked that "right is grounded in the fact that we have the free use of a thing, whereas law is what enjoins or forbids the doing of a thing" (p. 111). On this understanding, for one to have a right to do so-and-so is for the relevant laws of obligation to *permit* one to do so-and-so. But obviously God's right to command obedience of us cannot be understood as consisting in God's being permitted to do so by the laws of obligation, if the laws of obligation are just God's laws. Locke offers no alternative analysis, however;[132] and I fail to see what alternative analysis he could offer. There is, here, a deep fissure in Locke's theory.

It is important to realize that the very same rule for action which occurs in divine law might also occur in civil and social law; when that is the case, and the question is raised why the rule should be followed, one might reply by appealing to any one of the statuses that it has – or to all of them.[133] Furthermore, people may disagree on the status of some rule for action; one person may think it belongs to divine law; another, only to civil or social law. To deny that a rule for action has the status of divine law is tantamount, on Locke's view, to denying that it specifies a moral *obligation*;[134] those who deny that there are any divine laws

---

[132] See, for example, IV,xiii,3, where Locke just asserts that whoever has "the idea of an intelligent, but frail and weak being, made by and depending on another, who is eternal, omnipotent, perfectly wise and good, will certainly know that man is to honour, fear and obey God, as that the sun shines when he sees it. For if he hath but the ideas of two such beings in his mind, and will turn his thoughts that way, and consider them, he will as certainly find that the inferior, finite, and dependent, is under an obligation to obey the supreme and infinite, as he is certain to find, that three, four, and seven, are less than fifteen, if he will consider, and compute those numbers." Perhaps so! But there is no way in which Locke can account for the fact here "perceived."

[133] And it is because, if a rule for action is a law, there is always something (of one or the other of three sorts) which accounts for its being a law, that "I think, there cannot any one moral rule be proposed whereof a man may not justly demand a reason . . . should that most unshaken rule of morality, and foundation of all social virtue, *That one should do as he would be done unto*, be proposed to one, who never heard it before, but yet is of capacity to understand its meaning; might he not without any absurdity ask a reason why? And were not he that proposed it, bound to make out the truth and reasonableness of it to him? So that the truth of all these moral rules, plainly depends upon some other antecedent to them, and from which they must be deduced" (I,iii,4). Locke regards this as a reason for concluding that moral laws are not innate in us.

[134] Cf. *Essay* I,iii,6: "the true ground of morality; which can only be the will and law of a God, who sees men in the dark, has in his hand rewards and punishments, and power enough to call to account the proudest offender."

whatsoever tacitly deny that there are any moral obligations. Nonetheless, something which *is in fact* a divine law may still be acknowledged by them as a law – i.e., as either a civil or social law.

That men should keep their compacts, is certainly a great and undeniable rule in morality: But yet, if a Christian, who has the view of happiness and misery in another life, be asked why a man must keep his word, he will give this as a reason: Because God, who has the power of eternal life and death, requires it of us. But if an Hobbist be asked why; he will answer: Because the public requires it, and the Leviathan will punish you, if you do not. And if one of the old heathen philosophers had been asked, he would have answered: Because it was dishonest, below the dignity of a man, and opposite to virtue, the highest perfection of human nature, to do otherwise. Hence naturally flows the great variety of opinions, concerning moral rules, which are to be found amongst men, according to the different sorts of happiness, they have a prospect of, or propose to themselves ... But yet I think it must be allowed, that several moral rules may receive, from mankind, a very general approbation, without either knowing, or admitting the true ground of morality; which can only be the will and law of a God. (1,iii,5 and 6)[135]

That there are civil and social laws is obvious. Locke took it as scarcely less obvious that there is divine law – "that law which God has set to the actions of men, whether promulgated to them by the light of nature, or the voice of revelation" (II,xxviii,8). Both reason and revelation tell us that we have obligations to God. And as to how, from the other side, we come to believe that some rule for action is an obligation, i.e., that it is something God requires of us, Locke's answer is that we come to believe this in many ways: by believing our teachers on their sayso, by accepting revelation, and so on:

I doubt not, but without being written on their hearts, many men, may, by the same way that they come to the knowledge of other things come to assent to several moral rules, and be convinced of their obligation. Others also may come to be of the same mind, from their education, company, and customs of their country; which, persuasion however got, will serve to set conscience on work, which is nothing else, but our own opinion or judgment of the moral rectitude or pravity of our own actions. (1,ii,8; cf. *Essays*, p. 129)

---

[135] Cf. *Reasonableness*; *Works* VI,144: "Those just measures of right and wrong, which necessity had anywhere introduced, the civil laws prescribed or philosophy recommended, stood on their true foundations. They were looked on as bonds of society, and conveniencies of common life, and laudable practices. But where was it that their obligation was thoroughly known and allowed, and they received as precepts of a law; of the highest law, the law of nature? That could not be, without a clear knowledge and acknowledgment of the law-maker, and the great rewards and punishments, for those that would, or would not obey him."

The interesting question, though, is whether we can *know* – know in Locke's strict sense of "know" – that some rule for action is a moral obligation. Can we *know*, about some rule for action, that it is a law of God for us? Locke's answer is Yes: We can, in principle, arrive at a knowledge of many, if not all, of our moral obligations. We do not, indeed, come into the world knowing them; what is innate in us is not the knowledge of moral obligations but the capacity for coming to know moral obligations: "[T]he goodness of God . . . hath furnished man with those faculties, which will serve for the sufficient discovery of all things requisite to the end of such a being" (i,iv,12). The faculties required include our capacity for demonstration; moral obligations cannot be known intuitively. They are not self-evident. "[M]oral principles require reasoning and discourse and some exercise of the mind, to discover the certainty of their truth. They lie not open as natural characters ingraven on the mind . . . these moral rules are capable of demonstration: and therefore it is our own faults, if we come not to a certain knowledge of them" (i,iii,1).[136]

Locke consistently used the expression "law of nature" to mean a law of moral obligation which can in principle be known by Reason. Accordingly, summarizing his discussion of how authentic knowledge of moral obligation is attainable, he says that "There is a great deal of difference between an innate law, and a law of nature; between something imprinted on our minds in their very original, and something that we being ignorant of may attain to the knowlege of, by the use and due application of our natural faculties. And I think they equally forsake the truth, who running into the contrary extremes, either affirm an innate law, or deny that there is a law, knowable by the light of nature; i.e., without the help of positive revelation" (i,iii,13).

To say that something is a law of nature, meaning by "law of nature" what Locke means by it, is not to imply that everybody, or indeed, *anybody*, *knows* it to be a law of obligation. Locke's repeated references in the *Second Treatise* to laws of nature do not carry the implication that laws of nature are, by a *consensus gentium*, known to be laws of obligation. It is true that God's laws for our lives, to be genuine laws for us, must be *promulgated* – made available to us by Reason or revelation. But we may correctly *believe* of some rule for action that it is

---

[136] Cf. a passage already cited in another context: "Another reason that makes me doubt of any innate practical principles, is, that I think, there cannot any one moral rule be proposed, whereof a man may not justly demand a reason: which would be perfectly ridiculous and absurd if they were innate, *or so much as self-evident*" (i,iii,4; my italics).

a law of God without *knowing* that it is. Alternatively, we may not believe that it is a law of any sort; or we may believe that it is a law, but not a divine law, not a law of moral obligation. The existence of God, says Locke, "is so many ways manifest, and the obedience we owe him, so congruous to the light of Reason, that a great part of mankind give testimony to the law of nature: But yet I think it must be allowed, that several moral rules, may receive, from mankind, a very general approbation, without either knowing, or admitting the true ground of morality; which can only be the will and law of a God, who sees men in the dark, has in his hand rewards and punishments, and power enough to call to account the proudest offender" (1,iii,6).

Though he never doubted that some if not all moral obligations can in principle be demonstrated, and thereby known, Locke readily conceded that almost nothing had yet been done on this project; few of the requisite demonstrations had yet been offered. Possibly it is just "too hard a task for unassisted reason to establish morality, in all its parts, upon its true foundations, with a clear and convincing light" (*Reasonableness*; *Works* vi,139).[137] Or perhaps the reason that "the knowledge of morality, by mere natural light . . . has but a slow progress" is not to be found in the fact that it is beyond the unaided ability of human beings to accomplish it as a whole, but is rather "to be found in men's necessities, passions, vices, and mistaken interests, which turn their thoughts another way . . . the designing leaders, as well as the following herd, find it not to their purpose to employ much of their meditations this way" (vi,140). Whatever "the cause, it is plain in fact that human reason, unassisted, failed men in its great and proper business of *morality*. It never, from unquestionable principles, by clear deductions, made out an entire body of the *law of nature*" (vi,140).

---

[137] One of the points Locke makes in his discussion of these issues in *Reasonableness* is that sometimes one's abilities are such that one is able to construct a proof by following suggestions, but not able to construct that proof without having those suggestions. So too, one may be able to follow a proof, without having been able, even with hints and suggestions, to construct it oneself. Either way, one is able, solely by the use of reason, to come to know the conclusion, namely, by following the demonstration; even though one is not able, without suggestions, or even with suggestions, to construct the proof oneself. It was Locke's view that Scripture provides us with suggestions for how to construct a *scientia* of morality; he speculates that without those suggestions, it might have been impossible. When Locke defines a "law of nature" as an obligation which can in principle be known by unaided Reason, I suspect that he does not have in mind anything at all about the conditions for discovering the relevant demonstrations; he means only to say that there exist (whether any human being has ever been aware of them or not) arguments for those laws of obligation which human beings are capable of "perceiving" to be demonstrative.

Locke himself began the project of constructing the desired *scientia* of moral obligation, intending it as the conclusion of his *Essay*; eventually, however, he gave up and suppressed what he had written, remarking, in a letter to his young friend William Molyneux, that "I thought I saw that morality might be demonstratively made out; yet whether I am able so to make it out, is another question."[138] This passage has sometimes been interpreted as expressing uncertainty as to whether a *scientia* of morality with any significant amplitude really is possible. I think that reading it within the context of the letter as a whole makes clear that that is not how it should be interpreted; nor does any other passage in Locke, of which I am aware, warrant the conclusion that he had serious doubts on the matter. In the letter, he is simply expressing the doubt that *he himself* has the intellectual powers necessary for the task. Immediately after the sentence quoted he says that "Everyone could not have demonstrated what Mr. Newton's book hath shown to be demonstrable."

We can glean, from various sources, evidence of Locke's intimations as to how the demonstration would have to go. Starting from intuitive knowledge of one's own existence, coupled perhaps with sensitive knowledge of the existence of material objects (and other persons?), it would proceed to offer a proof of the existence of a Creator of these entities. Proofs concerning the nature of God would then be offered, from which the conclusion would be drawn that God issues rules for the action of God's rational creatures,[139] and that they have the obligation to obey those rules. From the nature of God we would then infer that these commands are for the happiness of God's creatures.[140]

---

[138] *The Correspondence of John Locke*, ed. E. S. De Beer, vol. iv (Oxford, Clarendon Press, 1979), p. 524, # 1538.

[139] Cf. this passage from MS Locke c 28, p. 152, printed in Peter King, *The Life of John Locke* (2 vols., London, Henry Colburn and Richard Bentley, 1830), vol. ii, p. 133: "to establish morality therefore upon its proper basis and such foundations as may carry an obligation with them we must first prove a law which always supposes a law maker one that has a superiority and right to ordain and also a power to reward and punish according to the tenor of the law established by him. This Sovereign Law Maker who has set rules and bounds to the actions of men is god their maker whose existence we have already proved. The next thing then to show is that there are certain rules, certain dictates which it is his will all men should conform their actions to, and that this will of his is sufficiently promulgated and made known to all mankind."

[140] The divine law, "in its true notion, is not so much the limitation *as the direction of a free and intelligent agent* to his proper interest, and prescribes no farther than is for the general good of those under that law" (*Second Treatise*, §57; *Works* iv,370). Cf. MS f 4, fol. 145, printed in King, *Life of Locke*, vol. i, pp. 228–9: God is "eternall and perfect in his own being"; "therefore all the exercise of that power must be in and upon his creatures, which cannot but be employed for their good and benefit as much as the order and perfection of the whole can allow to each individual in its particular rank and station."

We would then go on to discuss the nature of human beings, and what it is that gives human beings happiness;[141] and we would attempt, rather early, to derive the principle that *one should do as he would be done unto*, since it is "the most unshaken rule of morality, and foundation of all social virtue" (1,ii,4).[142] In short, a "rational ethics" would be constructed by reflecting on what a good God, who cares about the happiness of each of God's human creatures, would ask of them.

In a striking anticipation of Kant's opposition to utilitarian ethics, Locke holds that it will turn out that there are some duties such that it is impossible to be a human being and not have those duties. In the *Essays on the Law of Nature* he remarks that "human nature must needs be changed before this law can be either altered or annulled . . . this law does not depend on an unstable and changeable will, but on the eternal order of things . . . And this is not because nature or God (as I should say more correctly) could not have created man differently. Rather, the cause is that, since man has been made such as he is, equipped with reason and his other faculties and destined for this mode of life, there necessarily result from his inborn constitution some definite duties for him, which cannot be other than they are. In fact it seems to me to follow just as necessarily from the nature of man that, if he is a man, he is bound to love and worship God and also to fulfil other things appropriate to the rational nature, as it follows from the nature of a triangle that, if it is a triangle, its three angles are equal to two right angles . . . natural law stands and falls together with the nature of man as it is at present" (199–201).

---

[141] Cf. Colman's summary of the main elements of Locke's thought here: "In Locke's theory, then, the will of God is the form of the law of nature; it makes the directives of morality to be laws binding mankind. Human nature provides the necessary terminative element in the law of nature, for what God wills men to do is somehow incorporated in the way he has made them. Locke's theory of moral obligation may be summed up thus: God's will is necessary and sufficient to place men under an obligation; the facts of human nature are necessary and sufficient to delimit the obligations men are placed under" (*Locke's Moral Philosophy*, p. 42).

[142] Various commentators (e.g., Tully, in "Governing Conduct") argue that Locke was a voluntarist in his moral theory. I do not doubt that Locke thought God could have created human beings whose happiness was achieved somewhat differently from how ours is achieved – though Locke was impressed by the variety of the ways in which actual human beings do find their happiness (see esp. II,xxi,54–5, 65). Nonetheless, it is clear that Locke thought it to be *necessarily true* that the rules for action which God lays down as laws to human beings are laws which promote human happiness. (He does not, with any consistency, state the goal any more precisely than that.) He says that "the duties of [the divine] law, arising from the constitution of [God's] very nature, are of eternal obligation; nor can it be taken away or dispensed with without changing the nature of things" (*Reasonableness*; *Works* VI,112); and "that God himself cannot choose what is not good; the freedom of the almighty hinders not his being determined by what is best" (II,xxi,49).

In three different places in Book IV of the *Essay,* Locke speaks of his vision of a *scientia* of moral obligation. One of those can serve as a sketch of the picture I have drawn:

The idea of a supreme being, infinite in power, goodness, and wisdom, whose workmanship we are, and on whom we depend; and the idea of ourselves, as understanding, rational beings, being such as are clear in us, would, I suppose, if duly considered, and pursued, afford such foundations of our duty and rules of action, as might place morality amongst the sciences capable of demonstration: wherein I doubt not, but from self-evident propositions, by necessary consequences, as incontestable as those in mathematics, the measures of right and wrong might be made out. (IV,iii,18)

The other two passages, however, give a very different impression of how the *scientia* of moral obligation would be structured. One of them goes like this:

This gave me the confidence to advance that conjecture . . . that morality is capable of demonstration, as well as mathematics. For the ideas that ethics are conversant about, being all real essences, and such as I imagine have a discoverable connexion and agreement one with another; so far as we can find their habitudes and relations, so far we shall be possessed of certain, real, and general truths: and I doubt not, but if a right method were taken, a great part of morality might be made out with that clearness, that could leave, to a considering man, no more reason to doubt, than he could have to doubt of the truth of propositions in mathematics, which have been demonstrated to him. (IV,xii,8)[143]

As examples of propositions which will occur in this projected *scientia,* Locke cites *Where there is no property, there is no injustice,* and *No government allows absolute liberty* (IV,iii,18; perhaps, in IV,iv,8, he intends *Murder deserves death* as another example).

This alternative description of the project of a *scientia* of moral obligation is obviously very different from the previous description. Rather than constructing a long proof, moving from one's own existence, to God's existence, to God's nature, to our nature, to what yields us happiness, thence to rules of obligation, one simply offers necessary, analytic and synthetic, truths pertaining to moral concepts – constructing demonstrations of those necessary truths whenever one does not intuitively "perceive" them to be true. The analogue to pure

---

[143] Cf. IV,iv,7: "moral knowledge is as capable of real certainty, as mathematics. For certainty being but the perception of the agreement, or disagreement of our ideas; and demonstration nothing but the perception of such agreement, by the intervention of other ideas, or mediums, our moral ideas, as well as mathematical, being archetypes themselves, and so adequate, and complete ideas, all the agreement, or disagreement, which we shall find in them, will produce real knowledge, as well as in mathematical figures."

mathematics, as Locke understood that, is obvious. After all, says Locke, moral concepts are like mathematical ones in being "mixed modes"; being such, they are "combinations of several ideas, that the mind of man has arbitrarily put together, without reference to any archetypes . . . Accordingly, since the precise signification of the names of mixed modes, or which is all one, the real essence of each species, is to be known, they being not of nature's, but man's making, it is a great negligence and perverseness, to discourse of moral things with uncertainty and obscurity" (III,xi,15).

I know of no place in which Locke explains the discrepency between these two ways of describing the project of a *scientia* of morality; so we are left to speculate. My speculation is that Locke saw two different projects in the region: call them the *theistic project* and the *archetypal project*. The archetypal project is entirely hypothetical: If there were a situation in which there was no property, that would be a situation in which there was no injustice; if there were a situation of absolute liberty, that would be a situation in which there was no government; if some killing constituted murder, that killing would merit the death penalty. Extremely interesting things might turn up in this project, just as extremely interesting things turn up in pure mathematics. But from the archetypal project we do not learn what are in fact our moral obligations – that is, what God does in fact require of us. To learn that where there is no property, there is no injustice is not to learn what God requires and forbids of us with respect to property – nor, indeed, is it to learn whether there is any property. To learn that murder deserves death is not to learn what sort of penalty God requires for killing a fellow human being – nor is it to learn whether there have ever been any killings which are murders. The full picture, then, is that the archetypal project is not only of interest in its own right but an indispensable ancillary to the more comprehensive theistic project. Various abstract relations among moral concepts are mapped out in the archetypal project; in the theistic project, those concepts are used and their inter-relationships appealed to in the course of establishing our obligations. And to show that some action is obligatory is perforce to make clear a motivation for performing it.[144]

After being frustrated in his attempts in the late 1680s and early 1690s to construct a *scientia* of moral obligation – frustrated, apparently, in both the archetypal project and the theistic project – Locke seems

---

[144] Colman, *Locke's Moral Philosophy*, pp. 167–76, offers a somewhat different speculation as to what Locke had in mind.

to have desisted from such attempts during the last decade of his life and excused himself, to those who inquired, by suggesting that the project lay beyond his abilities.[145] He offered another excuse as well: The existence of the Christian revelation has taken away the urgency. Responding to William Molyneux' request that he write a treatise on morals, Locke said that "Did the world want a rule, I confess there could be no work so necessary, nor so commendable. But the Gospel contains so perfect a body of ethics, that reason may be excused from that inquiry, since she may find man's duty clearer and easier in revelation than in herself."[146] Anyone who wishes his rules to pass for authentic laws

must show that either he builds his doctrine upon principles of reason, self-evident in themselves, and that he deduces all the parts of it from thence, by clear and evident demonstration; or must show his commission from heaven, that he comes with authority from God to deliver his will and commands to the world. In the former way nobody that I know before our Saviour's time, ever did or went about to give us a morality. It is true, there is a *law of nature*; but who is there that ever did, or undertook to give it us all entire, as a law; no more nor no less than what was contained in, and had the obligation of, that law? Whoever made out all the parts of it, put them together, and showed the world their obligation? Where was there any such code, that mankind might have recourse to as their unerring rule, before our Saviour's time? If there was not, it is plain there was need of one to give us such a morality; such a law, which might be the sure guide of those who had a desire to go right; and, if they had a mind, need not mistake their duty; but might be certain when they had performed, when failed, in it. Such a *law of morality* Jesus Christ hath given in the New Testament; but by the latter of these ways, by revelation, we have from him a full and sufficient rule for our direction, and conformable to that of reason. But the truth and obligation of its precepts have their force, and are put past doubt to us, by the evidence of his mission. (*Reasonableness*; *Works* vi,142–3)

Christian philosophers have much outdone those who came "before our Saviour's time" in the project of demonstrating "a true and complete morality" (*Reasonableness*; *Works* vi,140). That is to be

---

[145] Colman, *ibid.*, pp. 169–70, remarks, correctly, I think, that "There are in fact two parts to Locke's envisaged demonstration of morality. The first concerns the existence of a moral law which imposes an obligation on all mankind. Carrying this through involves a proof of God's existence (sketched in the fourth book of the *Essays* and set out in detail at iv,x in the *Essay*), a proof that He does intend us to conform our actions to a law, and an analysis of the concept of obligation. Given the existence of the law, the second part of the demonstration is to make out its content, or determine beyond doubt the correct measures of right and wrong. Locke would consider the first of these parts to have been substantially completed in the *Essay*. It was this second to which his friend William Molyneux and others urged Locke to turn his hand."

[146] *The Correspondence of John Locke*, ed. E. S. De Beer, vol. v (Oxford, Clarendon Press, 1979), p. 595; # 2059.

explained by noticing that propositions and arguments which one did not oneself think of may be "seen" to be true or cogent when someone else mentions them. "A great many things which we have been bred up in the belief of from our cradles, and are notions grown familiar, (and, as it were, natural to us under the Gospel,) we take for unquestionable obvious truths, and easily demonstrable, without considering how long we might have been in doubt or ignorance of them had revelation been silent" (*Reasonableness*; *Works* VI,145). Nonetheless, the amplitude of the body of ethics presented in revelation goes well beyond what even Christian philosophers, working with the suggestions of Scripture, have been able to demonstrate.

Even more important, in Locke's view, than the relative completeness of the ethic presented in the gospels is the fact that in this form of presentation it has proved much more accessible to, and much more persuasive for, the bulk of humankind than it would be if presented in the form of a demonstration. It is "a surer and shorter way to the apprehensions of the vulgar, and mass of mankind, that one manifestly sent from God, and coming with visible authority from him, should, as a King and Lawmaker, tell them their duties, and require their obedience, than leave it to the long and sometimes intricate deductions of reason, to be made out to them. Such strains of reasonings the greatest part of mankind have neither leisure to weigh, nor, for want of education and use, skill to judge of" (*Reasonableness*; *Works* VI,139). "You may as soon hope to have all the day-labourers and tradesmen, the spinsters and dairy-maids, perfect mathematicians, as to have them perfect in ethics this way: hearing plain commands is the sure and only course to bring them to obedience and practice: the greatest part cannot know, and therefore they must believe" (*Reasonableness*; *Works* VI,146).[147]

---

[147] A central thesis in C. B. MacPherson's interpretation of Locke's political theory (*The Political Theory of Possessive Individualism* [Oxford, Oxford University Press, paperback, 1964]) is that "Locke assumed in his own society a class differential in rationality which left the labouring class incapable of a fully rational life, i.e. incapable of ordering their lives by the law of nature or reason" (p. 232). MacPherson goes on to argue that Locke assumed a differential of natural rights corresponding to this differential of rationality. In support of his claim that Locke assumed a differential of rationality between the laboring class and the leisured property class, MacPherson cites those passages in which Locke says that the members of the labouring class barely have time to "raise their thoughts above" the demands of subsistence. MacPherson then interprets the point of passages in *Reasonableness*, such as the one I have just quoted in the text above, as "that without supernatural sanctions the labouring class is incapable of following a rationalist ethic. He only wants the sanctions made clearer. The simple articles he recommends are not moral rules, they are articles of faith. They are to be believed. Belief in them is all that is necessary, for such belief converts

It goes without saying that few people have found Locke's proposal for a true science of ethics plausible. His application to morality of the practice he proposed has in that way experienced a fate strikingly different from his application to revealed religion of the practice. Though in this latter area, too, what we have from Locke's hand is more project than accomplishment, nonetheless his evidentialist model for the relation of faith and reason has proved enormously compelling among the intelligentsia of the modern West.

III IMPLEMENTATION OF THE VISION

At the very heart of Locke's model of the responsible believer was a preachment, an exhortation: We ought so to discipline ourselves that, for those propositions of sufficient "concernment" to us, we take Reason as our guide. The "we" here is Everyman: everyone who has

the moral rules of the Gospel into binding commands . . . The greatest part of mankind, Locke concludes, cannot be left to the guidance of the law of nature or law of reason; they are not capable of drawing rules of conduct from it" (p. 225). This is a deep, albeit subtle, misinterpretation of Locke. The fact that Scripture attaches divine sanctions to the law of God is nothing peculiar to Scripture. Locke's view is that a rule for action is a *law specifying obligations* just in case it is God's will for our lives and has divine sanctions attached. Such a law may be either a law of nature, or promulgated in Scripture, or believed on probabilistic evidence, or handed down by tradition, *or all of these*. It is a law of nature if it *can be demonstrated* by "unaided" Reason. Further, Locke thinks that even the best philosophers have come far short of developing a complete science of morality by unaided Reason, let alone developing one which is widely intelligible and convincing. Scripture in its completeness and its persuasiveness is superior to what *anyone* has been able to achieve. Thus Scripture is not just advantageous for the laboring class; it is advantageous for all human beings. Further, believing Scripture is itself to be done in accord with the dictates of Reason. But lastly, what about Locke's supposed assumption of a differential rationality and differential set of natural rights? Locke did indeed think that if one has no access to the moral law, one has no obligations and fewer natural rights; he thought that infants and small children and "mad" persons were in that position. But there are *various* modes of access to that law: demonstration, entitled belief which makes no appeal to Scripture, entitled belief which does make appeal to Scripture. Each of these makes use of Reason in its own way. And Locke thought that one or the other mode was available "even" to the members of the laboring class. What they do not have time for is the following out of complicated demonstrations, and the pursuit of "natural philosophy." Further, nobody whatsoever has the time to conduct his or her understanding aright with respect to more than a fraction of his or her beliefs. In short, one cannot arrive at the conclusion that Locke regarded members of the laboring class as having fewer natural rights from the premises that MacPherson appeals to. Infants and mad persons do; it's not at all clear that those who have to spend almost all their time working do. Perhaps I should add that I find Locke's smug and arrogant attitude toward the laboring class thoroughly offensive. My point has been that MacPherson's attempt to show that Locke grounds that attitude in his overall system fails.

some modicum of Reason and Will, everyone who is a sane, mature human being. Locke's philosophy was, by inner intent, a *public* philosophy. His proposal was a proposal for the reform of the doxastic practices of all of us.

Locke composed his book accordingly.[148] An *essay* he called it, not a treatise; and he wrote in "the plain style," not the style of the learned. He was convinced – as he makes abundantly clear – that all too often the jargon of academia is the enemy of good philosophy, the "hindrance of true knowledge" (*Essay*, Epistle to the Reader, p. 10 [16–17]). Knowledge "certainly had been very much more advanced in the world if the endeavours of ingenious and industrious men had not been much cumbred with the learned but frivolous use of uncouth, affected, or unintelligible terms, introduced into the science, and there made an art of, to that degree, that philosophy, which is, nothing but the true knowledge of things, was thought unfit, or uncapable to be brought into well-bred company, and polite conversation" (p. 10 [5–11]).

A philosophy written in a style fit for well-bred company and polite conversation – that was Locke's goal. It was for "men of [his] own size" (p. 8 [21]). Accordingly, not only did he adopt the plain style; he allowed himself to be more diffuse than "men of large thoughts" will approve of. To men of his own size "perhaps it will not be unacceptable, that I have taken some pains, to make plain and familiar to their thoughts some truths, which established prejudice, or the abstractness of the ideas themselves, might render difficult" (p. 8 [22–25]). In short, says Locke, "my appearing . . . in print, being on purpose to be as useful as I may, I think it necessary to make, what I have to say, as easy and intelligible to all sorts of readers as I can. And I had much rather the speculative and quicksighted should complain of my being in some parts tedious, than that anyone, not accustomed to abstract speculations, or prepossessed with different notions, should mistake, or not comprehend my meaning" (p. 9 [6–11]).

But if Locke meant his philosophy for the educated leisured public, and if at the core of that philosophy was a preachment, then he must have judged something amiss in public life. What was that? We know

---

[148] On the motivations behind the style of the *Essay*, see "Intentions and Audience," in Wood, *The Politics of Locke's Philosophy*. And on the style of the *Essay*, see Rosalie Colie, "The Essayist in his *Essay*," in John W. Yolton (ed.), *John Locke: Problems and Perspectives* (Cambridge, Cambridge University Press, 1969).

the answer: People did not conduct their understandings in the right way – not in science, not in religion, not in politics, not in ethics, not even in practical affairs. In the opening of the small book which Locke published as a supplement to his *Essay* and which he called *The Conduct of the Understanding*, he classifies under three headings the principal "miscarriages that men are guilty of in reference to their Reason" (§3; *Works* II,325). To these three he shortly (§6) adds a fourth.[149]

One of the common miscarriages is *shortsightedness*. We tend to "see but one side of the matter: our views are not extended to all that has a connection with it" (§3; II,326). "The faculty of reasoning seldom or never deceives those who trust to it, its consequences from what it builds on are evident and certain, but that which it oftenest, if not only, misleads us in, is, that the principles from which we conclude, the grounds upon which we bottom our reasoning, are but a part; something is left out which should go into the reckoning to make it just and exact" (§3; II,326–7). In some people this shortsightedness is like a disease. "They canton out to themselves a little Goshen in the intellectual world, where light shines, and, as they conclude, day blesses them; but the rest of that vast expansum they give up to night and darkness, and so avoid coming near it" (§3; II,327).

A second miscarriage in the use of Reason is permitting *passion* to play a role in the conduct of one's understanding. We have met this miscarriage earlier, in our discussion of the wounds of the mind: Instead of cultivating "indifference" to everything but truth in the conduct of their understandings, people allow passions to play their distorting role. They "put passion in the place of Reason, and . . . neither use their own, nor hearken to other people's, Reason any

---

[149] Later in the book, after discussing the importance of practice and habituation, Locke introduces and discusses a rather long list of vices which hinder the ability and inclination to apply the practice which he is recommending – tossing in here and there mention of some virtues necessary to the practice. "There are," he says, "several weaknesses and defects in the understanding, either from the natural temper of the mind, or ill habits taken up, which hinder it in its progress to knowledge. Of these there are as many, possibly, to be found, if the mind were thoroughly studied, as there are diseases of the body, each whereof clogs and disables the understanding to some degree, and therefore deserves to be looked after and cured. I shall set down some few to excite men, especially those who make knowledge their business, to look into themselves and observe whether they do not indulge some weaknesses . . . in the management of their intellectual faculty, which is prejudicial to them in the search of truth" (*Conduct*, §12; *Works* II,349).

farther than it suits their humor, interest, or party" (§3; II,326).

A third miscarriage is also familiar: Our education leads us to take as unquestionably true certain *principles*, and to judge the truth of other things by reference to these – this in spite of the fact that they "are not self-evident, and very often not so much as true" (§6; II,333).

But the first miscarriage which Locke cites is the one which has been a constant presence throughout our discussion: the influence of *tradition*, especially in the form of partisanship. It is the miscarriage "of those who seldom reason at all, but do and think according to the example of others, whether parents, neighbors, ministers, or who else they are pleased to have an implicit faith in, for the saving of themselves the pains and trouble of thinking and examining for themselves" (§3; II,326).

Earlier I called attention to the fact that between the medievals and Locke something happened which has proved of fateful significance for us in the modern West, and by now for the rest of the world: Whereas tradition had once been regarded and treated as a repository of wisdom, Locke unwaveringly saw it as a source of error and vice. The *Essay* and the *Conduct* are an unrelenting attack on tradition. Tradition is up against the wall. Words are all too often the enemy of good philosophy (III,x; IV,iii,30). Tradition is always the enemy of doing our best. To do our best, we must liberate ourselves from the grip of unexamined tradition and allegiance to unquestioned authority, coolly assessing the tenability of every tradition and authority from outside all traditions and authorities. The counterpart to Locke's attack on tradition was his celebration of the sovereign individual who, freed from distorting passion and principle, sits in judgment on tradition, "inquiring directly into the nature of the thing itself, without minding the opinions of others" (*Conduct*, §35; *Works* II,382). In Locke's epistemological thought, as well as his political thought, the sovereign individual occupies center stage. We would make greater progress, he says,

in the discovery of rational and contemplative knowledge, if we sought it in the fountain, in the consideration of things themselves; and made use rather of our own thoughts, than other men's to find it. For, I think, we may as rationally hope to see with other men's eyes, as to know by other men's understandings. So much as we ourselves consider and comprehend of truth and reason, so much we possess of real and true knowledge. The floating of other men's opinions in our brains makes us not one jot the more knowing, though they happen to be true. What in them was science, is in us but opiniatrety, whilst we give up our assent only to reverend names, and do not, as they did, employ our own Reason to understand those truths, which gave them reputation. (1,iv,23)

Locke uses this same point to defend the thesis which he propounds in the *Conduct* that "there is no part wherein the understanding needs a more careful and wary conduct than in the use of books" (§24; II,364). Books, after all, are among the principal bearers of tradition. "Books and reading are looked upon to be the great helps of the understanding and instruments of knowledge" (§24; II,364). They may well be that. But if the reader believes what the writer says on the writer's untested sayso, he will always believe it in a way inferior to that of the writer. If the writer knew, the reader merely believes. If the writer's belief was supported by strong evidence, that of the reader is supported by rather weak evidence.

The mistake here is, that it is usually supposed that by reading, the author's knowledge is transferred into the reader's understanding; and so it is, but not by bare reading, but by reading and understanding what he writ. Whereby I mean not barely comprehending what is affirmed or denied in each proposition . . . but to see and follow the train of his reasonings, observe the strength and clearness of their connection, and examine upon what they bottom . . . Knowing is seeing; and if it be so, it is madness to persuade ourselves that we do so by another man's eyes . . . Until we ourselves see it with our own eyes, and perceive it by our own understandings, we are as much in the dark, and as void of knowledge as before, let us believe any learned author as much as we will. Euclid and Archimedes are allowed to be knowing, and to have demonstrated what they say: and yet whoever shall read over their writings without perceiving the connection of their proofs, and seeing what they show, though he may understand all their words, yet he is not the more knowing. He may believe, indeed, but does not know what they say. (*Conduct*, §24; II,365; see also §§20, 24)

Locke was not under the illusion, however, that his writings would by themselves accomplish the goal of reforming how his fellow countrymen and women conducted their understandings; neither did he think that a bevy of similarly hortatory books would accomplish this goal. Such books can present *rules* for the direction of the mind, accompanied by defenses of the rules and exhortations to follow the rules, along with advice concerning their application. But "Nobody is made anything by hearing of rules, or laying them up in his memory . . . and you may as well hope to make a good painter or musician, extempore, by a lecture and instruction in the arts of music and painting, as a coherent thinker, or a strict reasoner, by a set of rules, showing him wherein right reasoning consists" (*Conduct*, §4; *Works* II,333). It is *practice*, not the propounding and hearing of rules, that generates right conduct: "As it is in the body, so it is in the mind; practice makes it what it is" (*Conduct*, §4; *Works*, II,333). It is no accident, then, that Locke called his book *The Conduct of the Understanding*, not *Rules for the Direction of the Mind*.

Would you have a man write or paint, dance or fence well, or perform any other manual operation dexterously and with ease, let him have never so much vigor and activity, suppleness and address, naturally, yet nobody expects this from him unless he has been used to it, and has employed time and pains in fashioning and forming his hand or outward parts to these motions. Just so it is in the mind: would you have a man reason well, you must use him to it betimes; exercise his mind in observing the connection of ideas, and following them in train. . . . we are born to be, if we please, rational creatures, but it is use and exercise only that makes us so. (*Conduct*, §6; II,337)

And how do we gain the practice required for the right conduct of the understanding? By *education*. Referring to the four miscarriages that we have noted Locke says that "These are the common and most general miscarriages which I think men should avoid or rectify in a right conduct of their understandings, and should be particularly taken care of in education. The business whereof, in respect of knowledge, is not, as I think, to perfect a learner in all or any one of the sciences, but to give his mind that freedom, that disposition, and those habits that may enable him to attain any part of knowledge he shall apply himself to, or stand in need of, in the future course of his life" (*Conduct*, §12; II,348).

I observed, in our discussion of Locke's wounds of the mind, that his recommendations for the cure of such wounds seemed curiously bland compared to their seriousness. There is nothing in Locke like Descartes's Therapy of Doubt. But now at last it becomes clear that we were looking in the wrong place. We were expecting Locke to urge on us some therapeutic regimen. There is, indeed, a bit of that. But mainly the counterpart in Locke to Descartes's Therapy of Doubt is not a similar regimen for curing the mind's wounds, but an educational program inculcating the habits required for rightly conducting the understanding. Locke's *Thoughts on Education* should be seen as the counterpart to those passages in Descartes where Descartes outlines, recommends and practices his Therapy of Doubt.[150] Descartes proposed therapeutic medicine, Locke, preventative.

The new educational practice is to be aimed at children, since adults who have been mis-educated are usually too set in their ways for much to be done about them – another reason, perhaps, why Locke says so little, when discussing the wounds of the mind, concerning the cure for the wounds. Much better to prevent the wounds than try to cure them:

> the reason why they do not make use of better and surer principles, is because they cannot: But this inability proceeds not from want of natural parts . . . but for want of use and exercise. Few men are from their youth accustomed to strict reasoning, and to trace the dependence of any truth in a long train of consequences to its remote principles, and to observe its connection; and he that by frequent practice has not been used to this employment of his understanding, it is no more wonder that he should not, when he is grown into years, be able to bring his mind to it, than that he should not be on a sudden able to grave or design, dance on the ropes, or write a good hand, who has never practised either of them . . . What then! can grown men never be improved or enlarged in their understandings? I say not so; but this I think I may say, that it will not be done without industry and application, which will require more time and pains than grown men, settled in their course of life, will allow to it, and therefore very seldom is done. (*Conduct*, §6; II,335)

Just as education in the right conduct of the understanding will focus especially on children, so, conversely, the education of children will focus mainly on such education. Other habits must be acquired than those necessary for rightly conducting the understanding. But these latter are fundamental: "Due care being had to keep the body in strength and vigor, so that it may be able to obey and execute the orders of the mind; the next and principal business is, to set the mind right, that on all occasions it may be disposed to consent to nothing, but what may be suitable to the dignity and excellency of a rational creature" (*Some Thoughts*, 31; *Works* VIII,26–7). "For [Reason], as the highest and most important faculty of our minds, deserves the

---

[150] Locke's *Some Thoughts Concerning Education* has now been edited for the Clarendon Press Edition of his works by John W. and Jean S. Yolton (Oxford, 1989). In addition to the Yoltons' introduction to their critical edition, see the introduction by James L. Axtell to his critical edition, *The Educational Writings of John Locke* (Cambridge, Cambridge University Press, 1968). The commentary on *Some Thoughts* by Nathan Tarcov, *Locke's Education for Liberty* (Chicago, University of Chicago Press, 1984), is also worth consulting. However, the best account of the relation between Locke's thoughts on education and his epistemology is now Peter Schouls' *Reasoned Freedom*, Part C.

greatest care and attention in cultivating it; the right improvement, and exercise of our Reason, being the highest perfection, that a man can attain to in this life" (*Some Thoughts*, 122; *Works* VIII, 118).

I have contended that Locke's philosophy was, by inner intent and by mode of presentation, a public philosophy, calling people to release themselves from the grip of tradition and passion, from inculcated principles and shortsightedness, urging on them a program of self-mastery, and more importantly, of child education. Though he does not often emphasize the point, Locke realizes that this public philosophy implies a social vision. Adequate inquiry which is at all extensive requires leisure; and within the space of leisure, it requires *peace, humanity, and friendship*. What, then, about those poor wretches, of whom Locke spoke so smugly and coolly, whose entire lives must be spent in manual drudgery? Are they not to enjoy the social utopia of peace, humanity, and friendship? Locke thought that even they had sufficient time, on Sundays and holidays, to reflect on elementary matters of morality and religion; so presumably for them those days are to be days of peace, humanity, and friendship. The point is that for all of us there are clearings in the thicket of our practical duties where we can concern ourselves with truth alone. For some, those clearings are cramped; for certain leisured members of society, they are expansive. But whether large or small, for life in those clearings peace, humanity, and friendship are required:

Since therefore it is unavoidable to the greatest part of men, if not all, to have several opinions, without certain and indubitable proofs of their truth; and it carries too great an imputation of ignorance, lightness, or folly, for men to quit and renounce their former tenets, presently upon the offer of an argument, which they cannot immediately answer, and show the insufficiency of it: it would, me thinks become all men to maintain peace, and the common offices of humanity, and friendship, in the diversity of opinions, since we cannot reasonably expect, that any one should readily and obsequiously quit his own opinion, and embrace ours with a blind resignation to an authority, which the understanding of man acknowledges not. For however it may often mistake, it can own no other guide but Reason, nor blindly submit to the will and dictates of another. (IV,xvi,4)[151]

Our expectations must be modest, however, even for a society which supports a sizeable group of leisured persons and creates the social conditions necessary for satisfactory inquiry and reflection. The

[151] See also IV,xx,4, where Locke says that what is needed is "the liberty and opportunities of a fair enquiry."

ancient and medieval ideal of insight by Reason into the essences of things must be renounced; "our faculties are not fitted to penetrate into the internal fabric and real essences of bodies." Instead of affording us insight into the reality surrounding us, Reason mainly offers us the guidance of probability for our making and doing in the midst of that reality. I think I may conclude, says Locke, "that morality is the proper science, and business of mankind in general; (who are both concerned, and fitted to search out their *Summum Bonum*,)." That is what holds for humanity in general. And as for leisured people: "several arts, conversant about several parts of nature, are the lot and private talent of particular men, for the common use of humane life, and their own particular subsistence in this world." It is to the "common use of humane life," and Yes, to the admiration of nature's Creator, that the new natural philosophy makes its principal contribution. "I readily agree" says Locke, that "the contemplation of [God's] works gives us occasion to admire, revere, and glorify their author: and if rightly directed, may be of greater benefit to mankind, than the monuments of exemplary charity." "All that I would say," he adds, "is, that we should not be too forwardly possessed with the opinion, or expectation of knowledge, where it is not to be had" (IV,xii,11–12). Our study of nature is not for the sake of contemplation. Our study of nature is in the service of our *praxis* and our *poiesis*, of our doing and our making; its results seldom reach beyond probability.

I close by noting a feature of Locke's writing which has perplexed a good many of his readers. Several times over we have noted Locke's conviction, shared by the Royal Society group in general, that words as we receive them are the enemy of good philosophy. "Students, being lost in the great wood of words," do not know where they are. Only if we put words aside and set before our mind's eye the very ideas themselves can we avoid "that perplexity, puddering, and confusion, which has so much hindered men's progress in other parts of knowledge" (IV,iii,30).

What is worst in words, if understanding is our goal, is figurative speech. Figurative speech has its place in discourse meant to give "pleasure and delight"; it is out of place, and worse than out of place – obstructive – in discourse meant to inform or instruct:

Since wit and fancy finds easier entertainment in the world, than dry truth and real knowledge, figurative speeches, and allusion in language, will hardly be admitted, as an imperfection or abuse of it. I confess, in discourses, where we seek rather pleasure and delight, than information and improvement, such ornaments as are borrowed from them, can scarce pass for faults. But yet, if we would speak of things as they are, we must allow, that all the art of rhetoric, besides order and clearness, all the artificial and figurative application of words eloquence hath invented, are for nothing else but to insinuate wrong ideas, move the passions, and thereby mislead the judgment; and so indeed are perfect cheat: and therefore however laudable or allowable oratory may render them in harangues and popular addresses, they are certainly, in all discourses that pretend to inform or instruct, wholly to be avoided. (III,x,34)

It is ironic that the rhetorical power of this harangue by Locke against figurative speech should in good measure depend on its vivid metaphors: "dry truth," "insinuate wrong ideas," "move the passions," "perfect cheat." And in general, the persuasive power of Locke's writing depends heavily on his extraordinary gift for metaphor: "the white tablet of the mind," "the state of nature," "the candle of the Lord," "cantoning a little Goshen for themselves in the intellectual world." How are we to explain the dissonance: harangues against metaphor by one of the greatest creators of metaphor in the English philosophical tradition? Was Locke oblivious to the fact that he was using metaphors? How, then, to explain such extraordinary obliviousness? Was his goal in writing to give pleasure and delight rather than inform and instruct?

An answer, of sorts, is to be found in *Conduct of the Understanding*, §32: Though philosophers must bring themselves to the point where they *think* without metaphor, they may nonetheless *speak* metaphorically:

But it is one thing to think right, and another thing to know the right way to lay our thoughts before others with advantage and clearness, be they right or wrong. Well-chosen similes, metaphors, and allegories, with method and order, do this the best of anything, because being taken from objects already known, and familiar to the understanding, they are conceived as fast as spoken; and the correspondence being concluded, the thing they are brought to explain and eludicate is thought to be understood too. Thus fancy [i.e., imagination] passes for knowledge, and what is prettily said is mistaken for solid. I say not this to decry metaphor, or with design to take away that ornament of speech; my business here is not with rhetoricians and orators, but with philosophers and lovers of truth; to whom I would beg leave to give this one rule whereby to try whether, in the application of their thoughts to anything for the improvement of their knowledge, they do in truth comprehend the matter before them really such as it is in itself. The way to discover this is to observe whether, in the laying it before themselves or others, they make use only of borrowed representations, and ideas foreign to the things, which are applied to it by way of accommodation, as bearing some proportion or imagined likeness to the subject under consideration. Figured and metaphorical expressions do well to illustrate more abstruse and unfamiliar ideas which the mind is not yet thoroughly accustomed to; but then they must be made use of to illustrate ideas that we already have, not to paint to us those which we yet have not. Such borrowed and allusive ideas may follow real and solid truth, to set it off when found; but must by no means be set in its place, and taken for it. If all our search has yet reached no farther than simile and metaphor, we may assure ourselves we rather fancy than know, and have not yet penetrated into the inside and reality of the thing. (II,378)

Locke's image of his own work, which he wishes us to share, is that first there was the non-pictorial thought, then there was the pictorial writing. The truth is that the thought itself is pictorial and metaphoric. The mind, says Locke, "perceives" agreements and disagreements among its ideas, those agreements and disagreements themselves being "luminous." These metaphors of perception and luminosity are deeper than any others in Locke. I have made no attempt in my discussion to eliminate them. For the pictures are not decorative features of Locke's presentation of his thought but an indispensable feature of the thought itself. Locke thought in pictures and metaphors. We all do. It was one of his gifts to have done his thinking in pictures which proved fruitful for himself and compelling for others.

CHAPTER 2

Hume's attack: why implementing Locke's practice is not always doing one's best

As I proceeded down the path of trying to discern what Locke was getting at in his discussion concerning the governance of belief and to uncover his motives for trying to get at it, I have offered, at various points, what is perhaps more a "rational reconstruction" than an interpretation, strictly speaking. When doing so, I have often brought twentieth-century discussions of the same issues into the conversation. And every now and then I have stopped to ask whether some claim or assumption that Locke made was true, often bringing contemporary discussions into the conversation at those points as well. Often, indeed, it was contemporary discussions which suggested the question. I have considered, for example, whether we human beings do in fact possess the powers of immediate awareness and of will which Locke's proposed method, or practice, presupposes. My conclusion was that, on these matters, Locke's proposal holds up better than a typical, late-twentieth-century, philosopher would initially have supposed.

However, my central goal on this occasion is not so much to critique as to understand this central part of the culture of modernity. Thus I have said *almost* nothing, and *will* say nothing more, about Locke's overarching strategy of trying to cope with fractured tradition by escaping from all untested tradition and going to "the things themselves." I believe that such escape is impossible. But many others have argued this point in recent years; on this occasion I will not add to what they have said.

Before we leave our grappling with Locke's thought I do wish, though, to appraise what he says on one, absolutely central, issue. Locke claimed that trying one's best to get in touch with reality on some matter, and then responding appropriately to the results thereof, requires trying to apply his principles of evidence, appraisal, and proportionality. I wish to ask whether he was right about even the first step in his three-step procedure; along the way, some considerations will arise pertaining to the other steps as well.

It was Hume who first saw the issues here with clarity, and who argued with great power that for many facts of several different sorts, Locke's method does not give us our best access. Hume went for the jugular; Thomas Reid joined him for the kill. So I propose considering the most fully developed of Hume's arguments on this score: his argument that while inductive inference, even at its best, is not a case of applying Locke's principles, it nonetheless provides us with our best access to a wide range of facts to which Locke's method, as it turns out, gives us no access at all. I shall then add to Hume's argument some comments of my own.

To the fourth edition of his *Essay* Locke added a chapter which he called "Of the Association of Ideas." He had noticed that not only persons of too much self-love, but "men of fair minds, and not given up to the overweening of self-flattery," also frequently display a wounding of the mind. In "many cases one with amazement hears the arguings, and is astonished at the obstinacy of a worthy man, who yields not to the evidence of Reason, though laid before him as clear as daylight" (II,xxxiii,2). This may rightly be called "by so harsh a name as *madness*, when it is considered, that opposition to Reason deserves that name" (II,xxxiii,4). Locke observes that the particular wound he has in mind can rightly be ascribed to education and prejudice. But he has come to believe, he says, that to say this is not to get to "the bottom of the disease, nor [to show] distinctly enough whence it rises, or wherein it lies" (II,xxxiii,3). The cause is that ideas acquire a connection in the mind quite other than their intrinsic agreement and disagreement. They become *associated* by *custom*: "ideas that in themselves are not at all of kin, come to be so united in some men's minds, that 'tis very hard to separate them, they always keep in company, and the one no sooner at any time comes into the understanding but its associate appears with it; and if they are more than two which are thus united, the whole gang always inseparable show themselves together" (II,xxxiii,5).

Locke's description of the injurious effects of custom on the mind rises to eloquence:

That which thus captivates their Reasons, and leads men of sincerity blindfold from common sense, will, when examined, be found to be what we are speaking of: some independent ideas, of no alliance to one another, are by education, custom, and the constant din of their party, so coupled in their minds, that they always appear there together, and they can no more separate them in their thoughts, than if they were but one idea, and they operate as if they were so. This . . . is the foundation of the greatest, I had almost said, of all the errors in the world; or if it does not reach so far, it is at least the most dangerous one, since so far as it obtains, it hinders men from seeing and examining . . . This . . . confusion of two different ideas, which a customary connexion of them in their minds hath to them made in effect but one, fills their heads with false views, and their reasonings with false consequences. (II,xxxiii,18; cf. *Conduct*, §41)

Confusing the association of ideas produced by custom with the agreement and disagreement that they possess intrinsically is "a weakness to which all men are so liable," "a taint which so universally infects mankind," and so much sets "us awry in our actions, as well moral as natural, passions, reasonings and notions themselves" (II,xxxiii,8) that extremely great care must be taken "in its prevention and cure" (II,xxxiii,4).

What Hume showed in his frontal attack on the Lockian vision was that the association of ideas, which Locke says we must do our best to set off to the side as we try to conduct our understanding aright, lies at the very foundation of our practice of induction; and that this, in turn, is indispensable to human, and indeed animal, existence. Human life rests at bottom not on Reason in particular, nor insight in general, but on the association of ideas by habit.

Hume had no substantial disagreements with Locke on the nature of *knowledge* and *science* (i.e., *scientia*). To see this, we must begin with an item of terminology. Locke grouped together all mental objects as *ideas*. Hume called them all, instead, *perceptions*. But Hume then went on to distinguish, among perceptions, those which he called *impressions* and those which he called *ideas*. We shall not go wrong if we think of Hume's ideas as our present-day *concepts*. Few of us would nowadays accept Hume's *theory* of concepts (taking his theory of ideas to be his theory of concepts). But what we would cite as *examples* of concepts are pretty much what Hume cites as *examples* of ideas.

Now for the Lockianism. There are, says Hume, various types of relations holding among ideas. "These relations may be divided into two classes: into such as depend entirely on the ideas, which we compare together, and such as may be changed without any change in the ideas" (*T* 69).[1] In other words, some of these relations hold

---

[1] I shall be quoting from the Selby-Bigge edition of Hume's *Treatise of Human Nature* (Oxford, Clarendon Press, 1951 repr.), and from P. H. Nidditch's revision of the third edition of the Selby-Bigge edition of Hume's *An Enquiry Concerning Human Understanding*. I shall abbreviate page references to these editions as *T* and *E* respectively.

necessarily; some, only contingently. Those of the former sort "can be the objects of knowledge and certainty" (*T* 70). "All certainty arises," says Hume, "from the comparison of ideas, and from the discovery of such relations as are unalterable, so long as the ideas continue the same" (*T* 79). When we do have knowledge of the necessary relations among our ideas, it is because of the workings of "intuition" and "demonstration" (*T* 70).

Hume thinks that necessary relations among ideas are all of one or the other of four fundamental types. And these four, he says, "are the foundation of science" (*T* 73). His view in the *Treatise* is that only algebra and arithmetic can "be esteemed a perfect and infallible science" (*T* 71). He explicitly argues that geometry does not qualify. Clearly it is *applied* geometry on which he has his eye. Perhaps he himself eventually realized this; for in the later *Enquiry Concerning Human Understanding* he cites geometry along with algebra and arithmetic as a "science." It is worth quoting what he says there:

All the objects of human reason or enquiry may naturally be divided into two kinds, to wit, *Relations of Ideas*, and *Matters of Fact*. Of the first kind are the sciences of Geometry, Algebra, and Arithmetic; and in short, every affirmation which is either intuitively or demonstratively certain. *That the square of the hypotenuse is equal to the squares of the two sides*, is a proposition which expresses a relation between these figures. *That three times five is equal to the half of thirty*, expresses a relation between these numbers. Propositions of this kind are discoverable by the mere operation of thought, without dependence on what is anywhere existent in the universe. Though there never were a circle or triangle in nature, the truths demonstrated by Euclid would for ever retain their certainty and evidence. (*E* 25)

Hume had little interest, however, in knowledge – less even than Locke. Having said that "all the objects of human reason or enquiry" are either (necessary) relations of ideas or (contingent) matters of fact, he rushes quickly from relations of ideas to matters of fact. And then, in turn, he quickly remarks that it is "a subject worthy of curiosity, to enquire what is the matter of that evidence which assures us of any real existence and matter of fact, beyond the present testimony of our senses, or the records of our memory" (*E* 25). What Hume had in mind by "the present testimony of our senses" is, I think, what in other passages he calls "impressions of sensation and reflection"; thus what he proposes inquiring into is "the nature of that evidence which assures us of any real existence and matter of fact" beyond present and remembered subjective experience.

It is characteristic of human beings and animals, says Hume, that upon perceiving an event of one type they believe that an event of some other type has occurred or is occurring or will occur. No such belief-dispositions are innate in us. Instead, we have an innate disposition for the formation of such belief-dispositions. And that innate disposition-to-form-such-belief-dispositions is activated, by experience, to produce different specific belief-dispositions, the particular belief-dispositions produced depending on the particular experience activating that basic-disposition. In short, the presence in us of inductive belief dispositions is the consequence of learning, not of being innately endowed with such dispositions.

What sort of experience activates that innate disposition to form these belief-dispositions? Only one sort, says Hume: the experience of a correlation of spatio-temporally contiguous events. To put it roughly: It is one's experience of a regular correlation, between spatio-temporally contiguous events of type A and of type B, which produces in one the disposition, upon perceiving an event of type A, to believe that there is or was or will be also an event of type B.

All belief of matter of fact or real existence is derived merely from some object, present to the memory or senses, and a customary conjunction between that and some other object. Or in other words; having found in many instances, that any two kinds of objects – flame and heat, snow and cold – have always been conjoined together; if flame or snow be presented anew to the senses, the mind is carried by custom to expect heat or cold, and to *believe* that such a quality does exist, and will discover itself upon a nearer approach. This belief is the necessary result of placing the mind in such circumstances. It is an operation of the soul, when we are so situated, as unavoidable as to feel the passion of love, when we receive benefits, or hatred, when we meet with injuries. (*E* 46)[2]

Though in general the correlation between A-type events and B-type events must have been experienced a number of times before the belief-disposition is produced, Hume grants that in certain cases just one such experience is sufficient. Furthermore, he thinks that in general the more often a correlation has been experienced, the

[2] Cf. 87: "'Tis therefore by EXPERIENCE only, that we can infer the existence of one object from that of another. The nature of experience is this. We remember to have had frequent instances of the existence of one species of objects; and also remember, that the individuals of another species of objects have always attended them, and have existence in a regular order of contiguity and succession with regard to them. Thus we remember to have seen that species of object we call flame, and to have felt that species of sensation we call *heat*. We likewise call to mind their constant conjunction in all past instances."

stronger is "the impulse or tendency to the transition" (T 130); and in turn, the stronger that impulse, the more firmly is the belief held when the belief-disposition is triggered – up to, no doubt, some maximal firmness for such beliefs (T 130–1). What happens if the correlation experienced is *fairly* regular but not invariant? Then the belief-disposition will be weaker, and the belief produced will be less firm, than they would have been if the experienced correlation had been invariant. Roughly speaking, the further from invariant the experienced correlation, the weaker the disposition and the less firm the belief. If one has over and over experienced that nineteen out of every twenty ships which sail from a harbor eventually return, then upon seeing another ship sail out of the harbor, one will be quite strongly inclined to believe quite firmly that it will return (T 134ff.). Though Hume introduces various refinements into this general picture (cf. especially his discussion of "the probability of chances" and of "unphilosophical probability"), a review of the psychological literature produced since his day would, of course, lead one to introduce many more.

Certain matters Hume leaves obscure; for example, the role of *belief* in the formation of these belief-dispositions, and in their activation once they have been formed. Hume recognizes that beliefs are sometimes components in the activating experience; but he offers no general theory on the matter, and does not speak consistently. Other crucial matters simply escape his attention – for example, the fact that an indefinite number of distinct inductions are compatible with any given set of experiences. What determines, then, *which* belief-disposition will get formed? And when various dispositions have been formed, what determines which will get activated on a given occasion?

I think it can be said, however, that introducing into Hume's account the necessary refinements, clarifications, and elaborations will not diminish the power of his attack on Locke's system. We all do engage in *the practice of induction*. One can concede that point, without agreeing with Hume that *every* disposition to believe the occurrence of some event which is activated by experiencing the occurrence of another is produced in us by the observation of some regularity. One can hold that some such belief-dispositions are produced by something else in experience, even that some are innate. Neither need one accept Hume's description of the nature of belief and the manner of its formation. It will be sufficient to grant that we *do* engage in the practice of induction – that upon perceiving one event we believe the occurrence of another even when we discern no logically/ontologically necessary relation between the two, and that sometimes the mechanisms for such belief-formation work as Hume suggests.

What is it that Hume wishes to say about this practice of induction? The conventional interpretation has been that he wishes to say that the beliefs produced by the practice lack "justification"; and that, derivatively, the practice itself lacks "justification." Ian Hacking, for example, in *The Emergence of Probability*, describes Hume as holding that "Our expectations are formed by custom and habit, but lack justification."[3] And again, "expectation about the future is unjustified."[4] Though Hacking is certainly one of our most clear-eyed and perceptive historians, he is not, indeed, a "professional" historian of modern philosophy. But many "professional" historians have spoken the same way. Richard Popkin, for example, says that it was Hume's view of ordinary matter-of-fact beliefs that they are *groundless*, have *no ground*, are *unfounded*, lack *justification*, have no *foundation*.[5]

What is it that Hacking, Popkin, and others have had in mind when they have said that, on Hume's view, beliefs formed by the practice of induction lack justification? That is by no means clear. One course to take here would be to bring more interpreters into the discussion and then to explore various possibilities as to what they might mean. But I see no way of interpreting what might be meant which does not conflict with one or more of four fundamental facts about Hume's thought. So rather than considering various possibilities as to what Hume's interpreters might mean by "justification," let us take note of these fundamental facts.

First, Hume held that once an inductive belief-disposition has been produced in us, then, if the event which activates that disposition occurs, the corresponding belief follows automatically, without the working of volition. And not only are inductive beliefs not formed by the will; we cannot by acts of will prevent their formation if the belief-disposition has been formed and the activating event occurs. All we can do by act of will to get rid of the belief is change the regularities in our experience.

Secondly, Hume points to a continuum of degrees of "evidence," offers his own demarcation of different gamuts on the continuum, and *places probabilities and (causal) proofs on the positive end of the continuum.*

Thirdly, Hume speaks of *just* inferences – that is, in contemporary

---

[3] (Cambridge, Cambridge University Press, 1975), p. 176.   [4] *Ibid.*, p. 181.
[5] Richard Popkin, *The High Road to Pyrrhonism* (San Diego, Austin Hill Press, 1980), pp. 57,133,141,145.

English, of *justified* inferences. "The only connexion or relation of objects, which can lead us beyond the immediate impressions of our memory and senses, is that of cause and effect; and that because 'tis the only one, on which we can found a just inference from one object to another" (*T* 89). And again, "I shall allow, if you please, that the one proposition may justly be inferred from the other; I know, in fact, that it always is inferred" (*E* 34). It should also be noted that after reviewing various "kinds of probability," i.e., various manifestations of our practice of induction, Hume says that these "are received by philosophers, and allowed to be reasonable foundations of belief and opinion" (*T* 143).[6]

And fourthly, Hume says that the practice of induction "*informs* us of existences and objects, which we do not see or feel" (*T* 74; my italics). Elaborating this point, he says in another place that "Here, then, is a kind of pre-established harmony between the course of nature and the succession of our ideas; and though the powers and forces, by which the former is governed, be wholly unknown to us; yet our thoughts and conceptions have still, we find, gone on in the same train with the other works of nature. Custom is that principle, by which this correspondence has been effected; so necessary to the subsistence of our species, and the regulation of our conduct, in every circumstance and occurrence of human life" (*E* 54–5).[7]

In short, Hume regards many of the *beliefs* produced by our practice of induction as having a certain (positive) degree of "evidence," and many of our inductive *inferences* as just and reasonable. And he thinks that much of the time our inductive practice maps or mirrors what transpires in nature itself. Now whatever may be meant in saying of Hume that on his view our inductive practice and the

---

[6] I take Hume to be hinting, in these passages, at an account of justifiedly held belief quite different from anything Locke would have affirmed. The clearest expressions of this account that Hume ever gives in his published works – and they are quite unclear – are to be found in Book I, Part IV, Section IV [*Of the modern philosophy*] of the *Treatise*, and here and there in the *Dialogues concerning Natural Religion*, where he speaks of the "irregular inference." What is clear, in spite of the unclarity, is that it is a "proper functioning" account. In calling it this, I mean both to allude to the fact that it is an immediate predecessor of Reid's account, and to indicate that Alvin Plantinga's "proper functioning" theory of *warrant* is the most recent, and far and away the most sophisticated, manifestation of a line of thought adumbrated by Hume. See Plantinga, *Warrant and Proper Function* (Oxford, Oxford University Press, 1993).

[7] On the surface reading of this passage, Hume believed that natural objects possessed causal powers. A recent defense of the thesis that the surface reading is the correct reading is Galen Strawson, *The Secret Connexion: Causation, Realism, and David Hume* (Oxford, Clarendon Press, 1989). A vigorous defense of the "Old Hume" against this "New Hume" is Kenneth P. Winkler, "The New Hume," in the *Philosophical Review* 100, 4 (October 1991).

beliefs produced thereby are *unjustified*, it is to say, at a minimum, that on his view there is something intrinsically wrong or deficient about that practice and about those beliefs. But in the light of the passages cited, I think we must conclude that Hume did not believe that – unless, of course, one regards a belief's having a degree of "evidence" less than the highest as a deficiency in it.

What, then, *did* Hume wish to say about this practice and the beliefs it produces? Pretty clearly he had two closely connected main points in mind. He insisted that the practice of induction is not a manifestation of Reason but of that very different dynamic of belief-formation which Locke called *custom* and which he warned us so firmly against. And secondly, Hume contended that the Lockian practice gives us access to those facts to which induction gives us access only if we make use of a premise which is the product not of Reason or any other faculty of insight, but of habit or custom. In Hume's rhetoric one senses nostalgia for Locke's vision; he wishes it were true. But in fact Hume has broken with the Lockian vision in a fundamental way.[8]

Locke's principle of proportionality said that we ought to proportion the level of confidence we place in a proposition to its probability on our evidence concerning it, when that evidence attains the level of being satisfactory. The evidence is to consist of things that we intuitively or demonstratively "perceive" to be true; and it is Reason, says Locke, which informs us as to the probability of a proposition on a body of evidence.

Hume posed a simple but profound question to this Lockian vision: How are we to tell *when the evidence is satisfactory* – i.e., when it is a reliable indicator of the truth or falsehood of the proposition? Let us grant that it is Reason which tells us what degree of probability a proposition has on a given body of evidence. What tells us whether that evidence is satisfactory? Hume argued, decisively in my judgment, that within the Lockian vision no acceptable answer to this question is

---

[8] Thus I hold that Hume is a skeptic concerning inductive inference, his particular form of skepticism consisting in his affirmation of the two theses concerning the limits of Reason formulated in the text above. A similar interpretation of Hume as skeptic is developed in a (thus far) unpublished paper by Kenneth P. Winkler, "Hume's Skepticism." There has been a great flowering of discussions of Hume's skepticism in recent years. To cite only a few: Annette Baier, *A Progress of Sentiments* (Cambridge, Harvard University Press, 1991); T. Beauchamp and A. Rosenberg, *Hume and the Problem of Causation* (New York, Oxford University Press, 1981); Robert J. Fogelin, "The Tendency of Hume's Skepticism," in his *Philosophical Interpretations* (New York, Oxford University Press, 1992); and Barry Stroud, *Hume* (London, Routledge & Kegan Paul, 1977).

available. In particular, Reason is not capable of telling us when beliefs concerning present and remembered experience constitute satisfactory evidence for some proposition concerning (contingent) facts which we have not experienced and are not experiencing.

Reason, Hume assumes, is our faculty for apprehending necessary relations among propositions (and apparently for apprehending necessary truths in general). Locke held essentially the same view. Of course, Locke also held that Reason is our faculty for apprehending the probability of a proposition on a body of evidence; but he regarded that relationship as a species of necessary relation. Hume expresses no disagreement. So suppose I hear a certain noise and infer that a motor vehicle is going by on the street in front of my house. Can I arrive at that conclusion, from that experience, by Reason?

Certainly there is no *necessary* relation between that noise and a motor vehicle's going by, says Hume. It is not a necessary property of this noise that it is made by a motor vehicle going by, or that it is an accompaniment of that. The noise could have been made by something else; indeed, it is logically/ontologically possible that it was not caused by anything at all. In short, there is here no "relation of ideas" susceptible of being intuited or demonstrated.

> 'Tis easy to observe, that in tracing this relation, the inference we draw from cause to effect, is not derived merely from a survey of these particular objects, and from such a penetration into their essences as may discover the dependence of the one upon the other. There is no object, which implies the existence of any other if we consider these objects in themselves, and never look beyond the ideas which we form of them. Such an inference would amount to knowledge, and would imply the absolute contradiction and impossibility of conceiving any thing different. (*T* 86–7)

What, then, accounts for my inference, if I do not, by Reason, penetrate into the essence of this noise so as to be able to discern that it *must* have been made (or at least accompanied) by a motor vehicle going by? Well, remember what we have already seen about the workings of our practice of induction: It is because I have often experienced a noise of this *sort* being made by a motor vehicle going by that I now infer, upon hearing this particular noise, that a motor vehicle is going by. Perhaps, then, these present and remembered facts function for me as *evidence*; and perhaps my Reason tells me that this evidence logically supports the conclusion that probably a motor vehicle is going by. Perhaps, in turn, it is my Reason telling me this that produces in me the belief that a motor vehicle is going by.

What, on this construal, would the argument look like? Something like this:

1. I have noted in the past an invariant correlation between noises of a certain sort and a motor vehicle going by;
2. The noise I am presently hearing is of that sort;
C. Hence it is highly probable that a motor vehicle is going by.

But the argument as it stands is obviously not deductively valid, says Hume; the premises do not entail the conclusion. Since the correlations I happen to have noticed may not be representative of reality in general, there is nothing impossible about the premises being true and the conclusion false. Reason, which, to say it once again, is our faculty for apprehending necessary truths, does not enable us to conclude, just from these premises, that the conclusion is true.

As to past *experience*, it can be allowed to give *direct* and *certain* information of those precise objects only, and that precise period of time, which fell under its cognizance: but why this experience should be extended to future times, and to other objects, which, for aught we know, may be only in appearance similar; this is the main question on which I would insist. The bread, which I formerly eat, nourished me; that is, a body of such sensible qualities was, at that time, endued with such secret powers: but does it follow, that other bread must also nourish me at another time, and that like sensible qualities must always be attended with like secret powers? The consequence seems nowise necessary. At least, it must be acknowledged that there is here a consequence drawn by the mind; that there is a certain step taken; a process of thought, and an inference, which wants to be explained ... When a man says, *I have found, in all past instances, such sensible qualities conjoined with such secret powers*: And when he says, *Similar sensible qualities will always be conjoined with similar secret powers*, he is not guilty of a tautology, nor are these propositions in any respect the same. You say that the one proposition is an inference from the other. But you must confess that the inference is not intuitive; neither is it demonstrative: Of what nature is it then? (*E* 33–7)

It is not difficult to see what sort of premise must be added to the argument as it stands to make it deductively valid. If we add a premise to the effect that my sample was and is representative, and thus, reliable – *was* representative of frequencies in reality up to this time, and, assuming the uniformity of the past with the present on these matters, *remains* representative – then we have a valid argument. Hume, focusing on the latter of these two points, puts it like this: "If reason determined us, it would proceed upon that principle, *that instances, of which we have had no experience, must resemble those, of which we have had experience, and that the course of nature continues always uniformly the same* (*T* 89). The entire argument would then look like this:

1*. I have noted in the past an invariant correlation between noises of a certain sort and a motor vehicle going by.
2*. My sample of the correlation of events of these sorts was and is representative.
3*. The noise I am presently hearing is of that sort.
C*. Hence, it is highly probable that a motor vehicle is going by.

Our project, to repeat, is to discover whether I am or can be "determined by reason to make the transition" (*T* 88) from hearing this noise to the conclusion that it is very probable that a motor vehicle is going by. Reason now tells me that the argument proposed is valid. And I know premise (1*) by way of memory of past experience, and premise (3*) by way of awareness of present experience (plus comparison with remembered experience). So the question focuses on the epistemological status of (2*).

Certainly this is not a necessary truth, knowable by intuition or demonstration. Hume does not focus on the fact that it is not necessary that my sample *have been* representative. He focuses instead on the fact that there is no necessity about present and future nature being uniform with nature of the past – which implies, of course, no necessity about such nature being uniform with *already observed* nature. "We can at least conceive a change in the course of nature; which sufficiently proves, that such a change is not absolutely impossible" (*T* 89).

> May I not clearly and distinctly conceive that a body, falling from the clouds, and which, in all other respects, resembles snow, has yet the taste of salt or feeling of fire? Is there any more intelligible proposition than to affirm, that all the trees will flourish in December and January, and decay in May and June? Now whatever is intelligible, and can be distinctly conceived, implies no contradiction, and can never be proved false by any demonstrative argument or abstract reasoning *a priori*. (*E* 35)

But obviously premise (2*) is also not a simple report of present or remembered experience. Perhaps, then, it is itself a contingent truth inferred from remembered or past experience. But if so, then the very questions we have posed concerning (1) now arise concerning (2*). Says Hume: "According to this account of things . . . probability is founded on the presumption of a resemblance betwixt those objects, of which we have had experience, and those, of which we have had none; and therefore 'tis impossible this presumption can arise from probability. The same principle cannot be both the cause and effect of another" (*T* 90).[9]

Hume's conclusion is that our actual practice of induction is not an exercise of Reason, nor can the beliefs which the practice produces in us be arrived at by arguments which Reason tells us are valid and whose premises are the deliverances of Reason, memory, and awareness. Always we shall have to add a premise which is the product not of Reason, memory, or awareness but of sheer habit, mere custom. "Reason can never show us the connexion of one object with another, though aided by experience, and the observation of their constant conjunction in all past instances" (*T* 92). "When we pass from the impression of one [object] to the idea or belief of another, we are not determined by reason, but by custom or a principle of association" (*T* 97).[10]

Many readers of Hume find something deeply counter-intuitive in his argument. As we accumulate more and more experience of nature and nature continues to prove uniform in its observed workings, does not *Reason* tell us that we are more and more entitled to believe that nature *throughout* is uniform with respect to such workings, present

---

[9] Cf. 37–8: "For all inferences from experience suppose, as their foundation, that the future will resemble the past, and that similar powers will be conjoined with similar sensible qualities. If there be any suspicion that the course of nature may change, and that the past may be no rule for the future, all experience becomes useless, and can give rise to no inference or conclusion. It is impossible, therefore, that any arguments from experience can prove this resemblance of the past to the future; since all these arguments are founded on the supposition of that resemblance."

[10] By saying that the belief arises "without any new reasoning or conclusion," Hume means that it "arises immediately." "Of this I can be certain," he says, "because I never am conscious of any such operation, and find nothing in the subject, on which it can be founded" (T 102). The claim that *custom* is a mode of belief-formation which operates immediately is then used by Hume as an argument for his claim that as a matter of fact, the practice of induction is not an exercise of Reason: "The custom operates before we have time for reflexion. The objects seem so inseparable, that we interpose not a moment's delay in passing from the one to the other. But as this transition proceeds from experience, and not from any primate connexion betwixt the ideas, we must necessarily acknowledge, that experience may produce a belief and a judgment of causes and effects by a secret operation, and without being once thought of. This removes all pretext, if there yet remains any, for asserting that the mind is convinced by reasoning of that principle, *that instances of which we have no experience, must necessarily resemble those, of which we have.* For we here find, that the understanding or imagination can draw inferences from past experience, without reflecting on it; much more without forming any principle concerning it, or reasoning upon that principle" (*T* 104). He does not wish to deny, however, says Hume, that "in other associations of objects, which are more rare and unusual, [the mind] may assist the custom and transition of ideas by this reflexion. Nay we find in some cases, that the reflexion produces the belief without the custom; or more properly speaking, that the reflexion produces the custom in an *oblique* and *artificial* manner."

and future nature uniform with past, and distant nature uniform with local?

What might Hume say, in addition to what he has already said, to get us to share his intuition on this matter? Perhaps something like this: We can, of course, discover that a larger later sample of correlations, call it *Beta*, exhibits the same invariance (or relative frequency) that our earlier smaller sample, call it *Alpha*, exhibited. Accordingly, if I later make an inference to non-sampled events, I do not have to be content with adding the premise that relative frequencies in sample *Alpha* are representative of relative frequencies in reality. I can instead add the premise that frequencies in sample *Beta* – a later and larger sample – are representative of frequencies in reality. But how do I know that *that* is true? The fact that frequencies in *Alpha* proved representative of frequencies in *Beta* – how does that prove that frequencies in *Beta* are representative of frequencies in reality in general? Of course, I can collect a yet larger sample, *Gamma*. I may discover that frequencies in *Beta* were representative of frequencies in *Gamma*. But suppose I infer to some event not included in *Gamma*. Then I shall have to assume that frequencies in *Gamma* are representative of frequencies in reality. By the very nature of the case, when I infer to the existence of some event beyond my sample, but on the basis of my sample, I must suppose that relative frequencies in the sample were and are representative of relative frequencies in reality without having confirmed that they are. We can confirm that one sample is representative of another sample. What we cannot do is confirm that our sample is representative of reality – without having sampled all the reality on the matter, in which case we no longer make an inductive inference *beyond* our sample but just report remembered and present experience. Unless, of course, it was the case, and we somehow knew it was the case, that there are insufficient unsampled cases to render our sample unrepresentative under even the worst scenario.

But perhaps this way of looking at the matter is still too quick to be persuasive. So let us arrive at Hume's point by looking a bit more deeply into probability and Locke's use thereof. And since Hume casts the argument in terms of relative frequencies and the determination of objective statistical probabilities, let us do so as well. Begin by distinguishing a number of closely related sorts of propositions concerning relative frequencies and probabilities. Suppose the candidate-preference of someone, call him Paul, in the 1992 US presidential election had been a matter of such concernment to me that I was required to try to do my best to get at the fact of the matter, which in this case is the (statistical) probability of the matter. And suppose that the only relevant thing I knew about Paul was that he was a registered Michigan voter. On Locke's view, the first step in doing my best in this case consists of forming a sample which constitutes satisfactory evidence as to Paul's preference. So suppose I take a sample of registered Michigan voters, a sample which is reliable in its amplitude and representativeness as to candidate-preference in this population; and suppose that, in this sample, 55 percent prefer Clinton and 45 percent prefer Bush. Consider then the following propositions:

1. The relative frequency, in this sample of registered Michigan voters, of those who prefer Clinton is ·55.
2. The probability on the evidence specified in (1), that in randomly selecting a member of the sample one will select one who prefers Clinton, is ·55.
3. The probability on the evidence specified in (1), that in randomly selecting a member of the wider population of registered Michigan voters one will select one who prefers Clinton, is ·55.
4. Each member of the sample is such that the probability on the evidence specified in (1), that that member prefers Clinton, is ·55.
5. Each member of the wider population of registered Michigan voters is such that the probability on the evidence specified in (1), that that member prefers Clinton, is ·55.
6. The objective statistical probability that, in randomly selecting a member of the sample, one will select one who prefers Clinton, is ·55.
7. The relative frequency in the wider population of those who prefer Clinton is ·55.
8. The objective statistical probability, that in randomly selecting a member of the wider population one will select one who prefers Clinton, is ·55.
9. Each member of the wider population is such that the objective statistical probability that that member prefers Clinton is ·55.
10. The objective statistical probability that Paul prefers Clinton is ·55 (Paul being a member of that wider population of registered Michigan voters).
11. Paul prefers Clinton.

We can agree that (1) entails (2) through (5). Indeed, even if this sample were not sufficient in amplitude and representativeness, as I have specified that it is, (1) would still entail (2) through (5). If a sample of registered Michigan voters yielded the relative frequency specified in (1), then the chance on that evidence of selecting someone who prefers Clinton, in randomly picking someone either from the sample or from the wider population, would be ·55. But the evidence might be very skimpy or skewed; and if one knew or believed it was, one would be well advised not to do much with (3) and (5).

Starting with (6) we move beyond claims as to what is probable *on this evidence* to claims concerning objective statistical probability. In (6), however, we have not yet moved outside the circle of evidence, with the consequence that (6) is also entailed by (1). Indeed, even if the sample were not reliable in its amplitude and representativeness, (6) would still be true for a sample which displayed the relative frequencies cited in (1).

But when with (7) we do move outside the circle of evidence, things are different. If the sample is representative – that is to say, if the relative frequencies in the sample match those in the population – then, but only then, will (7) and (8) also be true. Correspondingly – to move from logic to epistemology – only if one is entitled to believe that one's sample is representative is one entitled to believe (7) or (8) on the basis of one's sample. I have argued that Locke saw this point; hence his insistence that, before anything else, one make sure that one's evidence is satisfactory.

When we come to (9) and (10), yet a different consideration enters the picture. Propositions (9) and (10) are also statements of objective statistical probability. But whereas (8) speaks of the chance of picking out a Clinton-preferrer in randomly selecting someone from the population of registered Michigan voters, (9) and (10) speak of the probability, for a given person, *of that person* preferring Clinton. Proposition (10) actually picks out such a person, namely Paul, the person of concern in all this. Proposition (9) does not do that; instead it generalizes. It says that for any person you pick out from among registered Michigan voters, be it Paul or whoever, the probability *that that person* prefers Clinton is ·55.

But suppose that Paul – or anyone else from among the registered Michigan voters – is a worker for the Bush campaign in Lansing. The proportion of Clinton-preferrers among workers for the Bush campaign in Lansing was surely very low – say, 10 percent. On the other hand, Paul may have been one of those workers for the Bush campaign who became disillusioned with Bush – we are to suppose that the poll we are imagining took place just before the election. The relative frequency of Clinton-preferrers among registered Michigan voters who were workers for the Bush campaign in Lansing but became disillusioned would no doubt have been higher than 10 percent but still lower than 55 percent. The likelihood of Paul's preferring Clinton can be determined only by reference to the relative frequency of Clinton-preferrers in the intersection of all groupings to which Paul belongs which are *relevant to* his presidential preference.

Only if one's sample is satisfactory in relevance (with respect to Paul) as well as satisfactory in representativeness will it be the case that (10) is true if (1) is. And correspondingly, one would be entitled to believe (10) only if one knew or was entitled to believe that one's sample was thus satisfactory, plus knowing or believing with entitlement that the evidence was sufficiently ample. The sample which I have invited us to imagine is not good evidence for (9) and (10). To be entitled to believe either (9) or (10), one needs to know much more. I have assumed that Locke also saw this point. The point has destructive consequences for his position which he either overlooked or ignored, as I shall shortly point out. But his insistence that we must look for evidence *both pro and con* should, I think, be seen as an adumbration of the point.[11]

At other points, Locke was less perceptive. First, he not only insisted that one's level of confidence in a proposition be proportioned to its probability on satisfactory evidence; he insisted, so far as I can tell, that if the probability on such evidence is above ·5, then one should believe the proposition – or perhaps he just assumed that if one's level of confidence is above ·5, then one *will* believe. Either way, surely this is not correct. If the proposition that Paul prefers Clinton is just slightly more probable than not on some evidence, one would not automatically believe that proposition, nor do I see any reason to think that one should try to bring it about that one would believe it. There might be circumstances in which the best thing to do would be to bet on it; but that doesn't require believing it. One's level of confidence will and should be higher than that before one believes.

Secondly, Locke was mistaken as to the way in which inductive

---

[11] A useful discussion of many of the points rehearsed above is to be found on pp. 94–109 of L. Jonathan Cohen's book, *An Introduction to the Philosophy of Induction and Probability* (Oxford, Clarendon Press, 1989).

evidence entitles one to some level of confidence in a proposition. As Locke saw it, once one has collected evidence which is of a quality sufficient to bring it over the threshold level of reliability, one is then finished with considerations of quality. One then concerns oneself exclusively with the determination of relative frequencies in this satisfactory evidence. But surely this is not correct. Consider proposition (7), that the relative frequency in the wider population of those who prefer Clinton is ·55. On the evidence, this has a probability of 1·0; nothing could be more probable on that evidence. Locke instructs us then to believe this proposition with maximal firmness. But surely that would be a very stupid thing to do, because the evidence is not good enough for that. Another example to make the same point: Suppose that in some run of As which one samples, it turns out that all of them are Bs; the relative frequency of Bs among As is 1·0. In many cases it would be sheer folly to believe with maximal confidence that the probability that the next A will be a B is 1·0. Yet that is what Locke's rule instructs one to do. Only if it was somehow appropriate to have maximal confidence that the sample is representative would that level of confidence in that proposition be appropriate.

Or imagine two samples of registered Michigan voters, S and S*, both of which are above the threshold level of reliability, but with S* much more ample than S. If it is correct to think of us as having obligations to proportion levels of confidence, surely this difference is relevant to determining the entitled levels. Suppose, to be specific, that both S and S* show that 55 percent prefer Clinton, but that S is of 200 voters whereas S* is of 20,000. Surely the latter entitles me to believe both (7) and (8) with more confidence than the former – entitles me, that is, to believe with more confidence both that the relative frequency in the wider population of those who prefer Clinton is 55 percent, and that the probability is ·55 that in randomly selecting a member of the wider population, I shall select someone who prefers Clinton. So too, if my concern is Paul's preference and I have two samples, both of which meet the minimal reliability demands for representativeness and relevance-adequacy, but one of which is much more ample than the other, my confidence in the proposition that it is probable to such-and-such a degree that Paul prefers Clinton is rightly greater if my evidence is the more ample sample. In short, we are not finished with considerations of *quality* of evidence once we have determined that the quality is over the threshold of reliability. The rule that our level of confidence in a proposition is to be proportioned to its probability on satisfactory evidence gives radically mistaken advice.

So quality of evidence remains relevant. But reflection on the phenomenon of quality of evidence makes it clear that inductive inference is far from fitting into Locke's vision in the way he thought it did. Locke's aim was to ground our beliefs on insight. A proposition might have a high probability on fully reliable evidence and yet be false; thus the practice is not a guarantee of truth. Ideally, though, the possibility of error will be confined to that point. In our exposition of Locke we found him conceding that it cannot be confined to that point; our attempts to identify episodes of direct awareness are also fallible. But now it is clear that insight is lacking at crucial junctures in the process as well. It's not just that our attempts to identify episodes of insight are fallible; at crucial junctures we couldn't possibly have insight.

If one arrives at the point where one "sees" what are the relative frequencies in one's sample, then one is also in a position to "see" that (2) through (6) are true. But when one steps outside the circle of evidence, one goes beyond insight – unavoidably so. If one's sample is representative, then (7) and (8) will be true if (1) is. Furthermore, if one knows (or believes with entitlement) that (1) is true, *and also knows (or entitledly believes) that the sample is representative*, then one is also in a position to know (or believe with entitlement) (7) and (8). But if one doesn't know (or believe with entitlement) that one's sample is representative, one has no ground whatsoever for believing (7) or (8).

And now to come back to Hume: Hume's central point was that one can never "see" that one's sample is representative. Even if polling studies show that samples of this sort have always, in the cases studied, been representative, that falls short of enabling one to "see" that *this sample* is representative. The point about relevance is also relevant here. Sometimes some scientific (or homespun) theory assures one that in cases of the sort one is dealing with, no other factors are relevant than the ones of which one has already taken account. But often no such theory is available; and even when it is, we once again run into the problem of our inability to "see" that nature is uniform. The theory itself will simply have assumed that it is. That all the factors which are relevant *in this case* have been taken into account is something one can never just "see." But only if they have all been taken into account will it be the case that if (1) is true, (9) and (10) will be so also. And in the absence of knowing (or believing with entitlement) that they have been, one is not entitled to move, from one's knowledge (or entitled belief) of (1), to (9) and (10). We can put the point like this: Induction cannot be grounded in direct awareness. If we confined ourselves to direct awareness, we would never make inductive inferences. But, as Locke himself saw, we human beings cannot live without making such inferences. Our situation consigns us to going out beyond what direct awareness tells us has a probability of so-and-so on some body of evidence. If Reason be understood as a faculty of direct awareness, our situation consigns us to going out beyond the reach of Reason.

It was Thomas Reid's contribution to expand and systematize Hume's argument. No philosopher in Reid's day – nor in ours – has succeeded in showing that the existence of material objects is probable on evidence consisting exclusively of items of direct awareness which we can see to be satisfactory as evidence. The use of Locke's practice, if we require that we see that the evidence is satisfactory, will thus leave us with no beliefs about such objects. Yet we human beings have a very good mode of access to a great many such facts: we call it *perception*. So too, one's memory puts one in touch with a large body of facts which Locke's method, when insight into the satisfactoriness of the evidence is required, is incapable of reaching. It has even been argued in recent years – cogently, in my judgment – that we might well have faculties and practices which give us better access to certain facts *about God* than does the Lockian practice.[12] The basic point is the same in all these cases: We human beings are endowed with a variety of processes for immediate belief-formation which give us more reliable access to facts of various sorts than does the Lockian evidentialist practice with its base consisting exclusively of beliefs evoked by episodes of direct awareness. And as to *mediate* beliefs, recent discussions in philosophy of science suggest that there are bodies of facts to which modes of *mediate* belief-formation other than that which Locke proposes are our best modes of access.

I think one can see why Locke thought it self-evidently true that the best way to get in touch with those facts of which one cannot have direct awareness is to start with facts of which one does have direct awareness and then either construct deductive proofs or, where that proves impossible, follow the principles of evidence, appraisal, and

---

[12] See especially Alvin Plantinga, "Reason and Belief in God," in Plantinga and Wolterstorff (eds.), *Faith and Rationality* (Notre Dame, University of Notre Dame Press, 1983); and William P. Alston, *Perceiving God* (Ithaca, Cornell University Press, 1992).

proportionality. What could be a better way, more reliable and powerful, than this? Yet Locke was mistaken, and surprisingly so: For very many facts, we have better modes of access than this – better both in the sense of less often putting us out of touch with reality and in the sense of more often putting us in touch with reality.

But can we be *certain* of this, someone is sure to ask. If it is certainty we insist on, we are lost indeed. For we can be mistaken even in our attempt to pick out acts of direct awareness – even in our attempt to pick out cases of certainty!

CHAPTER 3

Locke's originality

John Locke, after distinguishing sharply between knowledge, on the one hand, and belief (opinion, assent) on the other, proceeded to offer a general ethic for the governance of our belief. "Reason must be our last judge and guide in everything," he said (IV,xix,14). Or more illuminatingly: Assent, "if it be regulated, as is our duty, cannot be afforded to anything, but upon good reason . . . For he governs his assent right, and places it as he should, who in any case or matter whatsoever, believes or disbelieves, according as reason directs him" (IV,xvii,24). We have seen that it is to all and only matters of maximal "concernment" that these ringing affirmations were meant to apply.

That there is a general ethic of belief, and that in this ethic Reason has a central role – once these convictions had been clearly formulated and persuasively propounded by Locke, they became prominent in the mentality of modernity. In that mentality, Locke's view as to the content of that ethic, and the proper role of Reason therein, became classic: For any proposition of maximal "concernment" which is not intuitively or demonstratively known to be true, Reason is to determine the probability of the proposition on satisfactory evidence, and we are to place a level of confidence in the proposition proportioned to what Reason tells us is that probability.

My thesis that Locke was the first great philosopher to propound this vision will strike many readers as perversely implausible. Is it not just a variant on Descartes's vision? Was not Descartes's Method the direct ancestor of Locke's proposed practice? Was not Descartes's *Rules for the Direction of the Mind* the direct ancestor of Locke's *Conduct of the Understanding*? I propose now to consider this issue of priority; and then, in the light of our analysis of Descartes's contribution, pinpoint more precisely than I have thus far the character of Locke's originality.

To prevent misunderstandings let me say emphatically here at the beginning, before we set out, that of course there are important similarities between Descartes's Method and Locke's proposed practice. But neither Descartes's Method nor Locke's practice was a free-standing entity; the Method was part of a project, the practice, part of a proposal. And my contention will be that when we take Descartes's *project* of "contemplation of the truth," along with the rules he proposed for that, and compare those, in the one direction, with the medieval *project* of *scientia*, and in the other direction, with Locke's *proposal* for a reformation in our way of conducting our understandings, it then becomes clear that Descartes's project is much more the continuation of the medieval project of *scientia* than the anticipation of Locke's proposal for governing the understanding. It should at once be added, however, that when we consider the *propaedeutic* Descartes recommends for those who wish to engage in that traditional project of *scientia*, and the *results* at which he himself arrived when pursuing the project, we catch sight of distinctly modern features. As to the results, Locke was speaking not only for himself but for others as well when he remarked, about Descartes, that "I must always acknowledge to that justly-admired gentleman the great obligation of my first deliverance from the unintelligible way of talking of the philosophy in use in the schools in his time" (First Letter to the Bishop of Worcester; *Works* III,48). Descartes is a bridge between an old world dying and a new world aborning.

The central point is this: Descartes never offered any general proposals for the governance of belief (opinion). Descartes was, of course, fully as aware as Locke of the cultural crisis at the founding of modernity – namely the anxiety of having to govern our belief in general, and settle our moral and religious quandaries in particular, when our once-unified tradition has fragmented into partisan quarrels. But the solution he proposed to that crisis – in so far as he did propose a solution – was that *scientia* be practiced on better grounds, with better preparation, and more expansively, than was currently being done. Edmund Husserl, who also supposed that a cultural crisis of roughly that sort could be met by the more resolute pursuit of *scientia*, is our preeminent contemporary Cartesian. Descartes did indeed have a "provisional moral code" for guiding his life so that he could work productively in the "contemplation of the truth." But he never proposed this code for everybody; and he never suggested that the code was based on "the deliverances of Reason." His true hope was that eventually a science of ethics could be developed. The first maxim of the code was "to obey the laws and customs of my country, holding constantly to the religion in which by God's grace I had been instructed from my childhood, and governing myself in all other matters according to the most moderate and least extreme opinions – the opinions commonly accepted in practice by the most sensible of those with whom I should have to live."[1] This maxim would not have appealed to Locke!

Far more prominent in Descartes's thought and writing than any such maxims was *the Method*, as he called it. But the Method was not for the governance of opinion but for the construction of *scientia*. Descartes took over intact the traditional medieval tripartite scheme of knowledge, faith, and opinion, offering no substantial innovation in how these are to be understood. His attention fell almost entirely on that species of knowledge which is *scientia*. His project was to work at that.

Locke, by contrast, discarded the tripartite scheme by treating faith as a species of belief (opinion). Then, convinced that *scientia* could never come to much, he paid it little attention. He offered no method for its construction. Instead he recommended the systematic pursuit by men of leisure of the new project which he called "natural philosophy." But natural philosophy, in his view, yields belief, not knowledge. It is not a form of *scientia*.

Descartes entitled his *Discourse*, "Discourse on the method of rightly conducting his reason and searching the truth in the sciences (*scientiae*)." Along the same line, Rule Three of his earlier but unpublished *Rules for the Direction of the Mind* reads as follows: "Concerning objects proposed for study, we ought to investigate what we can clearly and evidently intuit or deduce with certainty, and not what other people have thought or what we ourselves conjecture. For knowledge (*scientia*) can be attained in no other way" (CSM I,13). Again, the *Meditations* open with the words, "Some years ago I was struck by the large number of falsehoods that I had accepted as true in my childhood, and by the highly doubtful nature of the whole edifice that I had subsequently based on them. I realized that it was necessary, once in the course of my life, to demolish everything completely and start again right from the foundations if I wanted to

[1] J. Cottingham, R. Stoothoff, and D. Murdoch (tr.), *The Philosophical Writings of Descartes* (3 vols., Cambridge, Cambridge University Press, 1985 [vols. I and II], 1991 [vol. III]), vol. I, p. 122. All my citations from Descartes will be from these translations; the references will henceforth be incorporated into the text.

establish anything at all in the sciences (*scientiae*) that was stable and likely to last" (CSM II,12). And in his late unpublished dialogue, *The Search for the Truth*, Descartes has his spokesman in the dialogue, Eudoxus, say at one point: "I confess that it would be dangerous for someone who does not know a ford to venture across it without a guide, and many have lost their lives in doing so. But you have nothing to fear if you follow me. Indeed, just such fears have prevented most men of letters from acquiring a body of knowledge which was firm and certain enough to deserve the name 'science' (*scientia*)" (CSM II,408). I suggest that Descartes, throughout his career, had his eye on the construction of *scientia*. His Method was a method for the construction of that and that alone.

With a qualification to be mentioned later, Descartes took *scientia* to be what the high medievals (and Aristotle) took it to be – and what Locke still took it to be. The fundamental criterion is certitude: What is truly *scientia* will have certitude. "No act of awareness (*cognitio*) that can be rendered doubtful seems fit to be called knowledge (*scientia*)" says Descartes in his reply to the second set of objections to the *Meditations* (CSM II,103). In his discussion of Rule Two in *Rules for the Direction of the Mind* he says that "all knowledge (*scientia*) is certain and evident cognition" (CSM I,10). And in his discussion of Rule Three he speaks of what is desired as "so evident and certain as to be beyond dispute," "a knowledge of things with no means of being mistaken" (CSM I,14). Throughout his career, Descartes felt tension between the ideal of *scientia*, on the one hand, and the actual science which he developed, on the other; sometimes he argued that the actual science really did fit the ideal, and sometimes he conceded that it did not and proposed an adaptation of the ideal. But he never surrendered the ideal; Descartes, on this issue, was a conservative.[2]

Descartes appears, throughout his career, to have thought of *the (metaphysically) certain* as having two marks. It is incorrigible: "no means of being mistaken." And it is indubitable. A mode of apprehending a proposition is indubitable just in case a person, when apprehending the proposition in that mode, could never have a good enough reason for doubting it – that is, could never believe another proposition in such a way that one then had a good reason for

---

[2] For a detailed discussion which serves to confirm this judgment, see Daniel Garber, *Descartes' Metaphysical Physics* (Chicago, University of Chicago Press, 1992). The central thrust of Garber's conclusions is expressed in this sentence from his Afterword: "Though he tried as hard as he could to break with his teachers, the very conception of Descartes' project shows the extent to which he could not" (p. 305).

refraining from believing the original proposition.[3] (Shortly I shall call this *rational* indubitability, to distinguish it from psychological indubitability.) *Scientia* is to be built up from apprehensions which are incorrigible and indubitable.

As to "the actions of the intellect by means of which we are able to arrive at a knowledge of things with no fear of being mistaken: We recognize only two: intuition and deduction" (CSM 1,14). This is Descartes's claim in his early *Rules*. I see no evidence that he ever changed his mind on this; the only change is that in his later writings he speaks of "the natural light" rather than of intuition. Both intuition and deduction are thought of as apprehension, apprehension of propositions. The word *intueri* itself suggests apprehension.

What is it that characterizes those modes of apprehension of propositions in which intuition and deduction are at work – thus, those modes fit to lay at the foundation of *scientia*? Indubitability and incorrigibility, of course. But is there anything phenomenological or quasi-phenomenological about the state? Yes, indeed. When we apprehend a proposition *clearly* and *distinctly*, then intuition is at work.[4] Intuition, says Descartes, is "the conception of a clear and

---

[3] Cf. Harry G. Frankfurt, *Demons, Dreamers, and Madmen* (New York, Bobbs-Merrill, 1970), p. 27; and, especially, Edwin Curley, "Certainty: Psychological, Moral, and Metaphysical" in Stephen Voss (ed.), *Essays on the Philosophy and Science of René Descartes* (New York and Oxford, Oxford University Press, 1993). The point on which my account of Descartes's concept of metaphysical certainty differs most decisively from Curley's is that Curley's is entirely "internal," including no such objective phenomenon as incorrigibility. It seems to me that the evidence is in favor of Descartes's having wanted to include that; and my conclusion, that that is part of the concept, will be crucial to my subsequent argument. For the rest, the main issue between me and Curley in the accounts we offer is whether *good enough reason for* is ultimately reducible to *psychologically compelling reason for*. Is the appearance of normativity in the phrase "good reason" no more than an appearance? Curley's own view is that the supposition that it is no more than that is "a kind of naturalistic fallacy"; yet he concludes that that is how Descartes was thinking. I'm quite sure that Descartes did believe that what constitutes *good reasons* for us does depend, at bottom, on what the belief-forming faculties that God gave us compel us to believe. But my guess is that he would want to add to this something about *properly functioning* capacities, or about the capacities of a *properly formed* adult. That would be where the normativity comes in. Accordingly, I shall stick with the phrase "good reason" and not follow Curley in using only the notion of assent-compulsion in explicating Descartes's concept of metaphysical certainty.

[4] Harry Frankfurt's book, *Demons, Dreamers, and Madmen*, remains in my judgment much the best book on Descartes. From amidst the vast literature on Descartes, I shall pay it the particular honor of expressing agreement and disagreement. On pp. 123ff. of his book, Frankfurt suggests that Descartes in speaking of clear and distinct perception was not trying to pick out a certain phenomenology; rather, the concept of clear and distinct perception, says Frankfurt, just *is* the concept of entertaining a proposition in a way such that it is indubitable for one. Though this suggestion has some attractive features, it seems to me that certain texts are decisively against it. For example, when Descartes explains what he has in mind by clear and distinct perception in *Principles* 1:43–6, he uses very phenomenological language. Here is

attentive mind, which is so easy and distinct that there can be no room for doubt about what we are understanding. Alternatively, and this comes to the same thing, intuition is the indubitable conception of a clear and attentive mind which proceeds solely from the light of reason" (CSM 1,14). As examples of propositions which can be intuited, Descartes says that "everyone can mentally intuit that he exists, that he is thinking, that a triangle is bounded by just three lines, and a sphere by a single surface, and the like." And for those who grant that there are such perceptions but doubt that a *scientia* built up from them will come to very much, Descartes adds: "Perceptions such as these are more numerous than most people realize, disdaining as they do to turn their minds to such simple matters" (CSM 1,14).

Descartes's explanation of deduction in the *Rules* is parasitic on that of intuition:

The self-evidence and certainty of intuition is required not only for apprehending single propositions, but also for any train of reasoning whatever. Take for example the inference that 2 plus 2 equals 3 plus 1; not only must we intuitively perceive that 2 plus 2 make 4, and that 3 plus 1 make 4, but also that the original proposition follows necessarily from the other two. There may be some doubt here about our reason for suggesting another mode of knowing in addition to intuition, *viz.*, deduction, by which we mean the inference of something as following necessarily from some other propositions which are known with certainty. But this distinction had to be made, since very many facts which are not self-evident are known with certainty, provided they are inferred from true and known principles through a continuous and uninterrupted movement of thought in which each individual proposition is clearly intuited . . . Hence we are distinguishing mental intuition from certain deduction on the grounds that we are aware of a movement or a sort of sequence in the latter but not in the former, and also because immediate self-evidence is not required for deduction, as it is for intuition; deduction in a sense gets its certainty from memory. It follows that those propositions which are immediately inferred from first principles can be said to be known in one respect through intuition, and in another through deduction. But the first principles themselves are known only through intuition, and the remote conclusions only through deduction. (CSM 1,14–15)

What Descartes called the Method, from the time of the *Discourse* onwards, consists then of rules for constructing *scientia*, that is to say,

one example: "I call a perception 'clear' when it is present and accessible to the attentive mind" (CSM 1, 207). Further, it seems to me that regarding the concepts as identical renders unintelligible the "so . . . that" of Rule One in the *Discourse*: "to include nothing more in my judgment than what presented itself to my mind so clearly and so distinctly that I had no occasion to doubt it" (CSM 1,120).

rules for arriving at a body of propositions each of which has been intuited, or deduced from what has been intuited. A typical medieval would probably have found the second rule, the rule of *analysis*, a bit strange; but then, it's a good question how much attention Descartes himself paid to Rules Two through Four.[5] Rule One, on the other hand, follows from the very concept of *scientia*: "never to accept anything as true if I did not have evident knowledge of its truth: that is, carefully to avoid precipitate conclusions and preconceptions, and to include nothing more in my judgements than what presented itself to my mind so clearly and so distinctly that I had no occasion to doubt it" (CSM I,120).[6]

The faculty of intuition is at work in the clear and distinct apprehension of propositions – so we have found Descartes insisting. But are there not degrees of this, someone might ask – degrees of clarity and distinctness of apprehension? Perhaps so, says Descartes. But then we can add this: A law pertaining to the working of the human mind is that when our attention to a proposition attains a certain high degree of clarity and distinctness, then it is simply impossible to refrain from believing it. Over and over Descartes affirms this law: "my nature is such that so long as I perceive something very clearly and distinctly I cannot but believe it to be true" (CSM II,48). "All of us have been so moulded by nature that whenever we perceive something clearly, we spontaneously give our assent to it and are quite unable to doubt its truth" (CSM I,207).[7]

---

[5] See Garber, *Descartes' Metaphysical Physics*, chap. 2.

[6] The high medievals would have said that *scientia* proper consists only of propositions deduced from propositions intuited, and does not include those intuited. Though in one place Descartes acknowledges this usage (Second Set of Replies; CSM II,100), he himself does not, with any consistency, follow it. So I have chosen to speak as if Descartes would also include, within *scientia*, propositions intuited.

In his views (or assumptions) as to the sorts of propositions which are evident to one, Descartes differed from a high medieval like Aquinas. They agreed that necessarily true propositions which are self-evident *per se* may be evident to a person; but Aquinas' category of "propositions evident to the senses" would be vigorously disputed by Descartes. On the other hand, Descartes included among what is evident to a person various propositions concerning that person's states of consciousness; to the best of my knowledge, Aquinas never takes note of these – though if he had, he surely would have agreed with Descartes that they too are evident to the person.

[7] One of the most interesting affirmations of the Law of Assent occurs in Descartes's reply to the Second Set of Objections to the *Meditations* (CSM II,104): "some of these perceptions are so transparently clear and at the same time so simple that we cannot ever think of them without believing them to be true. The fact that I exist so long as I am thinking, or that what is done cannot be undone, are examples of truths in respect of which we manifestly possess this kind of certainty. For we cannot doubt them unless we think of them; but we cannot think of them without at the same time believing they are true, as was supposed. Hence we cannot doubt them without at the same time believing they are true; that is, we can never doubt them."

When this law – let us call it the *Law of Assent* – when this law of the mind comes into operation, then our faculty of intuition is at work.

There is, though, something profoundly implausible about the Law of Assent which, so far as I know, Descartes never notices – and which almost all his commentators overlook as well. Take any proposition which is self-evident to me. Descartes would describe the phenomenon of a proposition's being self-evident to me as my apprehending it so clearly and distinctly that I cannot refrain from believing it. Now let me consider the negation of that proposition. What reason could there possibly be for supposing that I don't also apprehend this proposition with full clarity and distinctness? I apprehend it so clearly and distinctly that I find myself compelled to disbelieve it.[8] Thus the law in the region, if there is one, is not the law that whenever we apprehend something with a certain high degree of clarity and distinctness, we are compelled to believe it, but rather that whenever we thus apprehend it, we are compelled to believe *or compelled to disbelieve* it. In all that follows, so far as I can tell, Descartes could have made the points he wants to make just as well if he had embraced this alternative law of assent. (That is not true for all of his thought.) Here, however, I shall not undertake to improve on Descartes; I shall expound his argument as he himself does, in terms of the Law of Assent.[9]

Repeatedly Descartes makes clear that in *scientia* there is no room for appeal to tradition or authority. In this, too, he is at one with the medievals; as he is in what he sees as the point, the benefit, of the pursuit of *scientia*: "human beings, whose most important part is the mind, should devote their main efforts to the search for wisdom, which is the true food of the mind" (Preface to the French edition of *The Principles*: CSM 1,180). Descartes's innovations begin when he reflects on the

[8] There comes to light here a deep difference between Locke and Descartes. Locke thinks in terms of "seeing" a proposition to be true; that consists, on his view, of "perceiving" that fact which makes the proposition true. Descartes does not think in terms of seeing a proposition to be true. Instead he thinks in terms just of "seeing" or "intuiting" propositions; and his claim is that, if one "intuits" a proposition with a certain high degree of clarity and distinctness, then one is compelled to believe it. From the very beginning, then, the question looms: Can I be assured that if I am compelled to believe some proposition, it is true? The notion of having direct awareness of certain of the facts of reality is simply not part of Descartes's thought. Thus I disagree with Aaron, *John Locke* (Oxford, Clarendon Press, 1971), who says that "Locke's intuitionism on the subjective side is identical with that of Descartes" (p. 221).

[9] The response I have often been offered to the point I make in the paragraph above, and typically offered by those commentators who notice the difficulty, is that Descartes is working with the notion of *clearly and distinctly apprehending that proposition P is true*, rather than *clearly and distinctly apprehending proposition P*. But if that were the case, the demon would be helpless in the face of our clear and distinct apprehensions.

potential extent of *scientia*; no medieval had such grand expectations concerning the potential scope of *scientia*: a great deal of natural science, philosophy, ethics, and beyond. And his innovations begin when he reflects how best to prepare ourselves for practicing *scientia*.[10]

Descartes was, of course, well acquainted with the scholastic conviction that the best preparation is to sift through the textual tradition dialectically. We must not, indeed, exaggerate the degree of consensus on this; already from the time of the *via moderna*, a good many scholastics denied that this is the best way to prepare oneself for engaging in, say, physics. Nonetheless, nobody proposed, for *scientia* in general, that the reading of texts be abolished as a preparatory discipline. However, Descartes's reflections had led him to the conviction that we do not approach the enterprise of distinguishing the certain from the uncertain – an enterprise which lies at the very foundation of the practice of *scientia* – with open minds. Quite to the contrary, we approach it with prejudgments, acquired from experience and social interchange, as to what we are certain of. These prejudgments are in good measure mistaken; and they inhibit our ability to distinguish reliably the certain from the uncertain. So how do we free ourselves from these mistaken *praejudicia*, so as to be able to construct a *scientia* of pure intuition and deduction – a body of certitude? It was Descartes's answer to this question that made the practice of *scientia* in his hands, in spite of all its continuities in concept and method with the medievals, nonetheless something new.

Already in the early *Rules* Descartes says that "We ought to read the writings of the ancients, for it is of great advantage to be able to make use of the labours of so many men . . . But at the same time there is a considerable danger that if we study these works too closely traces of their errors will infect us and cling to us against our will and despite our precautions" (CSM 1,13). In the late *Principles* he says that "Since we began life as infants, and made various judgments concerning the things that can be perceived by the senses before we had the full use of our reason, there are many preconceived opinions (*praejudicia*) that keep us from knowledge of the truth" (i,i; CSM 1,193). So as we prepare to engage in *scientia*, we need to be cured of the disease of mistaken preconceptions as to the locus of certitude. In his reply to Gassendi's objections to the *Meditations*, Descartes emphasized the difficulty of the cure:

---

[10] Also, I should add, in his recommendation that we follow the rule of analysis as we attempt to arrive at propositions on which intuition can go to work.

You say that you approve of my project for freeing my mind from preconceived opinions (*praejudicia*); and indeed no one can pretend that such a project should not be approved of. But you would have preferred me to have carried it out by making a "simple and brief statement" – that is, only in a perfunctory fashion. Is it really so easy to free ourselves from all the errors which we have soaked up since our infancy? Can we really be too careful in carrying out a project which everyone agrees should be performed? (CSM II,241–2)

The cure Descartes recommends is the Therapy of Doubt, to which I referred in the last section of Chapter 1. Here is one of his well-known recommendations of it:

In order to philosophize seriously and search out the truth about all the things that are capable of being known, we must first of all lay aside all our preconceived opinions, or at least we must take the greatest care not to put our trust in any of the opinions accepted by us in the past until we have first scrutinized them afresh and confirmed their truth. Next, we must give our attention in an orderly way to the notions that we have within us, and we must judge to be true all and only those whose truth we clearly and distinctly recognize when we attend to them in this way. (*Principles* 1,75; CSM 1,221)

The language Descartes uses in this passage suggests that the Therapy of Doubt is not the Method, but rather a therapeutic discipline to be undertaken before one can use the Method satisfactorily.[11] (Cf. CSM II,270, last paragraph; and CSM II,324.) In other passages Descartes speaks as if the Therapy and the Method were identical (see especially CSM II,407). I judge that a coherent interpretation requires that we treat them as distinct. The most decisive consideration is this: If we are apprehending, say, certain mathematical propositions clearly and distinctly, the Method tells us that we are allowed to accept them, whereas (as we shall see) the Therapy instructs us to doubt them.

The history of Descartes-interpretation makes it abundantly clear that Descartes invites being interpreted as holding that the goal of the Therapy is to free the mind from almost all assent – to vacuum it of almost all belief. If there were not that history, based on that ambiguity, I could at this point halt my discussion of Descartes and move on. That will not be possible. I shall have to argue that emptying the mind of almost all assent is not at all what Descartes

---

[11] Though I do not entirely agree with his understanding of the character and role of intellectual therapy in Descartes's thought, someone who has seen the importance of its role, especially in the *Meditations*, is Mike Marlies, "Doubt, Reason, and Cartesian Therapy," in Michael Hooker (ed.), *Descartes: Critical and Interpretive Essays* (Baltimore, Johns Hopkins Press, 1978), pp. 89–113.

thinks necessary for practicing *scientia* successfully; it is not an endeavor he ever recommended – if for no other reason than that he thought it had no chance whatsoever of succeeding. Indeed, I judge the traditional interpretation to be so entrenched that I shall have to go further yet and sketch the outlines, at least, of an alternative interpretation of what Descartes understood the goal of the Therapy to be.

There is a hermeneutical issue which is unavoidable at this point. It would be easy to cite passages in which Descartes speaks about doubt with words whose "plain sense" does not fit my interpretation of what he has in mind by doubt. It is from that "plain sense" that others have developed their different understandings of Cartesian doubt. So what leads me to violate that "plain sense"? Two considerations. I do not see how the "plain sense" interpretation can be fitted into an overall interpretation of Descartes which makes sense of his total project; and I propose that we prefer an interpretation which does make sense of his total project to one which does not. Secondly, and much more importantly, I think that we ought to follow Descartes's own guidelines as to the interpretation of such passages. In his letters, and especially in his replies to the objections to the *Meditations*, Descartes repeatedly calls attention to certain general indications he has planted in the text as to the nature of his project; he insists that these indications be treated as guidelines in interpreting his text. It turns out that following those guidelines often requires that we not go by the "plain sense of the text." Descartes regularly accuses his critics of ignoring the guidelines and – though he would not put it this way – of going instead by the "plain sense." I propose that we *do* follow Descartes's guidelines for the interpretation of his own texts; I think that it would be perverse not to do so, unless we have some indication that the stated guidelines are self-serving or deceptive. Of course the trouble arises from the fact that though Descartes wishes his texts to be *interpreted* in accordance with his guidelines, he himself seems to have *composed* a good deal of them without having those guidelines clearly in mind. If he had composed all of them with the guidelines clearly in mind, the "plain sense" interpretation would not so regularly be in tension with the interpretation which follows the guidelines, forcing us to decide which is to be preferred.

Descartes gives many descriptions of the Therapy of Doubt, the goal of which is to liberate us from our obstructive *praejudicia*. Here is one from the beginning of the *Principles*: "It seems that the only way of freeing ourselves from these opinions is to make the effort, once in the course of our life, to doubt everything which we find to contain even the smallest suspicion of uncertainty." Then, adding what already his original readers thought to be overkill, he says: "Indeed, it will even prove useful, once we have doubted these things, to consider them as false, so that our discovery of what is most certain and easy to know may be all the clearer" (CSM I,193). He goes on to say that, as the first step in the Therapy of Doubt, "our initial doubts will be about the existence of the objects of sense-perception and imagination. The first reason for such doubt is that from time to time we have caught out the senses when they were in error, and it is prudent never to place too much trust in those who have deceived us even once. The second reason is that in our sleep we regularly seem to have sensory perception of, or to imagine, countless things which do not exist anywhere; and if our doubts are on the scale just outlined, there seem to be no marks by means of which we can with certainty distinguish being asleep from being awake" (CSM I,193–4).

Yet, in the Synopsis to the *Meditations* Descartes says, about the arguments offered in the Sixth Meditation for "the existence of material things," that "the great benefit of these arguments is not, in my view, that they prove what they establish – namely that there really is a world, and that human beings have bodies and so on – since no sane person has ever seriously doubted these things" (CSM II,11). In his reply to Gassendi's objections to the *Meditations* he repeats the point: "Hence I point out in one passage that no sane person ever seriously doubts such things" (CSM II,243).

Here, then, is the question which every interpretation of Descartes must *face* rather than *avoid*: Descartes says that as the first step in the Therapy of Doubt, the therapy we must undertake so as to become able to apply the Method satisfactorily in the construction of *scientia*, we are to doubt the testimony of our senses that there is a material world. He makes clear that he views himself as having done this. Yet he also asserts emphatically that no sane person has ever seriously doubted these things; obviously he takes himself to be a sane person. What are we to make of this? I submit that unless we attribute the most appalling confusion to Descartes, we must interpret him as having two different things in mind by "doubt."

We can get at the same issue from a somewhat different angle. To engage in the Therapy of Doubt, let us remind ourselves, "is to make the effort, once in the course of our life, to doubt everything which we find to contain even the smallest suspicion of uncertainty." It consists of "rejecting everything in which I could discover the least occasion for doubt; for it is certain that principles which it was impossible to reject in this way, when one attentively considered them, are the clearest and most evident that the human mind can know" (CSM 1,183). But in his replies to the Second Set of Objections to the *Meditations*, Descartes says that "I should like you to remember here that, in matters which may be embraced by the will, I made a very careful distinction between the conduct of life and the contemplation of the truth. As far as the conduct of life is concerned, I am very far from thinking that we should assent only to what is clearly perceived. On the contrary, I do not think that we should always wait even for probable truths" (CSM II,106). But of course we cannot divide up propositions into two disjunct sets, those which in the conduct of life we decide whether or not to accept, and those which in the practice of *scientia* we decide whether or not to accept. The very propositions which for the conduct of life we must believe, for the contemplation of the truth, we must doubt. Neither is it the case that doubting and not doubting such propositions can be performed sequentially; since while a person is engaged in the contemplation of truth, he or she is also engaged in the conduct of life. While doubting that there is anything solid, as part of his or her contemplation of truth, a person must believe that he or she is seated on something solid. The conduct of life is not something one leaves behind as one contemplates the truth. The conduct of life *embraces* one's contemplation of the truth.

Perhaps if we try to recover what Descartes's experience would have been as he prepared to use the Method, we can discern what he has in mind. To get going, he must sort out the certain from the uncertain. So he asks himself: These beliefs of mine, based on perception and to the effect that there is this and that material object – do these beliefs have the requisite status of certitude? He has reason to think that they do not. Though up to this time he may have taken them as certain, that would have been a false *praejudicium*; reflection shows that they are not indubitable. But drawing this conclusion does not remove these beliefs from Descartes's mind. He still has them. It simply makes him doubt that these believings have the status requisite for *scientia*. It makes him doubt *that they are certain*. It removes whatever contrary *praejudicium* he may have had.[12]

---

[12] Frankfurt puts the point clearly, though I think that it does not have the determining role in his overall interpretation that it ought to have: "Descartes does not propose to make himself

I suggest that it is exactly this doubt which figures in the Therapy. Cartesian doubt is indeed suspension of assent. But to "doubt" P, as part of the Therapy of Doubt, is not to suspend one's belief that P but rather to suspend one's belief that one's mode of apprehending P is satisfactory for *scientia*. It is to suspend one's belief (if one had it) that P is certain for one. Cartesian doubt is second-order doubt: meta-doubt. It is not doubting those beliefs that play a role in *the conduct of life*, nor is it doubting those beliefs that play a role in the *practice of religion*. Neither is it suspending any second-order beliefs one might have about the satisfactoriness of those beliefs for the conduct of life or for the practice of religion. Nonetheless, it does involve *Cartesianly doubting* all the believings that occur in the conduct of life and in the practice of religion – doubting that they are satisfactory for *scientia*, doubting that they are the product of intuition and/or deduction. To say it again: "Doubting" a proposition, when engaging in the Therapy, is not withholding assent from *it* but withholding assent from the proposition that one's mode of entertaining it has the epistemic status needed for *scientia*: certainty, marked by indubitability and incorrigibility. Descartes never gives up his belief that there is an external world; neither, contrary to the great majority of his interpreters, does he think that he or anyone else *should* give it up. In fact he thinks that not having that belief is a mark of insanity. The "greatest benefit" of "such extensive doubt," says Descartes, "lies in freeing us from all our preconceived opinions (*praejudicia*), and providing the easiest route by which the mind may be led away from the senses" (Synopsis of the Meditations; CSM II,9).

This is not to say, of course, that Descartes thinks that the beliefs we presently have are all OK. Quite to the contrary; he thinks that they are riddled with error. But the task of dislodging those erroneous beliefs is not assigned to the Therapy of Doubt. The task of dislodging

into a *tabula rasa*, and the skepticism to which he commits himself is innocuously thin and undisruptive. Indeed it is inappropriate to describe it as skepticism at all. Consider the example of a mathematician who is, let us say, attempting to construct a system of arithmetic. If he has so far failed or neglected to establish that '2 + 2 = 4' is a theorem of his system, he will quite properly refuse to assume in his inquiry that the equation is true. This is hardly a case of skepticism, and it would be inane to argue, as it has been argued occasionally against Descartes, that the mathematician's refusal is insincere or that his project is absurd because it is psychologically impossible for him to cease believing that 2 + 2 = 4. The mathematician continues, of course, to 'believe' the equation, but he does not accord it a place in the system he is developing because it has not yet passed the tests for inclusion. Within the context of his theoretical work in arithmetic, then, he does not yet 'believe' that 2 + 2 = 4. When he undertook his work he 'overthrew' all such beliefs in the limited sense that he decided not to take their theoretical credentials for granted" (*Demons, Dreamers, and Madmen*, pp. 16–17).

our mistaken scientific beliefs falls to the construction of a new and better science; the task of dislodging our mistaken philosophical beliefs falls to the construction of a new and better philosophy; and so on. In the Sixth Meditation, Descartes gives detailed arguments against our present understanding of the nature of the external world and in favor of an alternative understanding.

But let us not live with the illusion that the Therapy is easy and pleasant, says Descartes. It is in fact "an arduous undertaking, and a kind of laziness brings me back to normal life. I am like a prisoner who is enjoying an imaginary freedom while asleep; as he begins to suspect that he is asleep, he dreads being woken up, and goes along with the pleasant illusion as long as he can. In the same way, I happily slide back into my old opinions and dread being shaken out of them, for fear that my peaceful sleep may be followed by hard labour when I wake, and that I shall have to toil not in the light, but amid the inextricable darkness of the problems I have now raised" (First Meditation; CSM II, 15). Descartes hints, in that last clause, that the Therapy is not only arduous but menacing in prospect. He opens his Second Meditation on this theme of menace: "So serious are the doubts into which I have been thrown as a result of yesterday's meditation that I can neither put them out of my mind nor see any way of resolving them. It feels as if I have fallen unexpectedly into a deep whirlpool which tumbles me around so that I can neither stand on the bottom nor swim up to the top" (Second Meditation; CSM II, 16).

Probably no one likes to have one's *praejudicia*, concerning what is and isn't certain for one, disturbed; the Therapy of Doubt will always be unpleasant. What makes it menacing, though, is the radically skeptical grounds for doubt that occurred to Descartes. We are to look around to see whether we can discover any grounds for doubting the certainty of one and another of our beliefs – or rather, of whole types of belief. Apparently around 1628, after he had composed a good deal of the *Rules* and before he had composed the *Discourse*, a truly radical and menacing ground for doubt occurred to Descartes – perhaps suggested by the currents of skepticism flowing in France at that time.[13] Might it be the case that we are so constituted or influenced

---

[13] I accept E. M. Curley's argumentation on this point, in the second chapter of his *Descartes against the Skeptics* (Cambridge, Mass., Harvard University Press, 1978).

It appears that what contributed to Descartes's new line of thought was not just the emergence of his conviction that it was possible for the phenomenology of self-evidence to be evoked by our "intuition" of falsehoods, but the emergence of his conviction that there are no limits on God's omnipotence: Whatever is false, God could have made true, and whatever is

that the experience of a proposition's being self-evident to us, as that was traditionally characterized, is in fact (sometimes) evoked by our "intuition" of falsehoods rather than of truths? With just one crucial change in the traditional characterization of that experience: The experience of self-evidence was often described as including *just seeing* that the proposition in question *is true*. That has to go, to be replaced by the phenomenology of *seeming to see* that it *is true*. For if one actually sees that it's true, then it is true.

I have suggested that in his understanding of *scientia* and its method, as well as in his insistence on the importance of practicing *scientia*, Descartes was perpetuating a long tradition. His innovations are located in the grand expectations he had for the scope of *scientia*, and in the proposals he made for how we are to prepare ourselves for engaging in *scientia*. What led to the latter innovations was Descartes's conviction that we bring with us, to the practice of *scientia*, inhibiting and false *praejudicia* concerning what is and isn't certain for us, due in part, as it turns out, to our failure to imagine the truly radical possibilities. Let it be seen clearly that Descartes's conviction is *not* that the propositional contents of those believings of ours which we, in advance of practicing *scientia*, believe to be certain, are *false*. Though he did think that a good deal of what is read in texts is false – the vision of a textual tradition whose deep content is an articulated unity was no longer alive in him – he regarded the beliefs that we bring with us from experience (and religion) as in great measure true. The false and debilitating *praejudicia* from which we must be liberated are second-order beliefs about the certainty of our believings.

Though Descartes was carrying on the medieval Aristotelian project of *scientia*, nobody in the medieval tradition had suggested anything like Descartes's Therapy of Doubt as the appropriate preparation for engaging in the project. Nonetheless, the points Descartes has raised are not ones that a person in that tradition could dismiss out of hand. Even if one believes (as Descartes did not) that the textual tradition presents an articulate unified body of truth, it must be conceded that in great measure it does not present that truth in the mode of knowledge but in the mode of opinion, and usually without any clear demarcation of the one from the other; accordingly, immersing oneself in those texts is indeed likely to inculcate in one

true, God could have made false. But though this conviction is usually in the wings when Descartes sets forth his radical ground for doubt, it is not really essential to it; the evil genius might be doing its devilish work even though God was not thus omnipotent.

mistaken convictions as to what one is certain of. And as to the status of "intuition": The possibility that the phenomenology of self-evidence be evoked by falsehoods is something that has to be considered.

Was Descartes of the view that his contemporaries were peculiarly prone to those false inhibiting *praejudicia*? Well, in Part I of the *Discourse* he certainly makes clear his conviction that *scientia in his day* was in a state of severe crisis; and the wanderings he describes in that same part, as well as his own subsequent controversies, immersed him in the religious turmoil of Europe. Nonetheless, the disease the Therapy is meant to cure is a *human* disease. Post-Reformation Europe and its academies may have had an unusually severe case of the disease. But the disease is present in anyone who has sensory experience and reads books; and it works its debilitating effects on anyone who sets about trying to practice *scientia*.

Let me summarize the central points I have been making: The Method does not tell us to dissent from everything which is not the result of intuition and deduction. We cannot do that, says Descartes, nor should we try. The Method is rather a method for the acquisition of apprehensions which are purely the product of intuition and deduction; it is a method for the building up of true *scientia*. But since mistaken prejudgments, as to which of one's apprehensions are certain for one, will get in the way of satisfactory practice of the Method, the Therapy of Doubt is to be undertaken so as to clear away those confusions.

The claim has often been made that it is not clear in the *Meditations* whether Descartes meant his therapeutic doubt to apply even to the clear and distinct apprehension of propositions.[14] Certainly to confused apprehensions. But what about our apprehensions of simple mathematical propositions which are so clear and distinct that we cannot refrain from believing the propositions, and such that we cannot be in a situation where, while thus apprehending those propositions, we yet have good reason for doubting them? Is there any reason for Cartesianly doubting that such apprehensions are good enough for

---

[14] But see Descartes's recollection of his doubts, as found in the Fifth Meditation: "I can convince myself that I have a natural disposition to go wrong from time to time in matters which I think I perceived as evidently as can be" (CSM II,48). This certainly fits with what Descartes says near the end of the First Meditation, as he is bringing the process of doubting to its conclusion : "I . . . am finally compelled to admit that there is not one of my former beliefs about which a doubt may not properly be raised; and this is not a flippant or ill-considered conclusion, but is based on powerful and well thought-out reasons" (CSM II,14–15).

scientia? And let it be noted that Cartesian doubt can only be accomplished *for reasons.*

If one were to have a good reason for Cartesianly doubting propositions thus apprehended, it would have to be a reason for refraining from believing that such apprehensions are *incorrigible*. For we are now past the point of dubitability. If one apprehends a proposition clearly and distinctly, then one's situation *couldn't be* that of having good reason to refrain from believing it. "Whatever is revealed to me by the natural light . . . cannot in any way be open to doubt. This is because there cannot be another faculty both as trustworthy as the natural light and also capable of showing me that such things are not true" (*Meditations* III; CSM II,27). "In the case of our clearest and most careful judgments . . . if such judgments were false they could not be corrected by any clearer judgments or by means of any other natural faculty" (Second Set of Replies; CSM II, 102–3). Of course, Descartes is assuming here that by the natural light we can never intuit or demonstrate both a proposition and its contradictory. If that could happen, then one could be in a situation where one both apprehended a proposition clearly and distinctly and had good reason to refrain from believing it (not, of course, to believe its contradictory). Still, this question arises: Might an apprehension which is rationally indubitable nonetheless be an apprehension of a proposition which is false?

The scenario of the evil genius is designed to show that this could be, so far as one can tell at this point. (Descartes offers other, less arresting, scenarios for the same possibility.) If it is logically possible that there be such an evil genius, then it is logically possible that the rationally indubitable be false. And as long as we don't find it *in*dubitable that such an evil genius is logically impossible, just so long is it also not rationally indubitable for us that the rationally indubitable is incorrigible. And so, of course, not rationally indubitable that the rationally indubitable is certain.

Just as we are to imagine the demon as altering nothing in the phenomena of rational dubitability/indubitability, so also we are to imagine him as altering nothing in the phenomena of psychological dubitability/indubitability. The Law of Assent continues to operate. Thus it is that Descartes exclaims in the Third Meditation: "when I turn to the things themselves which I think I perceive very clearly, I am so convinced by them that I spontaneously declare: let whoever can do so deceive me, he will never bring it about that I am nothing, so long as I continue to think I am something; or make it true at some future time that I have never existed, since it is not true that I exist; or bring it about that two and three added together are more or less than five, or anything of this kind in which I see a manifest contradiction" (CSM II,25).

Whether or not the *Meditations* are unclear as to how far Descartes wishes to press the question of incorrigibility, *Principles* I,5 is entirely clear on the matter: He wishes to press it for clear and distinct apprehensions which compel belief – thus for those apprehensions which are rationally and psychologically indubitable. He wishes to press it, in short, for *all* apprehensions and believings. The fact that my attention to a proposition is so clear and distinct that I cannot refrain from believing it and can have no good reason for doubting it while thus apprehending it is apparently compatible with the falsehood of the proposition thus apprehended. We can imagine a scenario according to which this is how things would be. Hence we should at this point in our reflections Cartesianly doubt such apprehensions; i.e., refrain from believing that those apprehensions are certain, refrain from believing that they are satisfactory for the construction of *scientia*. For certainty, remember, requires incorrigibility as well as indubitability.

Our doubt will also apply to other matters which we previously regarded as most certain – even the demonstrations of mathematics and even the principles which we hitherto considered to be self-evident. One reason for this is that we have sometimes seen people make mistakes in such matters, and accept as most certain and self-evident things which seemed false to us. Secondly, and most importantly, we have been told that there is an omnipotent God who created us. Now we do not know whether he may have wished to make us beings of the sort who are always deceived even in those matters which seem to us supremely evident; for such constant deception seems no less a possibility than the occasional deception which, as we have noticed on previous occasions, does occur. We may of course suppose that our existence derives not from a supremely powerful God but either from ourselves or from some other source; but in that case, the less powerful we make the author of our coming into being, the more likely it will be that we are so imperfect as to be deceived all the time. (CSM I, 194)[15]

---

[15] It is passages such as this which persuade me that Descartes's concept of certainty cannot be explicated entirely in terms of indubitability; incorrigibility is also necessary for certainty. For neither here nor anywhere else does Descartes suggest that he has reason to refrain from believing that clear and distinct apprehensions are indubitable; what he suggests is that, at this stage in his reflections, he has reason to refrain from believing that they are incorrigible – but hence, reason to refrain from believing that they are certain.

Descartes rightly says that the second possibility raised is more important than the first. We do indeed make mistakes in what we take to be self-evident. But someone might insist that such mistakes can always be explained as the result of our failure to take accurate note of the presence or absence of the phenomenology of clarity and distinctness. The second possibility is the truly serious one: So far as one can tell at this point, it seems quite possible that there be something in our constitution, or some outside agent, bringing it about that we experience the phenomenology of intuition and deduction with respect to false propositions.

But now the Therapy of Doubt, introduced as preparation for engaging in the Method satisfactorily, threatens the Method itself – or strictly, the assumptions underlying the Method. For The Method tells us that if we are apprehending a proposition so clearly and distinctly that we cannot refrain from believing it, and more importantly, so clearly and distinctly that we couldn't have a good reason for doubting it while thus apprehending it – if our apprehension has *psychological*, but more importantly, *rational* indubitability – then it can be regarded as satisfactory for *scientia*. Then our apprehension is to be taken as certain. But now we have discovered that we, at this point in our reflections, have good reason to refrain from believing that this is correct. For even though such apprehensions be indubitable in both senses, we have good reason to refrain from believing that they are also *incorrigible*. But if not incorrigible, then not certain. Thus at this point in the argument we have good reason to refrain from believing that following The Method will yield *scientia*.

And if we have good reason to doubt that the Method yields *scientia*, then it *doesn't* yield *scientia*. This shows, of course, how Descartes understands the nature of *scientia* – shows that he is attaching a qualification to the traditional Aristotelian–medieval understanding of *scientia*. Nothing has been said to show that indubitability *does not* coincide with incorrigibility. For all we know at this point, a systematic pursuit of indubitability might in fact yield believings which are always true – hence fully certain. But we would still not have *scientia*. "The fact that an atheist can be 'clearly aware that the 3 angles of a triangle are equal to 2 right angles' is something I do not dispute. But I maintain that this awareness (*cognitio*) of his is not true knowledge (*scientia*), since no act of awareness (*cognitio*) that can be rendered doubtful seems fit to be called knowledge (*scientia*) . . . And although this doubt may not occur to him, it can still crop up if someone else raises the point or if he looks into the matter himself. So he will never be free of this doubt until he acknowledges that God exists" (CSM II,101).[16]

How are we to proceed? Well, we have to overcome this doubt that we have, concerning indubitable apprehensions, that they are true – this reason-grounded refraining from believing that apprehensions so clear and distinct that they are psychologically and rationally indubitable are also true. Suppose that I have a clear and distinct apprehension of some proposition; my present situation is such that I have a reason for doubting that, necessarily, that proposition is true. That doubt inhibits me from setting that proposition down as belonging to *scientia*. And even if it be the case that all clearly and distinctly apprehended propositions *are* true, nonetheless, they still don't belong to *scientia* if I have a reason-grounded doubt that they do. So to overcome my disability, and to make *scientia* itself a reality, this reason-grounded doubt must be removed. I have to "be free of this doubt." That is what Descartes proceeds to try to do – to remove this doubt.

How can that be done? Well, as we all know, Descartes proposes to do so by arguing for the existence of an all-powerful, all-knowing, all-good God, and then inferring that God would see to it that whatever we apprehend clearly and distinctly is true. But all that we can make use of in this argument is phenomena that the evil genius would not change – if there were an evil genius. The evil genius would not change any of the facts about dubitability and indubitability. The Law of Assent would still be operative: We still find ourselves compelled to believe propositions which we apprehend with a certain high degree of clarity and distinctness. And we still find that no way of apprehending propositions is more compelling than clearly and distinctly doing so. So these are the phenomena that we have to make use of. The demon may well have attached these phenomena to falsehoods; so we must beware of ever assuming, for some proposition which is clearly and distinctly apprehended, that he has not done so in this case. And certainly we must avoid assuming that he has not done so in any case.

So consider one of the propositions which Descartes introduces in

---

[16] Cf. Descartes's letter to Regius of May 24, 1640. Distinguishing *scientia from conviction*, he says: "I distinguish the two as follows: there is conviction when there remains some reason which might lead us to doubt, but knowledge [*scientia*] is conviction based on a reason so strong that it can never be shaken by any stronger reason" (CSM III,147).

the course of the argument: *that the cause of an idea has at least as much formal reality as the idea has objective reality.* Let us, for convenience' sake, call this proposition P. I dare say that most of us do not find P compelling even when we do clearly and distinctly apprehend it; but that, for our purposes, is neither here nor there. The question I must ask myself, as I contemplate whether or not to set P down as part of the argument, is whether I find myself compelled to believe P when I grasp it well. If I do, then I set it down. Suppose that I am like Descartes and do find myself compelled to believe this; accordingly, I set it down. But now somebody whispers in my ear: "Do you find yourself compelled to believe this other proposition, *that if you apprehend P so clearly and distinctly that you cannot doubt it, then P is true?*" My answer to this question, at this stage of the argument, is No. But the fact that my answer is No, at this stage of the argument, is irrelevant.

I suggest, in short, that Descartes's strategy for "removing the doubt" is to construct an argument which satisfies these two conditions:

(1) It has for its conclusion that any proposition apprehended so clearly and distinctly as to be rationally (and psychologically) indubitable is necessarily also true, i.e., incorrigible; and

(2) Its premises, and the proposition that the premises entail the conclusion, are apprehended so clearly and distinctly as to be rationally (and psychologically) indubitable.

Once Descartes has freed us from doubting the general thesis, that any proposition apprehended so clearly and distinctly as to be rationally and psychologically indubitable is true, then he has also freed us from doubting, concerning some particular proposition P which is apprehended so clearly and distinctly that it cannot be doubted, that P is true.

Supposing that an argument which satisfies these conditions can be found, its import remains to be clarified. But counter to the charges which have haunted Descartes's *Meditations* ever since their publication, there is nothing circular or question-begging either in the argument proper or in Descartes's strategy as a whole. When one clearly and distinctly focuses on the argument presented, the conclusion that clarity and distinctness of apprehension insures truth of the proposition apprehended is both rationally and psychologically indubitable: Descartes claims to have given an argument of that sort. His failure lies simply in the fact that his argument is not of that sort. It is not indubitable; it is not compelling; it does not satisfy the second condition above. Almost no one has thought that it does, other than Descartes himself.

Previously I sketched a scenario according to which we could have the phenomenology of clarity and distinctness (and compelled assent) with respect to falsehoods. It was the scenario of the powerful demon. Under the scenario, we are still compelled to believe propositions when we apprehend them clearly and distinctly. But the scenario enabled us to doubt, both in general and for specific cases, whether there is any necessary connection between indubitability and truth. Now, with the argument before us, we are in the position of not being able to believe that scenario, or any other similar scenario; we find ourselves compelled to believe that such scenarios are impossible. We cannot believe that there can be such a demon – for we are rationally and psychologically compelled to believe that there is an omni-benevolent, omniscient, omnipotent God who exists necessarily; and that necessarily this God will prevent any such demon's doings. Only if there were no necessarily existing God of this sort would a demon of the sort imagined be possible.

But no one can keep the argument in mind all the time. Can one *now* once again refrain from accepting its conclusion – *now* once again refrain from believing that, in general, clarity and distinctness of apprehension of a proposition (and compelled assent thereto) is a guarantee of its truth? No, says Descartes – not if one remembers that one did clearly and distinctly perceive the argument. Neither can one now doubt the truth of particular propositions which one remembers having demonstrated clearly and distinctly: "Even if I am no longer attending to the arguments which led me to judge that this is true, as long as I remember that I clearly and distinctly perceived it, there are no counter-arguments which can be adduced to make me doubt it, but on the contrary I have true and certain knowledge of it. And I have knowledge not just of this matter, but of all matters which I remember ever having demonstrated, in geometry, and so on. For what objections can now be raised?" (CSM II,48).[17]

---

[17] Cf. Reply to the Second Set of Objections to the *Meditations*, CSM II,104: "But we forget the arguments in question and later remember simply the conclusions which were deduced from them. The question will now arise as to whether we possess the same firm and immutable conviction concerning these conclusions, when we simply recollect that they were previously deduced from quite evident principles (our ability to call them 'conclusions' presupposes such a recollection). My reply is that the required certainty is indeed possessed by those whose knowledge of God enables them to understand that the intellectual faculty which he gave them cannot but tend towards the truth." Thus God is also a guarantor of the veracity of memory. See also Descartes's letter to Regius of May 24, 1640; available in Anthony Kenny, *Descartes: Philosophical Letters* (Oxford, Clarendon Press, 1970) pp. 73–4.

I have emphasized Descartes's introduction of the Therapy of Doubt as a strategy for getting rid of the mistaken *praejudicia* that hinder us in the practice of *scientia*. Pretty clearly, though, Descartes saw the Therapy, when combined with the *Meditations* argument, as serving another purpose as well; namely, the polemical purpose of beating the skeptic at his own game. Descartes regards himself as having brought his readers to the point where they can no longer doubt, either rationally or psychologically, the things that the skeptic says are questionable. More than that, the *Meditations* argument, following on the radical practice of the Discipline, plays the constructive role of making it indubitable that the Method is satisfactory for the construction of *scientia*. It is meant, in that way, to "establish" the foundations of *scientia*. (Of course, the *Meditations* argument itself is meant to satisfy, formally, at least the first rule of the Method.) It may be added that, in turn, Descartes saw the Method not only as the best strategy for building up *scientia*, but also as yielding a "critique" of those of our assent-forming faculties other than intuition and deduction. We discover, for example, that perception informs us about reality only to a limited extent.

We must beware, though, of conceding to Descartes's argument more significance than it actually has. In the course of the early stages of the argument in the *Meditations*, which culminates in the affirmation of the principle that the phenomenology of clarity and distinctness (and of compulsion to believe) is a guarantee of truth, Descartes observes that the *cogito ergo sum* is impervious to the wiles of the evil genius. It is impossible that one should be compelled to believe this when it is false. The indubitable is here incorrigible. Suppose that "there is a deceiver of supreme power and cunning who is deliberately and constantly deceiving me. In that case I too undoubtedly exist, if he is deceiving me; and let him deceive me as much as he can, he will never bring it about that I am nothing so long as I think that I am something" (CSM II,17).

Descartes makes no such claim about later premises in the argument. What he claims is just that if one follows the argument as a whole, then

(A) One is rationally and psychologically compelled to believe that necessarily whatever one is thus compelled to believe is true.

And if that claim were correct, Descartes would have accomplished exactly what he wanted to accomplish; namely, devise an argument which, for all who attend to the argument, removes the doubt that clear and distinct apprehensions of propositions are certain.

You and I want to say, in response, that from (A) it does not follow that

(B) Necessarily what one is thus compelled to believe is true.

To get to (B) from (A) we need a principle of elimination:

Compelled-P

Therefore, P.

But Descartes's argument does nothing to entitle us to this principle. The truth, we want to say, is that (A) is compatible with

(C) Sometimes what one is thus compelled to believe is false.[18]

Thus you and I want to say that Descartes's argument, if successful, would do no more than display "a demand of thought." Of all the commentators on Descartes, Frankfurt is the one who has seen most clearly this "Kantian" import of the argument. Descartes's argument, he says,

> is an attempt to show that there are no good reasons for believing that reason is unreliable – that the mistrust of reason is not supported by reason and that it is accordingly irrational . . . The point of Descartes's validation of reason is that if reason is properly employed – that is, if we give assent only to what we clearly and distinctly perceive – we are not led to doubt that reason is reliable. We are led, on the contrary, to assent to the propositions that God exists and that He guarantees the reliability of reason . . . no proposition entailing the unreliability of reason can be clearly and distinctly perceived.[19]

What must be noted, however, is that your and my conviction that (B) does not follow from (A), and that (C) is compatible with (A), reflects the fact that we do not find the argument compelling; correspondingly, our conviction that the argument, if successful, would merely display a "demand of thought," reflects the fact that you and I do not find the argument compelling. We find ourselves entirely capable, with the argument before us, of doubting its conclusion. By contrast, if we did find the argument compelling, we would not believe that (C) is compatible with (A).

---

[18] It was my colleague at Calvin College, Del Ratzsch, who suggested to me the precise point made in this paragraph.
[19] *Demons, Dreamers, and Madmen*, pp. 175–7.

So we must not expect to find Descartes conceding that his argument is nothing but a demand of thought. He was, indeed, looking for a demand of thought; that is what he needed at this point in the argument. But having, in his judgment, found it, he naturally enough does not believe that it is *merely* a demand of thought. Nonetheless, there is a fascinating passage in the Second Set of Replies in which, amidst a lot of bluster, Descartes is quite clearly giving expression to some unease over the import of the argument:

as soon as we think that we correctly perceive something, we are spontaneously convinced that it is true. Now if this conviction is so firm that it is impossible for us ever to have any reason for doubting what we are convinced of, then there are no further questions for us to ask: we have everything that we could reasonably want. What is it to us that someone may make out that the perception whose truth we are so firmly convinced of may appear false to God or an angel, so that it is, absolutely speaking, false? Why should this alleged "absolute falsity" bother us, since we neither believe in it nor have even the smallest suspicion of it? . . . It is . . . no objection for someone to make out that such truths might appear false to God or to an angel. For the evident clarity of our perceptions does not allow us to listen to anyone who makes up this kind of story. (CSM II,103–4)

My contention throughout has been that Descartes's main concern was *scientia*, or as he tends to call it in his later writings, "the contemplation of the truth." The Method is a method for the construction of *scientia*. And what I have called the Therapy of Doubt is, first of all, a therapy to be undertaken so that we can practice the Method satisfactorily. Whereas the center of Locke's concern was to give us rules for the regulation of *opinio*, Descartes, for *opinio*, gives us nothing more than a few limited, bland, and thoroughly conventional pieces of advice.

It would appear, however, that this interpretation is in flagrant conflict with what Descartes says in the Fourth Meditation. For there, in the context of inquiring how error in human belief is compatible with the existence of an omnipotent, omniscient, benevolent God, he says that "If . . . I simply refrain from making a judgment in cases where I do not perceive the truth with sufficient clarity and distinctness, then it is clear that I am behaving correctly and avoiding error. But if in such cases I either affirm or deny, then I am not using my free will correctly" (CSM II,41). He adds: "For it is surely no imperfection in God that he has given me the freedom to assent or not to assent in those cases where he did not endow my intellect with a clear and distinct perception; but it is undoubtedly an imperfection in me to misuse that freedom and make judgements about matters which I do not fully understand" (CSM II,42). Descartes gives no indication here that these claims are restricted to *scientia*. He appears to be claiming, in general, that if one assents to some proposition which one has not perceived with full clarity and distinctness, then one is misusing the faculties God has given one.

But if this were in fact the right interpretation, Descartes would regard himself and every other sane person as violating this fundamental human obligation. For, as we have seen, he thinks that every sane person believes various existential propositions about material bodies, even though these are not apprehended clearly and distinctly. So I think that the proper interpretation requires that we take with full seriousness the explanations and disclaimers that Descartes makes in his reply to the Second Set of Objections to the *Meditations*. I have already quoted part of the passage. Let me now quote the whole of it:

> I should like you to remember here that, in matters which may be embraced by the will, I made a very careful distinction between the conduct of life and the contemplation of the truth. As far as the conduct of life is concerned, I am very far from thinking that we should assent only to what is clearly perceived. On the contrary, I do not think that we should always wait even for probable truths; from time to time we will have to choose one of many alternatives about which we have no knowledge, and once we have made our choice, so long as no reasons against it can be produced, we must stick to it as firmly as if it had been chosen for transparently clear reasons. I explained this on p. 26 of the *Discourse on the Method*. For when we are dealing solely with the contemplation of the truth, surely no one has ever denied that we should refrain from giving assent to matters which we do not perceive with sufficient distinctness. Now in my *Meditations* I was dealing with the contemplation of the truth; the whole enterprise shows this to be the case, as well as my express declaration at the end of the First Meditation where I said that I could not possibly go too far in my distrustful attitude, since the task in hand involved not action but merely the acquisition of knowledge. (CSM II,106; see also Fourth Set of Replies; CSM II,172, and Fifth Set of Replies; CSM II,243)

We should assent to P *as satisfactory for scientia* only if it is clearly and distinctly apprehended. But what, you ask, about our actual assent to P? Believing that P is satisfactory for *scientia* is different from believing (assenting to) P. Further, it sometimes turns out that the very proposition, assent to which is indispensable for the conduct of life, is *not* apprehended in such a way that I am entitled to inscribe it in the book of science. Do I then, or do I not, actually assent to P? Descartes says Yes. (See, for example, CSM II, 106.) Nonetheless, his observations on the matter are seldom more than incidental. That, on my interpretation, is no accident. Descartes is simply not much interested in rules for regulating our *actual* assent to most propositions. He is interested in acquiring a systematic and productive body of propositions each of which we know to have been either intuited or deduced from what is intuited. Obviously such propositions, when found, will be assented to. But there are many other belief-forming faculties than intuition and deduction. Some of these others lead us to assent to propositions which later we intuit or deduce; some lead us to assent to propositions which we never do and never can intuit or deduce. In all of that, Descartes had no fundamental interest.

There is another theme in the Fourth Meditation on whose compatibility with my interpretation we must reflect, the theme of the radical freedom of the will. A key component in my overall interpretation has been my claim that Descartes embraces what I have called the Law of Assent: If one clearly and distinctly apprehends a proposition, it is psychologically impossible to withhold one's assent from it; "our mind is of such a nature that it cannot help assenting to what it clearly conceives."[20] Is this not incompatible with Descartes's claim that the will is no more limited in its freedom in human beings than in God? For Descartes held, after all, that for any proposition whatsoever, God can make it either true or false.

In a well-known passage from the *Principles of Philosophy*, Descartes says that "we possess only two modes of thinking: the perception of the intellect and the operation of the will"; and he asserted – implausibly in my view – that assenting to a proposition is a species of willing:

All the modes of thinking that we experience within ourselves can be brought under two general headings: perception, or the operation of the intellect, and volition, or the operation of the will. Sensory perception, imagination and pure understanding are simply various modes of perception; desire, aversion, assertion, denial and doubt are various modes of willing. (1,32; CSM 1,204)

Descartes then held that in every case of belief, both the intellect and the will are involved. We apprehend the proposition with more or less clarity and distinctness; that is a mode of intellect. And we assent to the proposition; that is a mode of volition. "Making a judgment," he says, "requires not only the intellect but also the will."

[20] Letter to Regius, May 24, 1640, in Kenny, *Descartes: Philosophical Letters*, p. 73.

In order to make a judgement, the intellect is of course required since, in the case of something which we do not in any way perceive, there is no judgment we can make. But the will is also required so that, once something is perceived in some manner, our assent may then be given. Now a judgement – some kind of judgement at least – can be made without the need for a complete and exhaustive perception of the thing in question; for we can assent to many things which we know only in a very obscure and confused manner. (*Principles* 1,34; CSM 1,204)

Concerning these two fundamental modes of mind, Descartes held that though the human intellect is limited, in the sense that for every human being there are many propositions which are simply beyond the scope of his or her consideration or the power of his or her grasp, the will is not similarly limited. "I cannot complain," he says, "that the will or freedom of choice which I received from God is not sufficiently extensive or perfect, since I know by experience that it is not restricted in any way" (Fourth Meditation; CSM II,39). Then he goes on to say:

It is only the will, or freedom of choice which I experience within me to be so great that the idea of any greater faculty is beyond my grasp; so much so that it is above all in virtue of the will that I understand myself to bear in some way the image and likeness of God. For although God's will is incomparably greater than mine, both in virtue of the knowledge and power that accompany it and make it more firm and efficacious, and also in virtue of its object, in that it ranges over a greater number of items, nevertheless it does not seem any greater than mine when considered as will in the essential and strict sense. This is because the will simply consists in our ability to do or not do something (that is, to affirm or deny, to pursue or avoid). (Fourth Meditation; CSM II,40)

What is it that Descartes is saying here? Perhaps something like this: Suppose that we grant that the object of intentions and undertakings is always to bring it about that a certain proposition be made true. Intending to get my letter to the box before the mailman comes amounts to intending to bring about the truth of the proposition that I get my letter to the box before the mailman comes. Now, Descartes believes that God has entertained and grasped vastly more propositions than any of us has. Thus there are many more propositions which can be the object of intentions and undertakings on God's part than on ours. The power of will is incomparably greater in God than in us "in virtue of its object, in that it ranges over a greater number of items." So also, there are many propositions whose truth God knows how to bring about and has the power to bring about, but for which we lack either the one or the other, either the knowledge or the power. The power of will is incomparably greater in God than in us also "in virtue of the knowledge and power that accompany it and make it more firm and efficacious." Thus God can *successfully* undertake many things that we cannot. In these ways, God's will is undeniably, and incomparably, more powerful than ours, says Descartes. But these differences do not speak to what the will is "in the essential and strict sense." They speak to differences in knowledge and to differences in power of implementation. By contrast, *willing as such* involves neither of these but consists simply in undertaking something; the will "consists in our ability to do or not do something."

Immediately, however, Descartes adds a crucial qualification, or explanation, to this last point; an explanation which makes clear that, for him, freedom of the will consists not of the liberty of indifference but in the liberty of spontaneity. This is what he adds:

> or rather, the will consists simply in the fact that when the intellect puts something forward for affirmation or denial or for pursuit or avoidance, our inclinations are such that we do not feel we are determined by any external force. In order to be free there is no need for me to be inclined both ways; on the contrary, the more I incline in one direction – either because I clearly understand that reasons of truth and goodness point that way, or because of a divinely produced disposition of my inmost thoughts – the freer is my choice. Neither divine grace nor natural knowledge ever diminishes freedom; on the contrary, they increase and strengthen it. But the indifference I feel when there is no reason pushing me in one direction rather than another is the lowest grade of freedom; it is evidence not of any perfection of freedom, but rather of a defect in knowledge or a kind of negation. For if I always saw clearly what was true and good, I should never have to deliberate about the right judgement or choice; in that case, although I should be wholly free, it would be impossible for me ever to be in a state of indifference. (Fourth Meditation; CSM II,40)

Descartes's thought appears to be this: If there are sufficient causal conditions for the occurrence of some undertaking, but those sufficient causal conditions include no "external force," then the undertaking is free even though the person could not have chosen otherwise.

The application to the matter at hand of this understanding of freedom is this: Descartes's claim, that we are all so constituted as to be compelled to assent to propositions that we clearly and distinctly apprehend, is not seen by him as incompatible with his claim that free will is involved in all cases of assent. For the compulsion is internal:

during these past few days I have been asking whether anything in the world exists, and I have realized that from the very fact of my raising this question it follows quite evidently that I exist. I could not but judge that something which I understood so clearly was true; but this was not because I was compelled so to judge by any external force, but because a great light in the intellect was followed by a great inclination in the will, and thus the spontaneity and freedom of my belief was all the greater in proportion to my lack of indifference. (Fourth Meditation; CSM II,41)[21]

There is one exception which Descartes himself introduced into the Method – an exception which he seems to have regarded as minor in scope of application but major in import. Repeatedly Descartes emphasizes that not only is the Method not meant for the conduct of life; it is also not meant for religious faith: "when I asserted that 'we should assent only to what we clearly know' this was always subject to the exception of 'matters which belong to faith and the conduct of life'" (CSM II,172). When it comes to faith, the rule is that we are to accept what is revealed by God: "if God happens to reveal to us something about himself or others which is beyond the natural reach of our mind – such as the mystery of the Incarnation or of the Trinity – we will not refuse to believe it, despite the fact that we do not clearly understand it" (*Principles* I,25; CSM I,201).

Our natural perceptual faculties produce in us apprehensions of, and assentings to, various propositions which we have neither intuited nor demonstrated. That is quite acceptable, says Descartes. What must be kept in mind, however, is that none of those apprehensions are good enough for *scientia*; any *praejudicia* we may have that these beliefs are certain must be overcome by the Therapy of Doubt. For the most part, the same is true of religious faith. Faith simply involves a different apprehension and belief-forming process from the workings of those faculties of intuition and deduction which yield *scientia*. What that process might be, Descartes tries briefly to explain in his reply to the

[21] A bit later Descartes adds: "this indifference does not merely apply to cases where the intellect is wholly ignorant, but extends in general to every case where the intellect does not have sufficiently clear knowledge at the time when the will deliberates" (CSM II,41). Compare *Principles* I,39: "the freedom which we experienced within us was nonetheless so great as to enable us to abstain from believing whatever was not quite certain or fully examined" (CSM I,206). And also from the Fourth Meditation: "For although probable conjectures may pull me in one direction, the mere knowledge that they are simply conjectures, and not certain and indubitable reasons, is itself quite enough to push my assent the other way. My experience in the last few days confirms this: the mere fact that I found that all my previous beliefs were in some sense open to doubt was enough to turn my absolutely confident belief in their truth into the supposition that they were wholly false" (CSM II,41).

Second Set of Objections to the *Meditations* (CSM II,205). It is indeed a process rather than a faculty or mechanism. It consists of God directly producing in us the firm conviction, concerning some proposition P, that God has revealed it; given our intuition that God cannot lie, that produces in us the belief that P.[22]

But to limit the scope of the Method to the practice of *scientia* is different from contending that, *in the practice of scientia*, there may be certain cases in which we are to employ some other rule than the Method. But that is exactly what Descartes contends. Specifically, if some item of the faith is intuited as contradicting some proposition which is entertained with the phenomenology of clarity and distinctness, and compelled belief, we should – or perhaps just shall – prefer the item of faith. We should or shall conclude that at this point the phenomenology of clarity and distinctness, and compelled belief, is deceptive, that there is a fluke in the workings of our faculties. We find ourselves with the belief that God has revealed P; but we apprehend clearly and distinctly, and are compelled to believe, both not-P, and that not-P contradicts P. In such a situation, our conviction that God has revealed P, plus our standing conviction that God cannot lie, should (or will) win out over our intuitions, leading us to believe P. Hence "above all else we must impress on our memory the overriding rule that whatever God has revealed to us must be accepted as more certain than anything else. And although the light of reason may, with the utmost clarity and evidence, appear to suggest something different, we must still put our entire faith in divine authority rather than in our own judgment" (*Principles* 1,76; CSM 1,221).

As I have already suggested, the interpretation of Descartes which I have presented is unconventional at several points; if that were not

[22] "Now although it is commonly said that faith concerns matters which are obscure, this refers solely to the thing or subject-matter to which our faith relates; it does not imply that the formal reason which leads us to assent to matters of faith is obscure. On the contrary, this formal reason consists in a certain inner light which comes from God, and when we are supernaturally illumined by it we are confident that what is put forward for us to believe has been revealed by God himself. And it is quite impossible for him to lie; this is more certain than any natural light, and is often even more evident because of the light of grace" (Reply to the Second Set of Objections to the *Meditations*; CSM II,105). Cf. Descartes's letter to Hyperaspistes of August 1641: "In the reply to the *Second Objections* I said 'enlightened by God, we trust that what is proposed for our belief has been revealed by him': but there I was speaking not of human scientific knowledge, but of faith. And I did not assert that by the light of grace we clearly know the very mysteries of faith – though I would not deny that this too may happen – but only that we trust that they are to be believed. No one who really has the Catholic faith can doubt or be surprised that it is most evident that what God has revealed is to be believed and that the light of grace is to be preferred to the light of nature."

so, it could, for the purpose of illuminating the relation of Descartes to Locke, have been very much abbreviated. Nonetheless, I have not tried to defend it against alternatives but have contented myself with referring to supporting texts and pointing to its overall coherence. In conclusion, though, I wish to consider the alternative interpretation offered by Bernard Williams on the central point of the nature of Cartesian doubt.[23] I choose Williams as a good representative of a fairly standard line of interpretation.

On my interpretation, to Cartesianly doubt some proposition P is not to suspend one's assent to P but rather to suspend one's assent to the proposition that one's mode of apprehending P *is satisfactory for the inclusion of P in scientia.* Thus I contend that, to understand Descartes, we must distinguish between those passages in which by "doubting" P he means no longer assenting to P, and those in which by "doubting" P he means Cartesianly doubting P. Williams interprets Descartes as uniformly meaning the same thing by "doubt" – namely, doubting P is suspending one's assent to P. He says that "the method of doubting everything until one reaches, if one can, something that cannot be doubted, is presented as a strategy, as a systematic way of achieving something which is Descartes' aim: this is to discover *the truth*" (p. 35). And then he continues: "the strategy is to aim for certainty by rejecting the doubtful. To *reject* the doubtful here means, of course, to suspend judgment about it, or at most to treat it as false for the purposes of the argument" (p. 36).

Williams is fully aware, however, of Descartes's Law of Assent: If we clearly and distinctly apprehend a proposition, we cannot refrain from believing it. He is also aware of the passages in which Descartes insists that no sane person has ever "seriously doubted" that "there really is a world, and that human beings have bodies and so on." So how does Williams fit all this together, given that, in what I have called the Therapy of Doubt, we *are* to doubt that there really is a world and we *are* to doubt propositions that we clearly and distinctly apprehend?

Williams' solution is to distinguish between two different modes of having propositions in mind: If we have a proposition clearly and distinctly in mind, we cannot suspend assent to it, whereas if we do not have that same proposition thus in mind, we can (provided a good enough reason is offered to us). And this is, indeed, an authentically

---

[23] Bernard Williams, *Descartes: The Project of Pure Inquiry* (Harmondsworth, Penguin, 1986 repr.).

Cartesian point. This is what Williams says:

Descartes says in the *Second Replies* of the things about which we can be perfectly certain, "we cannot think of them without believing them to be true," and he there claims that we cannot doubt them without thinking of them. From those premisses it follows, as he correctly points out, that we cannot doubt them. Yet it seems that there is something which counts as doubting even those propositions, so it must be possible for such a proposition to be sufficiently "before the mind" for one to entertain a doubt about it, but not be so clearly in view that one's belief in it is activated. This is not a very deep or difficult problem. All that is required is some way of referring to or indicating a proposition or idea of this kind without bringing it clearly to mind. A standard way of doing that will lie in deploying a word or sentence which expresses that idea or proposition, without, however, concentrating closely on what that word or sentence expresses. One can, granted this, entertain a doubt about an irresistible proposition, but only by not thinking about it clearly.[24]

Now, in the first place, Williams does not formulate his distinction so that it applies directly to Descartes's argument. Descartes, remember, "doubts" all propositions about a physical world which we take to have been acquired by way of our senses, and does so with two broad questions: Why trust that which has even once deceived one? And, how does one know that one was not dreaming instead of sensing? This way of dealing with the beliefs we acquired by way of what we took to be perception is scarcely "deploying a word or sentence which expresses that idea or proposition, without, however, concentrating closely on what that word or sentence expresses."

But no matter. The crucial issue is this: Williams interprets Descartes as saying that by the Therapy of Doubt we bring ourselves to the point where we really don't believe any of the things "doubted"; a state which, for many propositions, can only be achieved, he says, by not having the doubted proposition clearly in mind. On Williams' interpretation, the mind is (almost entirely) emptied of assent by the doubt Descartes recommends – vacuumed clean. On my interpretation, by contrast, the mind remains very full, since Cartesianly doubting a proposition does not consist of withdrawing assent from that proposition.

What is to be said for my interpretation on this point and against the Williams style of interpretation? Well, there is, for one thing, the

---

[24] "Descartes' Use of Skepticism," in Miles Burnyeat (ed.), *The Skeptical Tradition* (Berkeley and Los Angeles, University of California Press, 1983), pp. 345–6.

inherent implausibility of anyone's really believing that by those broad swipes that Descartes uses, one can bring oneself to the point of believing almost nothing. The situation does not change if one *dwells on* those broad swipes, as Descartes says we should (Second Set of Replies, CSM II, 94; see also First Meditation, CSM II, 15). What the meditating which Descartes recommends might have a chance of accomplishing – so it seems to me – is that for which Descartes on my interpretation proposed it: freeing us up from our *praejudicia* as to what we are certain of.

Secondly, and more importantly, there is Descartes's insistence that practicing his Therapy of Doubt does nothing to disturb the beliefs presupposed in the conduct of our lives. In particular, everybody always believes that he or she has a body. Williams interprets Descartes as meaning that one can switch in and out of believing that one has a body. That is not what Descartes says.

But thirdly, and most importantly: The Williams style of interpretation renders Descartes's strategy in the *Meditations* fundamentally confused. Let us suppose, for the sake of the argument, that doubting P is always to be understood as refraining from assenting to P. Descartes offers reasons for doubting P. And if I have a good reason for doubting P, then obviously I am not entitled to go ahead and believe P until that reason has been answered. Now, it turns out that even when we have not excluded the possibility of the demon, there are a few propositions of which we can be certain that if they are apprehended clearly and distinctly, they are true. Indeed, we can be certain that if they are apprehended *at all*, they are true. These propositions of the *cogito*-sort can be seen without further ado to be not only indubitable but incorrigible. But most of the propositions which Descartes uses in the argument stretching from the Second to the Fourth Meditation are not of that sort. About them Descartes instructs us, on the Williams interpretation, to doubt them, no longer to believe them. Hence they are not available to us for use in any argument. Williams replies: Yes; but when we apprehend them clearly and distinctly, we *cannot* refrain from believing them. But this is beside the point. If one has good reason not to assent to P but finds that in certain circumstances one cannot *avoid* doing so, then surely the right thing to do is to avoid those circumstances as much as possible, rather than getting oneself into those circumstances and concluding that in those circumstances one is entitled to assent to P.

The problem is an old one in Descartes interpretation. Commentators have seen that the doubt which Descartes urges is almost totally comprehensive in its scope; only a few beliefs of the *cogito*-sort escape. But they have also seen that we need to have more than such beliefs left over, after we have followed the instructions to doubt, if we are to construct the *Meditations* argument. Thus a dilemma: Either one grants the radical scope of the doubt that Descartes urges, and finds oneself without enough entitled assentings left over to construct the argument; or one reserves enough assentings for the construction of the argument, and limits the scope of the doubt Descartes recommends. The Williams style of interpretation is an attempt to escape this dilemma; it says that one can both follow the radical instructions for doubt and have sufficient propositions left over for the argument: In following the instructions, one thinks of propositions unclearly and indistinctly but yet sufficiently to doubt them; in constructing the argument, one thinks of them clearly and distinctly. But that proposal just overlooks the fact that the radical doubt leaves one without *title* to use, in the argument, the propositions one was instructed to doubt. One doesn't receive that title until the end of the argument, when the reason for the radical doubt has been answered and the instruction lifted.

One can only escape the dilemma by distinguishing *doubting P* from *Cartesianly doubting P*. Cartesian doubt leaves us with more than enough propositions to construct the argument; since, for most propositions, it never enjoins us to give up our assent to them – only to give up our assent to the proposition that our mode of believing them is certain.

But let us look at the central piece of textual evidence which Williams offers for his interpretation. Found in the Seventh Set of Replies, it goes as follows: "So long as we attend to a truth which we perceive very clearly, we cannot doubt it. But when, as often happens, we are not attending to any truth in this way, then even though we remember that we have previously perceived many things very clearly, nonetheless there will be nothing which we may not justly doubt so long as we do not know that whatever we clearly perceive is true" (CSM II,309).

It may be noticed that this passage is not explicitly incompatible with my interpretation. On my interpretation, Descartes in the first sentence is saying that when we clearly and distinctly attend to a proposition, we cannot refrain from believing it. In the second he says that so long as we do not know that the phenomenology of clarity and distinctness guarantees truth, there is no belief-state at all about which we cannot doubt that it has the highest epistemic status – certitude. But though the passage does not explicitly contradict my interpretation, nonetheless the point it seems to be making is the Williams point.

Let us consider the context in which the passage occurs. In the preceding paragraph, Descartes is making exactly the point on which I have grounded my interpretation; namely, that his "metaphysical" doubt does not change and is not meant to change anything in practical life. In the passage he expressed his annoyance that Father Bourdin would have thought otherwise:

I said at the end of the First Meditation that we may doubt all those things which we have not yet perceived with sufficient clarity, since our doubt is based on "powerful and well thought-out reasons." But I said this because at that point I was dealing merely with the kind of extreme doubt which, as I frequently stressed, is metaphysical and exaggerated and in no way to be transferred to practical life. It was doubt of this type to which I was referring when I said that everything that could give rise to the slightest suspicion should be regarded as a sound reason for doubt. But my friendly and ingenuous critic here puts forward as an example of the things that I said we could doubt "for powerful reasons" the question of whether there is an earth, or whether I have a body, and so on; the effect is that the reader, if he knows nothing of my "metaphysical" doubt and refers the doubt to practical life, may think that I am not of sound mind. (CSM II,308–9)

What then follows is the passage which Williams cites, and which I quoted above. The passage then continues as follows:

From the fact that at one point I said that there was nothing that we might not doubt – namely in the First Meditation, in which I was supposing that I was not attending to anything that I clearly perceived – he draws the conclusion that I am unable to know anything certain, even in the following Meditations. This is to suggest that the reasons which may from time to time give us cause to doubt something are not legitimate or sound unless they prove that the same thing must be permanently in doubt. (CSM II,309)

In the entire passage, then, Descartes makes these three points:

(1) "Metaphysical" or exaggerated doubt is not meant to change anything at all in practical life.
(2) One can emerge from metaphysical doubt. Metaphysically doubting some proposition is not a permanent condition, nor is it meant to be.

(3) We manage to metaphysically doubt those propositions whose clear apprehension compels assent by recalling the fact that we have had the experience of clear apprehension, and then taking note of the fact that we do not find ourselves compelled to believe that this coincides with incorrigibility.

Thus the passage as a whole is not just logically compatible with my interpretation, but supports it: "metaphysical" doubt does not alter those beliefs which are presupposed in practical life.

Still, why does Descartes draw the contrast between attending "to a truth which we perceive very clearly" and remembering "that we have previously perceived many things very clearly"? Well, on my interpretation, Cartesian (metaphysical) doubt does indeed involve a shift of focus. On the one hand, there is the phenomenon of one's assent being compelled by one's clear and distinct apprehension of such a proposition as $2 + 2 = 4$. On the other hand, to engage in Cartesian doubt of that belief is to raise a question about one's mode of apprehension of it, a question which requires recollection. It is to raise this question: Was one's assent-compelling, clear and distinct apprehension of this proposition a guarantee of its truth? But of course one means this question generally: In general, is our assent-compelling, clear and distinct apprehension of propositions a guarantee of their truth? Though I do not contend that Descartes's way of pointing to this change of focus is entirely lucid, it is also not entirely infelicitous. Cartesian doubt does involve the change of focus to which Descartes here points: One remembers that one has had clear and distinct, assent-compelling apprehensions and then asks whether those are incorrigible.

Why doesn't Descartes make the point more lucidly? I have contended that Descartes operates with a distinction between two types of doubt, and that recognizing this is fundamental to interpreting his thought. But when he tries to explain the distinction, he almost always says that metaphysical doubt is an extreme, exaggerated, kind of doubt – that its scope is much wider than ordinary doubt. Yet when someone draws what would seem to be the obvious implication, that in metaphysical doubt we withdraw assent from all, or almost all, the things that we customarily assent to, even from the existence of a world, Descartes always emphatically insists that that is not his meaning. It is true, of course, that we are to Cartesianly doubt many more propositions than we are to ordinarily doubt. But to cite that as *the* difference is misleadingly off-target.

I suggest that what we witness in Descartes's writings is the struggle to get clear on what exactly the project was to which he had committed himself. He was, in this respect, like all the great philosophers. In my discussion I have obliterated most signs of the struggle, instead offering, as it were, a "rational reconstruction" of the Cartesian project. And then secondly, and more specifically, I suggest that at the heart of, or near the heart of, Descartes's struggle, was the struggle to get clear on the distinction between certainty as a (high) degree of *truth-likelihood* and certainty as extremely firm *assent*. The distinction was made later in the century by the Royal Society group in England; though even by them, not with sure-handedness. Descartes, though groping for the distinction, was even less far along the road of making it with clarity than they were; there are passages in which one can see him shifting back and forth between the two senses. If this speculation is correct, then pretty much everything falls into place. Metaphysically doubting P is not suspending one's assent to P but wondering whether one's mode of believing P has the epistemic status of certainty – or more than wondering, having reasons which lead one to suspend for the time being one's belief on the matter. Usually, however, one's *assent* to P continues throughout the process of Cartesianly doubting whether the *truth-likelihood* of one's mode of assent to P is that of certainty.

II WHERE LOCKE WAS ORIGINAL

Locke's originality inheres in a new vision, propounded with persuasive articulateness, of what we human beings are to do with *doxa*, opinion. One of the images haunting Western thought is the image of the divided line presented by Plato in the sixth book of the *Republic*. Take a line, says Plato, which has been divided into two (unequal) segments. Let one segment represent the perceptible; the other, the intelligible. Then divide each of these segments in turn. Of that initial segment which represents the perceptible, let one part represent the appearances of perceptible things; the other, the perceptible things themselves. And of that initial segment which represents the intelligible, let one part represent things knowable only by inference from things known, perhaps with the assistance of perceptible illustrations; let the other part represent things knowable immediately and without the assistance of illustrations. We can then pair off modes of intellectual apprehension with these different parts of the line and what they represent. There will be imagining (*eikasia*) and believing (*pistis*) corresponding to the two parts of the first segment, these together constituting opinion (*doxa*); and there will be thinking (*dianoia*) and knowing (*episteme*) corresponding to the two parts of the second segment.

Plato's instruction, *take a divided line and let its parts represent*, opens with language which is non-evaluative. He does not say, let the *lower* part of the line represent . . . He says simply, "take a line divided into two unequal parts, one to represent . . ." But anyone who has read this far in the *Republic* knows Plato's assessment of *doxa* and *episteme*. And by the time we are instructed to pair off mental states or actions with the parts of the line and what they symbolize, the evaluation has become fully explicit: "take, as corresponding to the four sections, these four states of mind: *intelligence* for the highest, *thinking* for the second, *belief* for the third, and for the last *imagining*. These you may arrange as the terms in a proportion, assigning to each a degree of clearness and certainty corresponding to the measure in which their objects possess truth and reality" (VI.511; Cornford tr.).

Episteme is highest; *doxa*, in its two forms, is lowest. For *episteme* occurs when we are in touch with what is fully real: with the realm of the necessary, eternal, immutable. Plato postulated the presence in us human beings of a faculty which puts us in touch with necessity: the faculty of Reason. In the contemplation of the realm of the necessary by Reason is to be found our deepest human happiness; and only in the realm of the necessary shall we find stable standards of excellence by which to measure our human lives and actions. In the *Timaeus* Plato argued that apprehension of the contingent can never be certain; only apprehension of the necessary can be that. *Episteme* is certain; *doxa*, uncertain. For Plato, the "moral" was clear: We must aim at *theoria*, that is, at contemplation of the realm of the eternal and necessary, retaining *doxa* only so much as is unavoidable.

This complex of conviction and imagery, powerful though it has proved to be, was by no means all-conquering in the world of antiquity. In its fundamentals it was shared by Aristotle, though Aristotle's articulation of it differed significantly from Plato's. But the Stoics accepted it only in part, and the skeptics saw it as fundamentally misguided.

The skeptics, along with everyone else in antiquity, agreed that happiness, *eudaimonia*, was the goal of human existence. But they disputed the claim that happiness is to be found in the exercise of Reason, understood as awareness of the eternal and necessary.

Happiness is to be found in quietude, *ataraxia*, "an untroubled and tranquil condition of soul," as Sextus Empiricus described it.[25] One feature of experience that especially perturbs people and prevents them from attaining quietude is "the contradictions in things," and doubts as to which alternative we ought to accept (i.vi). Dogmatists, as Sextus calls them, are those who try to attain quietude by resolving these contradictions and settling these doubts. Skeptics regard that as futile. They try instead to achieve quietude by suspension of judgment, this being that "state of mental rest owing to which we neither deny nor affirm any thing" (i.iv). Skeptics do not, indeed, aim to suspend judgment concerning *every* proposition that crosses their minds. Specifically, they do not aim to suspend judgments concerning appearances. "Those who say that 'the Sceptics abolish appearances,' or phenomena, seem to me," says Sextus, "to be unacquainted with the statements of our School. For, as we said above, we do not overthrow the affective sense-impressions which induce our assent involuntarily; and these impressions are 'the appearances'" (i.x). "No one, I suppose, disputes that the underlying object has this or that appearance; the point in dispute is whether the object is in reality such as it appears to be" (i.xi). Beliefs about how things appear to us are ineliminable, but also certain; quietude is not threatened by them. But for every proposition that comes one's way concerning what lies beyond appearance, the goal is to neither believe nor disbelieve: suspend judgment.

Plato has been turned on his head. If there is anything stable and certain in our mental life, it is our knowledge of how things appear to be, says the skeptic. What is important, however, if we wish to attain quietude, is not to dwell on what we are certain of but to regulate all the rest of our mental life – Platonic *pistis*, *dianoia*, and *episteme* are all lumped together as uncertain. To regulate it with the goal of eliminating falsehood from our beliefs would be, however, to suffer anxiety, unease, lack of quietude. The *elimination* of belief, and disbelief, is the goal. The ancient skeptic proposed governing assent with the goal of eliminating assent to all propositions but those recording appearance.

It was the Platonic–Aristotelian option which above all shaped the Christian Middle Ages, sometimes in Stoicized form. Our deepest human happiness lies in our contemplation of the realm of the eternal

---

[25] *Outlines of Pyrrhonism* i.vi; tr. R. G. Bury in the Loeb Classical Library (Cambridge, Mass., Harvard University Press, 1955). All subsequent references will be to this volume.

and necessary; and within this, in our contemplation of the nature of God, God's nature being what is highest in the realm of the eternal and necessary. It is by the exercise of *intellectus* and reason, together yielding *scientia*, that such contemplation is to be attained. Faith is an adumbration of such contemplation.

But though the medievals were at one with Plato in their understanding and estimate of *episteme*, the attitude of most, and in particular of Aquinas, toward *doxa* was very different from that of Plato, akin rather to that of Aristotle. For at least with respect to that component of *doxa* which is one's intellectual inheritance, Aquinas by no means recommended or practiced *turning away*. Instead he recommended and practiced working through one's intellectual inheritance by the practice of dialectic. Dialectical appropriation of one's intellectual tradition is unmistakably inferior to *scientia*; nonetheless, it is far from worthless. At its best it even puts us in a position where we can see how to go on to attain *scientia*. Dialectic stands in relation to the practice of *scientia* as the Therapy of Doubt stands to that practice in Descartes, and as the proper education of children stands, in Locke's thought, to the doxastic practice he recommends for matters of maximal "concernment."

Beneath this structural similarity, though, there are deep differences of attitude toward the textual tradition. There is, in Aquinas, no alienation and estrangement from the two traditions which constituted his principal intellectual inheritance, the Christian and the ancient Greek. The relative indifference to tradition which characterized Descartes, and the sharp hostility to tradition which motivated Locke, have yet to put in their appearance. Especially helpful here is the discussion by Edmund F. Byrne in his book *Probability and Opinion: A Study in the Medieval Presuppositions of Post-Medieval Theories of Probability*.[26] Byrne deals especially with Aquinas' thought in his commentary on Aristotle's *Posterior Analytics*.

Opinion, for Aquinas, is the believing of a proposition without being certain of it. And it was Aquinas' view – or at least his *dominant* view – that one can be certain of a proposition only if it is necessarily true. Thus if the proposition believed is contingent, the believing is perforce a matter of opinion. When a proposition is entertained in the mode of opinion, whether it be itself necessary or contingent, Aquinas finds it often convenient to speak of the proposition as itself *opinion*.

[26] (The Hague, Martinus Nijhoff, 1968).

Obviously this is a relational concept; a proposition which is an opinion for one person may not be that for another.

Those who wish to engage in the practice of *scientia* have no choice but to begin from a situation which consists for the most part of opinion. We try to move from *opinion*, which is where we are, to *scientia*, where we hope to be. But all too obviously human beings disagree in their opinions. So what are we to do? Try gaining at once that better land of science? Not at all. Then stick with whatever opinions we ourselves happen to have acquired? Not that either. Aquinas' own practice was to attend to the opinions of the wise, the learned. Naturally some of those will be *common* opinions, shared by all, or almost all, normal adults. But if not, then one attends to "the best of what the best men think," as Byrne puts it (p. 97). Why that? Because – and this Aquinas never doubts – such opinions "cannot be totally false but must be at least partly true" (p. 108).

Aquinas speaks of the opinions of the wise as *probable*. So in answer to our question, "To which opinions should we attend?" he would be willing to say, "Attend to those which are probable." But what does he mean in calling such opinions "probable"? As Byrne describes Aquinas' thought and speech, saying of some proposition that it is "probable" "refers to the authority of those who accept the given opinion; and from this point of view 'probability' suggests *approbation* with regard to the proposition accepted and *probity* with regard to the authorities who accept it" (p. 188).

I think there is another, inherently more plausible, way of construing the Thomistic texts on this matter. Byrne takes the *meaning* of "probable" in Aquinas to be: opinion held by persons of probity. Given this understanding of "probable," one then justifies attending to such opinions by adding the premise that such opinions "cannot be totally false but must be at least partly true."[27] Perhaps, though, the core meaning of the word "probable" for Aquinas (strictly, of its Latin counterpart *probabilis*), was *likely to be true at least in part*. If so, then it did not belong to the meaning of the word "probable," but was instead a substantive thesis of Aquinas, that the opinions of "persons of probity" are likely to be at least partly true. One advantage of interpreting Aquinas' usage in this latter way is that it preserves his contrast between what is *probable* for a person and what is *certain*, a contrast blurred by Byrne's construal.

---

[27] p. 108; Hacking, *The Emergence of Probability* (Cambridge, Cambridge University Press, 1975), follows Byrne in this interpretation.

No large issues hang on this disagreement over the meaning for Aquinas of "probable"; the substance of Aquinas' thought can be expressed either way. Let me, though, use my own interpretation rather than Byrne's. On this interpretation, what has changed when we get to Locke is not the meaning of "probable"; both Aquinas and Locke think of the probable as that which is likely to be true, or likely to be true at least in part. What has changed is the *criterion* that we are to use for determining what is probable. Aquinas was of the view that we are to go to the best opinions of the best persons; Locke, to the evidence of "the things themselves."

But the opinions even of the wise are normally *only in part* true: witness the fact that even such opinions conflict. Appealing to the opinions of the wise does not deliver us from the conflict of opinions – because, in general, such an appeal does not reveal to us *which parts* of their opinions are true. So, having begun with probable opinions collected from the wise persons in our intellectual inheritance, what do we do next?

We engage in *dialectical reasoning*, in *argumentation* – which is, be it noted, distinct from *demonstration*. "One must go deeper than mere authority. The means of going deeper is dialectic" (Byrne, p. 140). The goal of dialectic is to discover, without leaving the realm of opinion, *what* there is of truth in the various opinions of the wise. One does so by trying to discern what is to be said in favor of each of the conflicting opinions. Likewise one draws out the consequences of each opinion and tries to discern what is to be said against it in the light of these consequences. And through it all one makes distinctions. The goal is to arrive at a sort of synthesis in which one incorporates whatever there was of truth in the conflicting opinions with which one was dealing.

Dialectical disputation . . . takes as its very point of departure the question that is raised by opposite opinions. Each of the opposed opinions consti-tutes one side of the dispute, and the disputation itself consists in the presentation and consideration of the arguments in favor of either side. The arguments thus presented in favor of one side or the other are "probable" . . . that is, probable inasmuch as they draw their conclusions from premises which are probable. The propositions which serve as premises are, in their turn, probable on the basis of widespread acceptance, or acceptance by some particular authority (whether an individual or a group), or, especially, acceptance by the opposition. In a certain sense, then, the whole purpose of the disputation is to build up the authoritative probability of one side or the other – or, what is even more desirable, of both sides. Indeed, this very concern for the strength of opposite claims is, as it were, the essence of dialectical disputation. For, the purpose of disputation as such is not the determination of truth; this is the function of demonstration, which, if possible, follows upon the preparatory consideration of dialectic. The purpose of disputation is rather to present as well as humanly possible the reasons for adhering to either of the two opposite opinions. For . . . it is presupposed that no opinion can be totally devoid of truth, especially if it is in some way probable . . . Thus, disputational procedure implies a kind of dialectic even in the Hegelian sense. For, it is out of the very opposition of the opposing views that a new and more adequate statement of the truth – a synthesis, if you will – is sought. And from this point of view each particular opinion is but a stage in the growth of men's knowledge – not taken by itself but precisely insofar as it is opposed to another opinion. To this extent, dialectical disputation implies intolerance of differing opinions. For, this very difference of opinion is itself an indication that there is a higher truth to be attained which will incorporate the relative merits of these lesser, more partial statements of truth. (Byrne, pp. 141–2, 166)

Aquinas saw clearly that dialectical reasoning remains within the sphere of opinion. The drawing of deductive inferences from opinion yields opinion. Yet, sometimes engaging in dialectical reasoning puts us within sight of something else; namely, the possibility of demonstration. This is the true goal of dialectical reasoning, in the sense that this is what one always hopes for – to see how to get beyond the opinions of human beings to the nature of things. By "demonstration one transcends the opinionative, the merely probable, and attains a certitude founded upon the necessary, that is, upon what cannot be other than it is" (Byrne, p. 186). Conversely, it was Aquinas' view that "in this vale of tears," where "truth may be determined only by way of demonstration . . . one can arrive at demonstration only by way of the preparatory clash of opposing opinions" (pp. 165–6).

The contrast with Descartes and Locke could not be sharper. What most impressed Descartes and Locke about the opinions of their fellow human beings was not that those of the wise contain a great deal of truth, but that, in general, they are riddled with error, with the consequence that our being reared in such a "climate of opinion" plants in us all sorts of harmful *praejudicia*. To practice *scientia* successfully, Descartes insisted, we must free ourselves from these *praejudicia*; we do so not by working through our intellectual inheritance in dialectical fashion but only by submitting the whole of it to the

Therapy of Doubt.[28] To the things themselves, said Locke![29]

The full originality of Locke's vision can now be spied. In Locke there is almost no echo of the long contemplative tradition. True knowledge, and hence true *scientia*, comes to very little. And in any case, what is known is not some realm of higher reality. It is simply the mind and its modifications. Locke was no more concerned than were the ancient skeptics to rise above *doxa*. *Doxa* is satisfactory for our life in the world; it is our God-given lot. But we must *regulate doxa*. Not

---

[28] Contrast what Descartes says in his letter of August 1638 to Hogelande: "I do not mean that one should neglect other people's discoveries when one encounters useful ones; but I do not think one should spend the greater part of one's time in collecting them. If a man were capable of finding the foundations of the sciences, he would be wrong to waste his life in finding scraps of knowledge hidden in the corners of libraries; and if he was no good for anything else but that, he would not be capable of choosing and ordering what he found" (in Kenny, *Descartes: Philosophical Letters*, p. 60).

[29] In my discussion of Aquinas, as indeed in my discussion of Descartes, I have sharply distinguished the *practice of scientia* from the preliminary exercises that must be undertaken if we are to engage successfully in that practice. Alasdair MacIntyre, in the discussion of Aquinas in his recent work *Whose Justice? Which Rationality?* (Notre Dame, University of Notre Dame Press, 1988), obliterates the distinction. His own evident resistance to thinking of Reason as a faculty which yields insight, plus his equally evident admiration for Aquinas, lead him to see in Aquinas only dialectic, not *scientia*.

MacIntyre imagines someone objecting to his account in the following words: Surely "rational justification, according to both Aristotle and Aquinas, is a matter of deducibility from first principles, in the case of derived assertions, and of the self-evidentness as necessary truths of these same first principles. So that your account of the rational justification of Aquinas' overall view is quite inconsistent with Aquinas' own account of rational justification" (pp. 172–3). MacIntyre's answer to the objection goes as follows: "Rational justification within a perfected science is indeed a matter of demonstrating how derivative truths follow from the first truths of that particular science, in some types of case supplemented by additional premises; and the justification of the principles of a subordinate science by some higher-order enquiry will be similarly demonstrative. First principles themselves will be dialectically justifiable; their evidentness consists in their recognizability, in the light of such dialectic, as concerning what is the case per se, what attributes, for example, belong to the essential nature of what constitutes the fundamental subject matter of the science in question" (p. 173).

But this is to confuse *scientia* itself with the dialectical preparation for engaging in *scientia*. What gives a first principle of a science its status of being *certain* for someone is simply that the person "sees" it to be true. There is no getting around Aquinas' repetitive references to insight. The fact that a principle is certain for someone, that someone "sees" it to be true, does not imply that it will hold up in every dialectical dispute; it implies only that if it does not hold up in some such argument, someone in the argument has somewhere made a mistake. Nor, conversely, does the fact that some thesis holds up in all dialectical arguments imply that it is certain for anyone. *Scientia* for Aquinas is not what survives the dialectical sifting of tradition but what *transcends* all such sifting. Aquinas is no Hegelian born out of season. Byrne's summary, though flamboyant, is accurate: "Thomas suffers incurably from an epistemic nostalgia for the beatific vision, wherein man's cognitional limitations will be filled up with the plenitude of divine omniscience. Any knowledge short of this, however solid in itself, is by comparison but a feeble preparation for the perfection that lies beyond. For, it is then that the opiniative, the probable, the conjectural, even that which is believed on faith, will give way to certain and total vision" (*Probability and Opinion*, p. 239).

regulate it with the skeptic's goal of eliminating *doxa* so as to attain quietude; regulate it rather with the goal of eliminating falsehood. The way to do this is not to appropriate our intellectual tradition in dialectical fashion. Tradition, after all, is filled with error, since human beings have for the most part not conducted their understandings aright. When some matter of high "concernment" is before us, opinion is to be regulated by collecting satisfactory evidence for the proposition in question; and then believing it on the evidence and with a firmness proportioned to what Reason tells us is the probability of the proposition on that evidence. This view, shared by Locke's Royal Society cohorts, but first given its articulate formulation by him, was historically novel, and extraordinarily persuasive. It became a prominent component in the mentality of Western modernity.

Of course, as I have repeatedly emphasized, there were also continuities. Locke continued to hold that we human beings have direct insight into some of the facts of reality, Reason being one of the faculties yielding such insight. This conviction was fundamental to his vision. Our opinions are to be grounded on and governed by insight. The lure of certitude has not ceased to beckon. And secondly, Locke continued the long eudaemonistic tradition; our goal as human beings is happiness. The ultimate reason for pursuing truth and seeking to avoid error is happiness. Regulated opinion will yield improvement in our living conditions, especially when it takes the form of the new natural philosophy; and it will acquaint us with the ways of obedience to God. Such obedience yields happiness. One does not, indeed, find Locke joining the ancient Hebrew songwriters in praise of the inherent delight of obeying the Torah of Jahweh. Rather, God has instituted God's law for our communal happiness in this life, and will reward our obedience to that law with happiness in the next, no matter what it may be that we with our own particular character find happiness in: even if "we suppose [human] relishes as different there as they are here, yet the manna in heaven will suit every one's palate" (II,xxi,65). The road to true happiness is the road which leads to a society whose members obey the law of God as they singly enjoy political liberty and jointly struggle to master nature. Regulated opinion is indispensable to such happiness.

CHAPTER 4

Locke and the making of modern philosophy

Locke intended his epistemology as a solution to the crisis of the fracturing of the moral and religious tradition of Europe at the beginnings of modernity. That was not his only intent; but it was prominent. Furthermore, Locke, so I have suggested, was the first of those whom we now number among the great philosophers of early modernity to address himself to this crisis, certainly the first to offer the sort of proposal that he did. He described a new doxastic practice; and he argued that we are all obligated to apply this practice in all cases of maximal concernment – in particular, to matters of religion and morality. On its negative side, the practice represents the radical rejection of unverified tradition. On its positive side, the practice resembles the method which Descartes and his high medieval forebears had recommended for the practice of *scientia* – with this important revision, that probabilistic inferences be allowed in addition to deductive.

These conclusions, along with others which have turned up in the course of our discussion, invite a telling of the story of early modern philosophy quite different from that which has become traditional. I propose in this last chapter to point out where and why the main traditional story must be discarded, to indicate some of the outlines of an alternative, more accurate story, and to show how Locke fits into this alternative story.

My story will remain radically incomplete, however; and that in two ways. I shall speak only about Descartes, Locke, and Hume; I shall say nothing at all about the place of such other undeniably great and influential early modern philosophers as Bacon, Malebranche, Spinoza, Leibniz, Hobbes, and Berkeley. And my story will concentrate only on the epistemological aspect of early modern philosophy. In that respect it wears a regrettably conventional appearance. "Regrettably," I say; for my own conviction is that ethical and social-political reflections occupied a far more prominent place in early modern philosophy than the traditional account acknowledges.

Locke's place in my story is prominent; but I shall not claim that Locke should be regarded as the father of early modern philosophy, or that he was the first truly modern philosopher, or that he was the first great modern philosopher, or anything else of the sort. I regard all such single-parent claims as misguided, for reasons that will become clear shortly. The full story of early modern philosophy requires the weaving together of a number of distinct story lines.

The most familiar story about the development we now call "early modern philosophy" is the rationalist/empiricist/synthesist story. Some time before that story emerged, Thomas Reid told a story about his predecessors under the rubric of "The Way of Ideas." I shall not address myself directly to either of those stories; instead I shall address myself to Hegel's story, and to a certain variant thereon. For not only has Hegel's story proved enormously influential; the familiar rationalist/empiricist/synthesist story should probably be seen as a (somewhat superficial) facet of Hegel's story.

Hegel asked what no one before him had asked: What makes recent philosophy *modern*, rather than merely *recent?* Of course, the Middle Ages had already used the contrast between *via moderna* and *via antiqua*, applying it to music and philosophy, for example. But Hegel had something different in mind. The *society* of recent times, Hegel believed, was in its foundations different from the society that preceded it. Its Spirit, its *Geist*, was different. Between the society of recent times and that which preceded it – not ancient, of course, but *medieval* – there was a fundamental breach, making present society not just present but *modern*. The culture of this new society both expressed what was new in this society and contributed to its formation. And philosophy is part of this new, distinctly modern, culture. Hence, *modern* philosophy.

"The principle of the modern world is freedom of subjectivity," says Hegel, "the principle that all the essential factors present in the intellectual whole are now coming into their right in the course of their development."[1] "In this principle all externality or authority is . . . superseded, for this is the principle, but also no more than the principle, of the freedom of spirit. It is the greatness of our time that this form, however little its self-understanding, still bears within it this

---

[1] *Hegel's Philosophy of Right*, tr. with notes by T. M. Knox (Oxford, Clarendon Press, 1952), p. 286.

[truth] that freedom – the peculiar possession of spirit – is acknowledged, that spirit is inwardly at home with itself [*in sich bei sich ist*] and has this consciousness within it."[2] Jürgen Habermas, in his discussion of Hegel's concept of modernity, suggests that "the term 'subjectivity' carried primarily four connotations [for Hegel]: (a) *individualism*: in the modern world, singularity particularized without limit can make good its pretensions; (b) *the right to criticism*: the principle of the modern world requires that what anyone is to recognize shall reveal itself to him as something entitled to recognition; (c) *autonomy of action*: our responsibility for what we do is a characteristic of modern times; (d) finally, *idealistic philosophy* itself: Hegel considers it the work of modern times that philosophy grasps the self-conscious (or self-knowing) Idea."[3]

As to origins: It was Hegel's conviction that this principle of subjectivity, which constitutes "the greatness of our time," was introduced into history by the Protestant Reformation:

We have already remarked upon the first manifestations of this principle, the principle of our own human thought, our own knowing, its activity, its right, its trust in itself. It is the principle of finding satisfaction in our own activity, reason, imagination, and so forth, of taking pleasure in our products and our work and deeming it permissible and justifiable to do so, indeed, regarding our own work as something in which we may and should essentially invest our interest . . . This validation of the subjective domain now needed a higher – indeed, the highest – confirmation in order to be completely legitimated and to become even the absolute duty. To attain to this level it had to be grasped in its purest shape.

The highest confirmation of this principle is the religious confirmation, when this principle of our own spirituality and our own autonomy is recognized in our relation with God and to God . . .

[2] G. W. F. Hegel, *Lectures on the History of Philosophy: The Lectures of 1825–1826*, vol. III, ed. R. F. Brown, tr. R. F. Brown, J. M. Stewart, and H. S. Harris (Berkeley, University of California Press, 1990), p. 257. Cf. Hegel, *Philosophy of Right*, p. 84: "The right of the subject's particularity, his right to be satisfied, or in other words the right of subjective freedom, is the pivot and centre of the difference between antiquity and modern times. This right in its infinity is given expression in Christianity and it has become the universal effective principle of a new form of civilization. Amongst the primary shapes which this right assumes are love, romanticism, the quest for the eternal salvation of the individual, etc.; next come moral convictions and conscience; and, finally, the other forms, some of which come into prominence in what follows as the principle of civil society and as moments in the constitution of the state, while others appear in the course of history, particularly the history of art, science, and philosophy." Cf. also p. 294: "The principle of the modern world requires that what anyone is to recognize shall reveal itself to him as something entitled to recognition."

[3] Jürgen Habermas, *The Philosophical Discourse of Modernity*, tr. F. Lawrence (Cambridge, Polity Press, 1987), p. 17.

This, then, is the great principle of [the Reformation], that all externality disappears at the point of the absolute relationship to God. All self-estrangement, with its consequent dependence and servitude . . . disappears.

This principle of subjectivity became a moment of religion itself and thereby attained to its absolute recognition . . .

The principle of the Reformation . . . was the moment of spirit's being-within-self, of its being free, its coming to itself. That is just what freedom means: to relate oneself to oneself, in the determinate content.[4]

This interpretation of the Reformation, so it seems to me, is a tangle of insight and error. But rather than entering that beckoning side path, let me go on to observe that it follows from Hegel's interpretation of modernity that what makes philosophy *modern*, as indeed what makes any cultural development *modern*, is that its theme is subjectivity; Hegel interprets modern culture as the culture of Protestantism. And though he regarded Francis Bacon and Jacob Boehme as important preparatory figures, "It is with Descartes that the philosophy of the modern period, or abstract thinking, properly begins."[5]

Now we come for the first time to what is properly the philosophy of the modern world . . . Here, we may say, we are at home and, like the sailor after a long voyage, we can at last shout "Land ho." Descartes made a fresh start in every respect. The thinking or philosophizing, the thought and the formation of reason in modern times, begins with him. The principle in this new era is thinking, the thinking that proceeds from itself. We have exhibited this inwardness above all with respect to Christianity; it is preeminently the Protestant principle. The universal principle now is to hold fast to inwardness as such, to set dead externality and sheer authority aside and to look upon it as something not to be allowed. In accordance with this principle of inwardness it is now thinking, thinking on its own account, that is the purest pinnacle of this inwardness, the inmost core of inwardness – thinking is what now establishes itself on its own account. This period begins with Descartes. What is deemed valid or what has to be acknowledged is thinking freely on its own account, and this can happen only through my thinking freely within myself; only in this way can it be authenticated for me. This means equally that this thinking is a universal occupation or principle for the world in general and for individuals. Human beings must acknowledge and scrutinize in their own thoughts whatever is said to be normative, whatever in the world is said to be authoritative; what is to rank as established must have authenticated itself by means of thought.[6]

Let us assume, for the moment, that Hegel is right about the fundamental principle of modernity – that it is the principle of the

---

[4] Hegel, *Lectures on the History of Philosophy*, vol. III, pp. 94–102.
[5] *Ibid.*, p. 108.   [6] *Ibid.*, pp. 131–2.

freedom of subjectivity. The preceding discussion then compels the conclusion that, whereas Locke was certainly a modern philosopher, Descartes was not yet one. For Descartes understood the project to which he devoted his endeavors, the project of *scientia*, as a project for the intellectual elite, not as "a universal occupation or principle for the world in general and for individuals." It was Locke, not Descartes, who insisted that all human beings whatsoever, provided just that they be sane adults, "must acknowledge and scrutinize in their own thoughts whatever is said to be normative, whatever in the world is said to be authoritative." It was Locke who insisted that, with respect to anything of maximal concernment to anyone whatsoever, "what is to rank as established must have authenticated itself by means of thought."

It will be said that this is going by the letter of Hegel's analysis rather than the spirit. Let it be conceded that Hegel was mistaken in attributing to Descartes the sort of universalism that he does – because, let it be conceded, Hegel failed to discern that Descartes's lifelong project was to renew and practice *scientia*. Nonetheless, there is a momentous difference between the medieval way and the Cartesian way of *carrying out* this common project: Whereas the medievals regarded a dialectical appropriation of the textual tradition as the best preparation for the practice of *scientia*, Descartes argued that the best preparation requires closing one's books and engaging instead in the Therapy of Doubt. In this difference, there is point to Hegel's comments.

There is indeed this difference between Descartes and the medievals; the difference is important, and was seen as important by Descartes's contemporaries and successors. Descartes's closing of the books is something distinctly modern. Nonetheless, it is worth noting that in Descartes's *reason* for rejecting the dialectical appropriation of the textual tradition as preparation for the practice of *scientia*, there was nothing specific to modernity. To practice *scientia*, one has to be able to discriminate between those propositions which are immediately certain for one and those which are not. What impressed Descartes was that experience and reading fill us with mistaken *praejudicia* as to what we are certain of; and that even when we do reflect on the matter, we pull back from the consideration of the truly radical possibilities. Accordingly, before doing anything else we must liberate ourselves from these *praejudicia* and these hesitations; Descartes was persuaded that the best way to do so was to engage in his Therapy of

Doubt, and to do so in truly radical fashion. I submit that, in principle, a medieval philosopher could have said exactly the same thing. No "principle of subjectivity" was coming to expression in this reason. Neither was there any acknowledgment of the development I have emphasized: the fracturing of the moral and religious tradition and the emergence of raging conflicts over biblical interpretation. The issue is simply this: When reading texts which are not specimens of *scientia*, one is likely to acquire mistaken *praejudicia* which inhibit one's ability to discriminate the certain from the uncertain. Does that danger outweigh the likely benefit of having one's imagination stimulated into discerning new ways of advancing *scientia*? Descartes emphatically thought that it did. The medievals thought that it did not. Therein lies the difference.

But doesn't the core of Hegel's claim still remain intact, his claim that Descartes was the first to construct a philosophy in which freedom of subjectivity is central? There is room for doubt. Obviously subjectivity occupies an important place in the overall argument and pattern of thought of the *Meditations*; and contrary to those who suggest that Descartes himself didn't believe much of the *Meditations*, it seems to me that Descartes believed all of it, and saw the arguments developed there as constituting an important link in his comprehensive project. Nonetheless, the suggestion that subjectivity was the organizing center of Descartes's philosophy goes much too far; in Descartes's work as a whole it occupies only a subsidiary, albeit important, place. Descartes's project, to say it once again, was the renewal and expansive practice of *scientia*, not the development of a philosophy of subjectivity. And as to content of his execution of that project, it was especially "first philosophy" and "natural philosophy" which occupied his attention. His largest and most mature book was *Principles of Philosophy*. The *Meditations*, which are, of course, the *locus classicus* for the Hegelian interpretation, were presented as meditations *on first philosophy*, that is, on metaphysics – though in fact they are more than that. It is we who find Descartes's Second Meditation the most important, fascinating, and suggestive thing he ever wrote. There is no evidence that Descartes regarded it thus.

Only when we come to Locke does the self occupy center stage. Locke offers no meditations on first philosophy; neither is he interested in elaborating "principles of philosophy." His main endeavor was an essay concerning human understanding. Whichever way we turn, if we accept Hegel's account of what makes philosophy modern, Locke proves to be the first great modern philosopher, not Descartes – though what pushed the principle of freedom of subjectivity to center stage in Locke's thought was not his Protestantism but his unwillingness simply to appeal to the texts, even the biblical texts, when at a standstill in answering questions about morality and revealed religion.

In Charles Taylor's book on Hegel, titled simply *Hegel*, and in his later book, *The Sources of the Self*, one finds an interpretation of early modern philosophy which is both a variation on, and an elaboration of, Hegel's account: a variation, in that Taylor offers a different account of the origins of the centrality of subjectivity in modern philosophy, an elaboration, in that Taylor articulates in his own way Hegel's notion of *freedom* of subjectivity.[7] Though it is the elaboration I mainly want to consider, we must begin with a word about Taylor's alternative view as to origins. Rather than adopting Hegel's thesis that the main source of modernity was the religious legitimation by Protestantism of freedom of subjectivity, Taylor adopts Max Weber's alternative account of the origin of modernity – or at least, one important strand of that account.

It was Weber's conviction that the essence of modernization is to be located in two related phenomena. First, in the emergence of *differentiated spheres*; specifically, in the emergence of the differentiated *social spheres* of economy and state, along with household, and in the emergence of the differentiated *cultural spheres* of science, art, and law and ethics. Secondly, in the spread of rationalized thought and action within these spheres. The fundamental dynamic of our modern, capitalist economies is rationalization, Weber thought, just as the fundamental dynamic of our modern, bureaucratic states is rationalization; so too, rationalization is what accounts for the fundamental character of modern science, oriented as it is toward prediction, grounded as it is in sensory experience, intertwined as it is with technology.

Not only does the dynamic of rationalization account for what takes place within these differentiated social and cultural spheres; it accounts as well, Weber thought, for their emergence. His argument comes in three parts, only two of which are explicitly developed in his published work, and only the first of which is mentioned directly by Taylor.

---

[7] Charles Taylor, *Hegel* (Cambridge, Cambridge University Press, 1975); and Charles Taylor, *Sources of the Self* (Cambridge, Mass., Harvard University Press, 1989).

Weber regarded it as characteristic of "primitive" religions for the participants in those religions to think of the world as filled with magical and sacred powers – to think of the world as *enchanted*. A condition of the emergence of modern society and culture is the disappearance of such a view; modernity presupposes the disenchantment, the *Entzäuberung* (literally, de-magicalizing) of the world. The world for a modern person is an inherently meaningless, indifferent terrain for action.

The displacement of "primitive" religions by the world religions was the first large step along the road to this disenchantment; that step, by now far back in the mists of history, already represented the dynamic of rationalization at work. For religions are attempts to find meaning in human existence; but the meanings proposed by the "primitive" religions always found themselves without a satisfyingly "rational" account of suffering and injustice.

The emergence of the world religions by no means represented the completion of disenchantment, however; the process continues to work itself out within these religions, the dynamic still being rationalization as the response to questions of theodicy. Though Weber apparently believed that the dynamic of rationalization operating within each world religion, as a sort of "internal logic," would eventually lead each of them to adopt a fully disenchanted view of the world, he clearly regarded the dynamic as operating most powerfully in religions exhibiting that particular configuration of attitudes and convictions which one finds in Judaism, Christianity, and (presumably) Islam.

World religions can be distinguished along three dimensions. Some, the theocentric, sharply separate the divine from the world; others, the cosmocentric, locate the divine within the world. Some, the world-affirming, see the world as basically good; others, the world-rejecting, see the world as basically bad. And some proclaim the active, "ascetic" life as the road to salvation, whereas others proclaim the contemplative, "mystical" life as being that. Weber speculated that the pressures of rationalization toward a disenchanted view of the world would be felt most powerfully in religions which are theocentric, world-rejecting, and ascetic; he interpreted Judaism and Christianity as exactly such religions. In Judaism and Christianity there was, he thought, a powerful critique of actions performed simply out of habit or affect, and a powerful pressure toward the formation of a generalized ethic of principle – the corollary of which, he thought, is that the world itself is viewed as devoid of meaning, spread before the agent simply as the objective terrain in and on which action obedient to God is to be performed. Weber regarded the lifestyle of the monks as the finest example in medieval times of this religious type; they were the *virtuosi* of the day. Their lifestyle was the most methodical, that is, the most *rationalized*.

A disenchanted view of the world is no more, however, than a *necessary* condition of the emergence of modernity. And what especially intrigued Weber was this question: How could our capitalist economy, with its inherently "unbrotherly" modes of operation, have emerged from the cradle of a religion whose ethic, though coupled with an increasingly disenchanted view of the world, was nonetheless an ethic of "brotherliness"? What convictions were available for legitimating capitalist entrepreneurialism? We all know Weber's answer: It was the English Puritans in particular, and the Calvinists in general, who first exhibited the fully methodical, fully rationalized character-formation of "inner-worldly asceticism" requisite for capitalist entrepreneurship; and they legitimated their actions by extruding the ethic of brotherliness from the economic sphere and putting in its place "the Protestant ethic," as Weber called it, according to which the believer's capitalist entrepreneurship is legitimated by its being the calling (*vocatio*) given him by God, with success therein being a sign of his belonging to the company of God's elect.[8]

There remains a crucial part of Weber's argument which was never fleshed out by him. To act and think as we do within our rationalized social and cultural spheres requires that we view and treat the world as disenchanted; Weber offered an account of how that came about. To act and think as we do in our capitalist economy requires that one

---

[8] I disagree at this point with the otherwise superb reconstruction of Weber's thought by Jürgen Habermas in *The Theory of Communicative Action: Vol. I, Reason and the Rationalization of Society*, tr. T. McCarthy (Boston, Beacon Press, 1984), pp. 143–271. Habermas interprets Weber as holding that the Puritans embodied the rationalized ethic of conviction belonging to the Christian worldview in their economic activity, thus transposing rationalization from the cultural into the social sphere. Weber's thought was decisively different. The rationalized ethic of conviction which is properly part of the Christian worldview is an ethic of "brotherliness." What operates in the economic sphere is something quite other than "brotherliness." Hence the tensions between the two which Weber so emphatically emphasizes in his famous chapter "Religious Rejections of the World and their Directions." This interpretation confronted Weber with his famous puzzle: Why would Christians ever have regarded such "unbrotherly" action as legitimate? His solution was to attribute to the Puritans, presumably in addition to their convictional ethic of "brotherliness," that very different ethic, if "ethic" it can properly be called, which he calls "the Protestant ethic," according to which God wants the elect to practice their "vocations" according to the laws of the relevant social sphere, whether or not such action is "brotherly."

shelve the Christian ethic of "brotherliness" when acting as an economic agent and legitimate one's actions by some other appeal; Weber offered an account of how that came about. But what leads to the differentiation of these spheres?[9] To that question, Weber gave no answer. We know enough about his style of thought, however, to know that if he had given an answer, the dynamic of rationalization would have figured prominently therein!

Taylor accepts at least the disenchantment component in Weber's picture of the origins of modernity. Rather than focusing on the modern economy, however, as Weber does, he focuses on the new science. And rather than emphasizing the tension among the differentiated spheres and the absence of meaning from all of them, as Weber does, he emphasizes that modern science depicts for us "a vision of things as devoid of intrinsic meaning, of the world as the locus of contingent correlations to be traced by observation, conforming to no a priori pattern." "I have spoken of this vision of the world as 'disenchanted' using Weber's term," he says. He goes on to suggest an alternative word, the word "objectified," "to cover this denial to the world of inherent meaning . . . The point of using this term is to mark the fact that for the modern view categories of meaning and purpose apply exclusively to the thought and actions of subjects."[10]

Taylor goes beyond Weber in suggesting that an essential corollary to this modern picture of an objectified world is a new notion of the self as a *self-defining subject*; "a disenchanted world is correlative to a

---

[9] There is one passage in Weber's chapter on "Religious Rejections of the World and their Directions" which contains a revealing hint, however: "an especially important fraction of all cases of prophetic and redemptory religions have lived not only in an acute but in a permanent state of tension in relation to the world and its orders . . . The more the religions have been true religions of salvation, the greater has this tension been . . . The tension has also been the greater, the more rational in principle the ethic has been, and the more it has been oriented to *inward* sacred values as means of salvation . . . Indeed, the further the rationalization and sublimation of the external and internal possession of – in the widest sense – 'things worldly' has progressed, the stronger has the tension on the part of religion become. For the rationalization and the conscious sublimation of man's relations to the various spheres of values, external and internal, as well as religious and secular, have then pressed towards making conscious the *internal and lawful autonomy* of the individual spheres; thereby letting them drift into those tensions which remain hidden to the originally naive relation with the external world." H. H. Gerth and C. W. Mills (eds. and trs.), *From Max Weber: Essays in Sociology* (New York, Oxford University Press, 1958), p. 328. The picture which comes through is the neo-Kantian picture, according to which there just are those "individual spheres" in the nature of things, with their "internal and lawful autonomy," rationalization being the dynamic which reveals those spheres and sets thought and action within them free from external domination, so that life within each can develop according to the "internal logic" of that sphere.

[10] Taylor, *Hegel*, p. 9.

self-defining subject."[11] "[T]he view of the subject that came down from the dominant tradition of the ancients, was that man came most fully to himself when he was in touch with a cosmic order, and in touch with it in the way most suitable to it as an order of ideas, that is, by reason . . . Now the shift that occurs in the seventeenth-century revolution is, inter alia, a shift to the modern notion of the self [as a self-defining subject]." Taylor goes on to suggest "that one of the powerful attractions of this austere vision [of the world not as a locus of meaning, but rather of contingent, de facto correlations], long before it 'paid off' in technology . . . lies in the fact that the winning through to a self-defining identity was accompanied by a sense of exhilaration and power, that the subject need no longer define his perfection or vice, his equilibrium or disharmony, in relation to an external order. With the forging of this modern subjectivity there comes a new notion of freedom, and a newly central role attributed to freedom, which seems to have proved itself definitive and irreversible."[12]

Whereas in his book *Hegel*, Taylor does little more to tie down this interpretation of early modern philosophy to the actual historical figures than to remark that it is this "notion which underlies Descartes's *cogito*,"[13] in the chapter "Locke's Punctual Self" from his recent book *The Sources of the Self*, he elaborates what he sees as Locke's contribution to the emergence of this modern notion of the self as self-defining subject, along the way explaining in more detail what he has in mind by "self-defining." Let me first state the core of his interpretation, using his own terminology; and then explain in more detail some of its parts, and offer my critique.

Locke, says Taylor, urged that we human beings "objectify" and "disengage" ourselves from the actualities of self and world to such an extent as to take up what may be described as the stance of a "punctual" self. He urged this both in the domain of action and in the domain of knowledge and belief, the point of the exercise being to gain mastery over one's self. Pervasive in Locke is the theme of *control*. In so far as one gains such control over one's self, one liberates oneself from the "objectified" actualities of self and world. Thus correlative to the theme of control is that of *freedom*. In urging all this, Locke worked, says Taylor, with a "procedural" understanding of rationality. As to what led Locke to such views, Taylor emphasizes two things:

---

[11] *Ibid.*, p. 8. [12] *Ibid.*, pp. 8–9. [13] *Ibid.*, p. 6.

Locke's mechanistic picture of the world, and his rejection of the traditional belief that there is an "inherent bent to the truth or to the good" in the human subject.[14]

Taylor is right to insist on the importance in Locke of the theme of self-mastery, and of its corollary, freedom; as he is right to insist on the importance of the theme of the self-discipline required by self-mastery and liberation. These themes have been prominent in my own discussion – though I would insist that if we are to understand Locke and not simply treat him as a Cartesian we must recognize that for him proper education was at least as important as self-discipline for bringing about the right conduct of the understanding. The social dimensions of Locke's thought go unacknowledged by Taylor. Nevertheless, it is indubitable that *governance* is a central theme in Locke's epistemology.

For the rest, however, Taylor's interpretation severely distorts Locke's thought, the distortion in great measure caused by the all-too-characteristic, near-total neglect of Book IV of the *Essay*. Let us begin with Taylor's claim that the tradition before Locke and Descartes operated with a "substantive" view of rationality, whereas they operated with a "procedural." (Taylor adds that almost everyone after Descartes and Locke has followed them in adopting the procedural understanding of rationality, so that this, in his view, is one of the hallmarks of modern thought.)

By the *substantive* view of rationality Taylor means the view that reason is a faculty for apprehending an objective order which includes norms for conviction and action. On this view, the extent to which a person is rational is determined by the "substance" of his or her convictions. In so far as those convictions are out of accord (do not correspond) with the objective order, that person's reason has not been at work. That person was and is not rational. As one would surmise, Plato is Taylor's favorite example of someone who held this substantive view of rationality – though he attributes it to the ancients in general. To see the good is to love it, Plato thought, and whoever loves it will embody it in his or her life; accordingly, not only does the substance of a person's convictions indicate to what extent he or she is rational, but the substance of a person's actions do so as well. Let me allow Taylor to state in his own words what he has in mind by the "substantive" view of rationality:

---

[14] Taylor, *Sources of the Self*, p. 164.

Reason is the capacity to see and understand . . . So to be ruled by reason is to be ruled by the correct vision or understanding. The correct vision or understanding of ourselves is one which grasps the natural order . . . So reason can be understood as the perception of the natural or right order, and to be ruled by reason is to be ruled by a vision of this order.

Plato offers what we can call a substantive conception of reason. Rationality is tied to the perception of order; and so to realize our capacity for reason is to see the order as it is. The correct vision is criterial. There is no way one could be ruled by reason and be *mistaken* or wrong about the order of reality. It makes no sense for Plato to imagine a perfectly rational person who would nevertheless have quite erroneous views about the order of things or the morally good.[15]

Once reason is substantively defined, once a correct vision of the order is criterial to rationality, then our becoming rational ought not most perspicuously to be described as something that takes place in us, but rather better as our connecting up to the larger order in which we are placed. Reason is our capacity to see being, illuminated reality. Just as the eye cannot exercise its function of seeing unless there is reality there and it is properly illuminated, so reason cannot realize its function until we are turned towards real being, illuminated by the Good. That is why reason has to be understood substantively, and why the vision of the true order is criterial for rationality.[16]

What, by contrast, is *procedural* rationality? Taylor's best description occurs in the context of his discussion of Descartes's mechanistic picture of the world and his body/mind dualism. These, says Taylor, cannot "but result in a very different notion of the self-mastery wrought by reason. This cannot mean what it meant for Plato, that one's soul is ordered by the Good which presides over the cosmic order which one attends to and loves. For there is no such order . . . The Cartesian option is to see rationality, or the power of thought, as a capacity we have to *construct* orders which meet the standards demanded by knowledge, or understanding, or certainty . . . If we follow this line, then the self-mastery of reason now must consist in this capacity being the controlling element in our lives, and not the senses; self-mastery consists in our lives being shaped by the orders that our reasoning capacity constructs according to the appropriate standards."[17] "What we are called on to do is not to become contemplators of order, but rather to construct a picture of things following the canons of rational thinking . . . Rationality is above all a property of the process of thinking, not of the substantive content of thought."[18]

If one were going to place much weight on this distinction between substantive and procedural rationality, one would have to clarify and

[15] *Ibid.*, pp. 121–2.   [16] *Ibid.*, pp. 123–4.   [17] *Ibid.*, pp. 146–7.   [18] *Ibid.*, p. 168.

articulate it a good deal more than Taylor does. But even without such development I think we can see clearly enough what Taylor has in mind to enable us also to see that it is simply not true that Locke and Descartes adopted a procedural view of rationality.

In the first place, the project of constructing something which one's reason tells one satisfies certain standards that one has set for oneself – the phenomenon of one's reason telling one this seems to be what Taylor means by "procedural" rationality – was far from absent in the tradition. Taylor neglects it; but surely the traditional project of *scientia* was exactly such a project. The tradition by no means thought that reason had only to do with contemplation, not at all with construction. Probably one should interpret Plato's remarks in Book VI of the *Republic* as advice concerning how one is to attain to a vision of the good rather than advice as to how one is to construct *scientia*. But by the time we get to Aristotle the project of constructing *scientia* is clearly in view. What must be added, though, is that the tradition would not be happy with Taylor's sharp contrast between construction and contemplation. *By* constructing *scientia* one contemplates the order of necessity.

On the other hand, there is no hope whatsoever of understanding Locke unless one realizes that reason for him is as much a faculty of *apprehension* as it was for the ancients, and that what reason apprehends is by no means just that some belief or action satisfies some standard one has embraced. Reason is that faculty whereby we apprehend necessities in general. Over and over, as we have seen, Locke uses the word "perceive" to describe what reason does. And he adamantly refuses to admit that reason can go wrong – or even that among our faculties there is any which can accurately mimic the phenomenology of reason. Hence it is as true for Locke as it was for Plato that failure to apprehend some item in the realm of necessity – whether or not that failure is accompanied by the *belief* that one has apprehended some such item – is a failure of reason, of rationality. The content, the "substance," of one's thought is a mark of the degree of one's rationality.

Of course, Locke was far from being a Platonist. Part of the difference lies in disagreement over the *ontological status* of that which reason apprehends. For Plato, what one apprehends by reason is mind-independent *ideai*. For Locke, what one apprehends by reason is one's mind and its modifications, including its ideas. With an eye on the ontological status of that which reason apprehends, one might say that Locke's picture of the self is that of the "claustrophobic" self.

Furthermore, Locke had a different understanding of the nature of norms. Counter to Taylor's interpretation, Locke clearly held that norms are among what reason apprehends. Locke's concept of a law of nature was that of a moral obligation apprehensible by reason. But Locke did not share Plato's conviction that the realm of necessity includes eternal, self-exemplifying virtues, and that all persons are of such a nature that for them to know these self-exemplifying virtues is to love and seek to imitate them. As to the former point, morality is grounded in the commands of God. As to the latter, Locke was Augustinian: One might by reason apprehend a law of nature without trying to obey it; between apprehension and intention comes will.

These observations suggest that Taylor's substantive/procedural distinction lumps together a number of distinct issues in such a way as to make the disjunction non-exhaustive. Locke holds neither a substantive nor a procedural view of reason. Plato and Locke share the conviction that reason is a faculty of apprehension; they share what might be called an *apprehensive* view of reason. They disagree on what it is that reason apprehends and what we are to do with its apprehensions. When Taylor speaks of "substantive" reason, he has in mind the *complex* view that reason is a faculty for apprehending an objective order of necessity incorporating paradigms for belief and action. If we are to understand what divides Locke from Plato, the issue must be divided. The decay of the conviction that we human beings have in us a faculty for apprehending necessary truths occurs *after* Locke; from Plato to Locke, almost everyone in the Western philosophical tradition shared this conviction. Without such apprehension, said Locke, we would be wandering in darkness.

Locke's innovation (shared with his associates in the Royal Society) is to be located in his view as to what we are to do with reason's deliverances. Here too, though, we must step carefully. Locke's innovation was not in his insistence *that* we should use reason's deliverances constructively – procedurally, if you will. All those who had recommended *scientia* had said the same. Locke's innovation lies in *what* it was he thought we should construct under reason's guidance. *Scientia*, of course; Locke never rejected the project of *scientia*. But he went on to suggest that when we are obligated to do our best in the governance of *beliefs*, then too we are to listen to the voice of Reason. Of course, one's listening to the voice of Reason and applying what one hears it saying, in accord with the principle of proportionality, might result in one's believing something false – since what is highly probable, and thus permissible to believe, might nonetheless be false. Thus what Taylor notes comes about: the "substance" (content) of one's beliefs is not always by itself an indicator of the extent to which one has been rational.

The other main part of Taylor's interpretation is the claim that Locke was more radical than anyone before him in the recommended scope of objectification, disengagement, and control – that Locke was as radical as anyone could possibly be. "The subject of disengagement and rational control," says Taylor, "has become a familiar modern figure . . . The key to this figure is that it gains control through disengagement. Disengagement is always correlative of an 'objectification' . . . Objectifying a given domain involves depriving it of its normative force for us."[19] On Locke's view, according to Taylor, "we are to wrest the control of our thinking and outlook away from passion or custom or authority and assume responsibility for it ourselves. Locke's theory generates and also reflects an ideal of independence and self-responsibility, a notion of reason as free from established customs and locally dominant authority."[20] "The disengagement both from the activities of thought and from our unreflecting desires and tastes allows us to see ourselves as objects of far-reaching reformation."[21] Indeed, so radical is Locke's proposal as to the proper scope of objectification, disengagement, and control that only a self which is a mere "point" could act thus: "The subject who can take this kind of radical stance of disengagement to himself or herself with a view to remaking, is what I want to call the 'punctual' self. To take this stance is to identify oneself with the power to objectify and remake, and by this act to distance oneself from all the particular features which are objects of potential change. What we are essentially is none of the latter, but what finds itself capable of fixing them and working on them. This is what the image of the point is meant to convey."[22]

Is it true that Locke recommended that we each engage in so radical a critique and control of self as to assume that one is nothing but the power to engage in such radical critique and control? Certainly not. Taylor correctly observes that to engage in critique and control of everything about the self presupposes aligning oneself "against any view which sees us as naturally tending to or attuned to

[19] *Ibid.*, p. 160.   [20] *Ibid.*, p. 167.   [21] *Ibid.*, p. 171.   [22] *Ibid.*, pp. 171–2.

the truth, whether it be of the ancient variety, that we are qua rational beings constitutionally disposed to recognize the rational order of things; or of the modern variety, that we have innate ideas, or an innate tendency to unfold our thought toward the truth."[23] It requires that "Instead of being swept along to error by the ordinary bent of our experience, we stand back from it, withdraw from it, reconstrue it objectively, and then learn to draw defensible conclusions from it."[24] But Locke does not deny, in this sense, the presence of an innate bent toward the truth in us. He affirms in us the presence of Reason. And never does he propose a critique of Reason; Reason cannot go wrong. In turn, Reason is for Locke just one of the faculties yielding insight. There is no significant difference between Locke and Plato on the presence in us of an innate bent toward the truth, or on where in us that bent is to be located. Or if there is a difference, Locke is not more radical, but less radical, than Plato. For Locke acknowledges insight into various contingent facts, whereas (perhaps) Plato did not. And as to the issue raised by Taylor of Locke's denial of innate ideas: Locke makes clear that though he denies innate ideas, he affirms innate *powers*. The workings of our innate powers, coupled with the impact of reality on us, account, he thought, for all our ideas.

If one wants to find in the seventeenth century a truly radical proposal for objectification, disengagement, and control, one would be well advised to look into the Calvinist movement. It was the Calvinists who insisted that we are "fallen" in all dimensions of our existence – including our Reason. We are, in this sense, "totally depraved." They insisted, accordingly, that for guidance in reform of self and world we must look outside ourselves, to the Word of God. Of course, they did not insist that everything in all our thoughts and actions, cultural products and social constructions, is bad. They did not, in this sense, believe that "there is no health in us." Rather, they held that only the Word of God provides us with a reliable criterion for sorting through what is good and bad.

Here, then, there is a truly radical disengagement. But these same Calvinists would have firmly rejected Taylor's conclusion that they were presupposing a purely punctual self. For they would have insisted that those dimensions of one's person which one subjects to critique nevertheless belong to one's self. So much, indeed, do they belong to one's self that one confesses before God all that is sinful in

---

[23] *Ibid.*, p. 165.   [24] *Ibid.*, p. 163.

them. The Calvinists did not make Taylor's (Hegelian?) move of regarding as belonging to the self only what is not subjected to critique, or only what is essential to the self. They made the Pauline/Augustinian move of confessing that the *real* self is a *fallen* self. The self they presupposed was not a punctual self but a self naked before the eyes of God.

Taylor's claim, that fundamental to modern philosophy is the notion of the self-defining subject as the corollary of Weber's disenchanted world, and that Descartes and Locke represent the initial development of this idea, cannot be sustained. The notion of the subject as self-defining comes after Descartes and after Locke. And to repeat a point made earlier: Not even is it the case that the self is central in Descartes's thought; in Locke's thought, Yes, in Descartes's, No.

Fundamental to Weber's interpretation of modernity is taking *societies* as one's basic entities, and then distinguishing within a given society various spheres of that society – various social spheres, and various cultural spheres. My own preference is for what has come to be called the "world-system" interpretation, according to which we discard *society* as our unit of analysis and work instead with economies, states, nations, and religious groupings as our units of analysis. What characterizes the social world of modernity is the emergence of economies which do not coincide with, but overlap, distinct states; indeed, that there is in general a striking lack of coincidence among economies, states, nations, and religious groupings in the modern world. Areas of the world displaying deep economic linkages are nonetheless under the sovereignty of different states; and within these states there are distinct nationalities and distinct religions. Conversely, members of the same nation find themselves under the sovereignty of distinct states, as do members of the same religion.

Part of what makes modern philosophy *modern* is that it deals with philosophical questions raised by this new social order. Locke's letters concerning toleration addressed questions raised by the emergence in England of distinct religious groupings within a single polity; his treatises concerning civil government addressed fundamental questions raised by the new economy and the new state. Furthermore, the placing of the self, and in particular, of the *volitional* self, on the agenda of modern philosophy is to be seen as a natural response to the centrality of volition in this new social order. The gradual loss of ascriptivism in capitalist economies means that the social roles one plays are more and more the consequence of choice (albeit often constrained choice) rather than ascription; and the fact that all about us are people of different religions, or of no religion, leads very many members of modern society to see themselves as faced with the need to choose.

But modernity is more than a new form of social order; modernity is also new forms of culture. Some of that culture can be seen as a response, in one way or another, to this new modern social order; such culture is then discernibly *modern*. Just above, I was assuming that to be true for some of the philosophical culture which has arisen in the modern period. But it would be "materialist" folly to think that culture is entirely to be accounted for as response to social events. Culture has its own dynamics. Part of what makes culture of the modern period very different from what preceded it is, for example, that our science, following in part its own internal dynamics, is very different. The philosophical career of Descartes was intimately interwoven with the emergence of our new science. That's what makes *him* a modern philosopher.

Let us beware, though, of following Weber in thinking of these intra-cultural developments as simply the slow, episodic working out of the "logic" of the matter. Descartes's deep, theologically grounded, and enormously influential intuition that something in nature is "conserved" – motion, he thought – was that a case of his discerning the "logic" of the matter? But more important: My claim has been that the Reformation produced a crisis in European culture (and a corresponding crisis in society). The way which European humanity had painstakingly developed of living with its textual inheritance was ripped in shreds. Weber assumes that, looking back over the sweep of history from the standpoint of modernity, we can discern a "logic" in the process and can identify for each stage a vanguard on whom the dynamics of rationalization worked most powerfully. In this way of thinking he was, of course, following Hegel; Hegel regarded Protestantism as the vanguard of modernity. It is now clear, from our vantage-point four centuries later, that it was not that. Protestantism has not proved to be the vanguard of the future with which everyone else eventually catches up; neither, *pace* the French Enlightenment thinkers, has secularism proved to be the vanguard with which everyone else eventually catches up. There is no vanguard; the others have not caught up, because they have not followed. The Catholics remain, and the Orthodox, and the Muslims – and that only begins the list. The Reformation did not represent a working out of the logic of the situation, but a cataclysm. Locke's epistemology was addressed to that cataclysm. That is what makes it modern. There is more to modernity than fractured moral and religious traditions; other philosophers have addressed themselves to other phases of modernity. Other things make them *modern*. But this – along with his treatment of religious toleration and of civil authority – is what makes Locke *modern*.

A final word: Locke's proposal will not do. Our problems with traditions remain, however. Traditions are still a source of benightedness, chicanery, hostility, and oppression. And our moral, religious, and even theoretical traditions are even more fractured today than they were in Locke's day. In this situation, examining our traditions remains for many of us a deep obligation, and for all of us together, a desperate need. But we shall have to acknowledge what the thinkers of the Enlightenment would have found appallingly unpalatable; namely, that examination of tradition can take place only in the context of unexamined tradition, and that in our examination, our convictions as to the facts are schooled by our traditions. The thinkers of the Enlightenment hoped to bring about a rational consensus in place of fractured tradition. That hope has failed. In my judgment it was bound to fail; it could not succeed.

Yet we must live together. It is to politics and not to epistemology that we shall have to look for an answer as to how to do that. "Liberal" politics has fallen on bad days recently. But to its animating vision of a society in which persons of diverse traditions live together in justice and friendship, conversing with each other and slowly altering their traditions in response to their conversation – to that, there is no viable alternative.

Index

247

CAMBRIDGE STUDIES IN RELIGION AND CRITICAL THOUGHT